An Educator's Guide to ADHD

An Educator's Guide to
ADHD

Designing and Teaching
for Student Success

Karen Costa

JOHNS HOPKINS UNIVERSITY PRESS | *Baltimore*

© 2026 Johns Hopkins University Press
All rights reserved. Published 2026
Printed in the United States of America on acid-free paper

9 8 7 6 5 4 3 2 1

Johns Hopkins University Press
2715 North Charles Street
Baltimore, Maryland 21218
www.press.jhu.edu

Library of Congress Cataloging-in-Publication Data

Names: Costa, Karen author http://id.loc.gov/authorities/names/n2020015193
    http://id.loc.gov/rwo/agents/n2020015193
Title: An educator's guide to ADHD : designing and teaching for student
    success / Karen Costa.
Description: Baltimore : Johns Hopkins University Press, [2026] | Includes
bibliographical references and index. |
Identifiers: LCCN 2025012419 | ISBN 9781421453507 paperback | ISBN 9781421453514 ebook
Subjects: LCSH: Children with attention-deficit hyperactivity disorder—Education |
    Attention-deficit hyperactivity disorder
    http://id.loc.gov/authorities/subjects/sh85063661
Classification: LCC LC4713.2 .C68 2025 | DDC 371.94—dc23/eng/20250617
LC record available at https://lccn.loc.gov/2025012419

A catalog record for this book is available from the British Library.

Special discounts are available for bulk purchases of this book.
For more information, please contact Special Sales at specialsales@jh.edu.

EU GPSR Authorized Representative
LOGOS EUROPE, 9 rue Nicolas Poussin,
17000, La Rochelle, France
E-mail: Contact@logoseurope.eu

If you feel you don't fit into this world, it's because you're here to create a new one.
                                                                —Ross Caligiuri

Every tree and plant in the meadow seemed to be dancing, those which average eyes would see as fixed and still.
                                                                —Rumi

Contents

Acknowledgments

Actress Niecy Nash gave a speech at the 2023 Golden Globes where she thanked herself first. It immediately went viral. I want what she has, as they say in many recovery spaces. I want to first thank myself, that brave, weird little girl who survived it all, often on her own. The brave, weird grown-up woman who refused to give up on finding answers. Who fought for a diagnosis. Who found people like her. Who still has a lot to learn, but is doing it from a newly solidified foundation of self-love and self-acceptance. I hope you'll consider thanking yourself first, too, once in a while.

To my husband, Andrew, and my son, Fred, who always support my dreams. I have won the life lottery with you. And of course, to Rocky, whose cuteness is the antidote to almost anything. To my mental and physical care team of doctors and my therapist, who got me through some of the hardest days. I cannot thank you enough for helping me return to myself. To my friends, who are a select group of kind and well-boundaried souls these days. Thank you for accepting me as I am. To Jim Lang and Derek Krisoff, who pointed at my ADHD work and asked for more. To my editor, Ezra Rodriguez, for your kind and clear direction. To my copyeditor, Debby Bors, for helping me put forward my best work. To artists and writers, who keep creating, despite it all. Your words and creations give us things to look forward to. They excite and inspire us. They help us to stay our most human. You teach us how to imagine something that doesn't exist and then to take the small, incremental, courageous steps to build this new thing. That's how we make art, but it's also how we can and will create a better world. To my fellow ADHDers: I love you and your beautiful brains, just as you are. Thank you.

An Educator's Guide to ADHD

Introduction

Imagine a house.

Now open up all the windows—no screens—just fresh air and exposure to the elements.

What would living in this house of wide open windows be like?

Let's start with the challenges. It would be noisier. Crickets would keep you up half the night. There could be lots of pollen drifting inside, especially in the spring. Wildlife might decide to become your roommate. The skunks and bears in my neighborhood would present particular challenges. Mosquitos would be most unwelcome. And, of course, any human animals with nefarious intentions could enter this house at any time, stealing or doing harm to its inhabitants. There are real and likely challenges we'd face in this house.

But there would be gifts too, wouldn't there? Fresh air. Cool breezes. Birdsong. We could lean our heads out of our windows to smell fresh flowers. There's good data that seeing and feeling the natural world boosts mood and focus, so we might expect to feel happier and less stressed. We would more easily connect to the natural world and our neighbors. When my neighbor, Sue, walks her golden retriever, Tucker, I could easily holler outside to ask her what book she's reading.

Serious challenges. Amazing gifts.

If you were the owner of this house, what might you do to mitigate those challenges without sacrificing too many of the gifts? You could shut the windows when you're not at home. You could also put screens on the windows to keep bugs and wildlife outside while keeping the fresh air flowing. You could also choose to leave some windows open and others closed. In short, you have lots of options to boost the benefits while lessening the negative impacts.

Now imagine that you get married, and your spouse comes to live with you. They tell you your open window habit is wrong, deficient, broken, and maybe even dangerous to yourself and others. "Close the windows," they tell you. "This is no way to live." Shutting the windows would address all the negatives, but you'd also sacrifice all the positives in the process (and be stuck with a jerk for a partner).

To live with the ADHD (which technically stands for "attention deficit hyperactivity disorder") neurotype is to live with a mind that is thrown wide open to the world. Oh, the many gifts! The things that we can realize, connect, create, and envision. We think and feel deeply and passionately. But the challenges exist, too; they are never-ending and relentless. Both of these things are true.

People with ADHD have long been told to close their windows to the world. To ignore and sacrifice our gifts. To act like "normal" neurotypical people. Thankfully, as more ADHDers are taking the lead in discussions and movements about ADHD, that history is gradually coming to an end. A new era is beginning, and I'm proud to be a part of it. It's time to learn how to keep our minds open in a way that serves our needs and desires, balancing our strengths and our challenges. And if you're new to my work, I use the word "our" because, like many of you and many of our students, I have ADHD.

This book guides educators to honor their ADHD learners' open minds, helping students realize and decide on solutions to keep their windows open while also keeping those pesky mosquitoes outside. I am so glad that you're here, because I believe that this strengths-based, challenge-aware approach to designing and teaching for ADHD learners is going to save lives. Shifting our understanding of ADHD will not only benefit ADHDers but society as a whole, which will benefit from the full display of our creative strengths.

In an era of increased recognition and diagnosis (both formal and self-made) of ADHD, our world needs educators who are ready to design and teach for ADHD learners' success just as they are, not how anyone else wants them to be. You are here because you've accepted the invitation to be one of those educators. Welcome. Come on inside. If you wish, go through the window instead of the door, because doesn't that sound like more fun?

Why This Book? Why Now?

If you work in education, particularly higher education, you've likely noticed an uptick in the number of learners who are disclosing to you that they have ADHD. A few factors contribute to this uptick: first off, yes, the number of folks being diagnosed with ADHD is growing, particularly among previously underrepresented groups like adult women.[1] Does this mean that more people have ADHD than in previous generations? Not necessarily. It means that more people are receiving diagnoses. Could rates of ADHD be increasing? Absolutely. But we know that, particularly among girls and adult women, ADHD has been woefully underdiagnosed.[2] I'll share more of my own diagnosis story later, but to summarize: I was diagnosed at age 40, despite having what I lovingly call "raging ADHD" since childhood. Our world ignores the needs of girls and women, and this is especially true of girls and women with ADHD.

Another factor in higher rates of ADHD is that social media has become a site for information sharing and disclosure of a variety of health and wellness concerns.[3] Today, more people write about their stories and struggles to help themselves and others get and stay well. As our society becomes increasingly online in nature, disclosures can require less effort than they did when made primarily face to face. With many students learning online, it can also be easier to disclose that you have ADHD in an email to your instructor or an introductory discussion post. Folks will discuss freely online what they can sometimes be more hesitant to share in in-person settings.

You might have heard critiques suggesting that ADHD is overdiagnosed, with many pointing to social media as the source of its rise. Since we're all about asking good, necessary questions here, my take is that the question, "Is ADHD being overdiagnosed?" is a terrible one. As Ellie Middleton, author of *Unmasked: The Ultimate Guide to ADHD, Autism, and Neurodivergence*, writes: "Society's answer to an increase in diagnoses shouldn't be, 'Oh my god, everyone has ADHD and autism now.' It should be, 'Oh my god, how did we manage to let so many people down?' "[4] I'd argue that a great question is: Now that we realize all the people we've let down, how will we support them better moving forward?

Finally, conversations about the connection between trauma and ADHD are growing, with some experts theorizing that ADHD is a sort of low-level, constant form of dissociation.[5] Essentially, the ADHD person's brain checks out from the present moment as a form of self-protection against trauma, often childhood trauma. While trauma is not new, I consider the recent COVID years to be what I call "The Great Amplifier." Going with this analogy of sound, this most recent global pandemic "turned up the volume" of trauma. As a result, we may be seeing a predictable uptick in ADHD diagnoses as folks struggle to protect themselves against that "noise."

As we navigate this era of increased diagnosis and awareness, what do we know about how many people have ADHD? Five percent of Americans having ADHD is a solid starting point that you can safely rely upon.[6] However, the CDC estimates that about 10% of American children have ever been diagnosed with ADHD.[7] Why is there a discrepancy between overall and childhood numbers? Some argue that as brains develop, ADHD symptoms can go into remission.[8] Many believe this is less about neurobiology and more about environment, once kids are out of the formal school setting; to the extent that people with ADHD can design their environments and careers to meet their needs, ADHD symptoms may become less disruptive with age.

Remember that girls and women are underdiagnosed. Consider further that data also indicates that Black children are "70% less likely to receive an ADHD diagnosis than white children."[9] Considering this data, I suspect 5% is the tip of the proverbial iceberg. When we talk about diagnosis rates and the stakes and impacts of ADHD, we must pay attention to whose voices are silenced in this research and do our part to start addressing this massive public health issue. But as a starting point, I'll use a 5%-10% estimate as a reasonable range. In a classroom of twenty-five students, you can expect that at least a couple of students have ADHD. Anecdotally, in recent classes I've taught with class sizes of about thirty students, I've had as many as ten students disclose an ADHD diagnosis, leading me to question the 5-10% estimate. Let's agree to keep a close eye on diagnosis rates and continue to wonder who's being left out of access to the correct care, which a diagnosis can often provide.

Two other common questions that we should also get out of the way from the start are: Is ADHD caused by modern life (i.e., screen culture), and is it a uniquely American phenomenon? The short answer to both those questions: No. Those are good questions, and they've been answered well by actual scientists, not some guy making an Instagram reel who's trying to sell you his favorite supplement. ADHD exists globally, and no significant cultural variations in its prevalence appear.[10]

Further, while it obviously wasn't called ADHD, evidence exists throughout history of people exhibiting ADHD traits, some as far back as 460 BCE.[11] Other researchers point to possible evidence of ADHD traits in the Bible and additional historical art sources.[12] In their article in *Attention Deficit and Hyperactivity Disorders* on the history of ADHD, Klaus Lange and colleagues offer a detailed analysis of psychiatric investigations of ADHD symptoms throughout the eighteenth and nineteenth centuries.[13]

Some have argued, quite convincingly, that Leonardo da Vinci (1452–1519) was a member of team ADHD.[14] In addition to being famous for his obvious creative genius, da Vinci was infamous for struggling to complete projects, even those that were immensely important to him. I think it's safe to say that neither TikTok nor the internet caused his condition. I understand the curiosity around ADHD's history and cultural influences, but I also believe they can distract us from doing the work of making a better world for ADHDers. In short, while we're seeing increased diagnosis rates, that does not mean ADHD is caused by screens or by American culture.

Another impetus for the timing of this book is that we are witnessing shifts in expectations and norms in classrooms across formal education. The old paradigm of the teacher as the authority figure in the classroom and the student as their devoted disciple has been dying for a while now. I would argue that COVID finally put it out of its misery. A fundamental shift has occurred in how power is distributed in the classroom. The pandemic gave many of us a feeling that we did not survive all of "that" to live lives of, as Thoreau would say, "quiet desperation." If we devote our time to something (a job, relationships, schooling), it better be worth our while. I suspect that this has influenced how folks with ADHD or suspected ADHD get their needs met in classrooms.

More folks are speaking up for themselves and asking for adaptability in how educators teach them. Some might see this as students being more "demanding." I hear that concern. We must support teachers. But teachers aren't the problem; they are integral to solutions, full stop. I also believe it's a positive development that more students are asking for and expecting support for their ADHD and other disabilities. These needs deserve attention, and as a society, we should invest more in helping teachers meet them—through smaller class sizes, additional paraprofessionals and tutors, and higher salaries for educators. My hope in publishing this book is that educators at all levels will feel supported and inspired to meet these societal shifts so that they can, in turn, support and inspire their students.

Now that I've made the case for why we need this book and why we need it now, it's time to explain why I'm the person who wrote it.

Why Me?

I have lived with ADHD for as long as I can remember, at the very least since childhood, if not since birth. I didn't receive a diagnosis until I was forty years old.

All my life, I've experienced a persistent sense of wrongness, a feeling that I am a square peg in a world of round holes. Anxiety? Giftedness?

Just plain weird? Fundamentally broken? Who knew? The first time I ever suspected that I had ADHD was about a year after I'd quit a full-time job (ADHD often reveals itself more loudly in significant life transitions). I was sitting on my floor with my laptop open in front of me, surrounded by journal articles, binders full of lesson plans, and Post-It notes, working on the hundredth idea that had come to me since I'd resigned.

Something isn't right. This doesn't feel right, I thought. Felt. Knew. Could I have ADHD? I had been taking a break from psychotherapy but decided this was a good reason to return. I attended my first appointment with a new therapist, ran through my life story in fifteen minutes, and then got to why I was there.

"I think I might have ADHD," I told her.

I described my history of what I'd always just called "zoning out." I have many murky memories of teachers, coaches, and other adults calling my name from what felt like another realm. I'd "come to" and look around at a sea of faces staring at me. I'd been lost in thought. There, but not really there.

I once drove a car out of gas when traveling home from college—not that I realized I was running out of gas and couldn't get to a gas station, but that the car started shaking while I was driving 65 miles per hour on the highway and then shuddered to a stop. Once, in my early twenties, I missed a flight home, but not because I was running late. Nope. I was at the gate, sitting in the correct waiting area an hour before takeoff. The airline staff made all the typical announcements. Everyone around me boarded. I was seated about thirty feet from the jetway. Once again, I "came to," looked around, and rushed to the desk in a panic. They were very sorry, but the door had closed. In my defense, I'd been reading a very juicy edition of *US Weekly*.

We didn't have time for much more in that first session, but these stories were enough for the therapist to suggest we continue the exploration the following week. "ADHD is definitely a possibility," she said.

I went to the local library the next day and found every book I could on ADHD, read through them all, and returned the next week to discuss a plan. I didn't know it then, but this is a phenomenon called hyperfocus.[15] It's often considered one of the greatest strengths of ADHDers, one we'll discuss in more detail later. The same brain, the same human that can drive a car out of gas, can also read three books on a topic that fascinates her in less than a week.

"Wow," the therapist said, after I rapidly regurgitated summaries of the three books in fifteen minutes. "I actually have ADHD myself, and those are some great ideas. I should really try some of those."

Here's where things became *almost* comical—or was it tragic?

I forgot that I had ADHD. I honestly forgot about it. Within days of that second therapy session, I was on to my next fascinating topic (the enneagram) and stopped seeing that therapist. I dove into another pile of personal development books, down the next rabbit hole, and into the next creative project. ADHD? Gone. Vanished. Disappeared.

Except, of course, ADHD wasn't gone at all. I lived with it for the next eight years, just as I'd done for decades prior. I had insufficient support for dealing with it. No words to put a name to the constant, daily challenges I faced, to the messy and beautiful ways my brain processed the world. With the idea of ADHD having faded away, I looked for other ways to fix myself. I got sober, which was a necessary fix but not the root issue. I started (and stopped and started) psychotherapy again for what several therapists told me was anxiety.

I was still often surrounded by laptops, binders, journal articles, notebooks, and Post-Its. I still bought a new planner every few months, convinced that the right one would finally get my brain on track. Boredom still made me feel like I was going to explode out of my skin. The most mundane tasks, such as cooking and cleaning, which many call "adulting," were the hardest. Remembering to take my vitamins every day? Impossible. Flossing? Forget it. And then came the worst part: the shame. *You're an adult. Get it together.*

Something isn't right. This doesn't feel right, I still thought. Felt. Knew. I had just turned forty and was tired of never feeling any sense of rightness in my brain or body.

On March 9, 2020 (yes, I got my ADHD diagnosis the same week that we went into COVID-19 lockdown), I co-led an Online Learning Consortium webinar with my pal Clea Mahoney on the topic of continuity of instruction during COVID-19. Over four hundred people attended to hear me speak as an expert on this topic.

Earlier in the day, I'd seen a psychologist specializing in ADHD. Publicly, I wanted everyone to see me as a capable helper available to help during this global crisis. And I was. Privately, I felt like the little five-year-old girl whose teacher yelled her name in class. "Karen! Where were you? Are you with us? Why aren't you paying attention?" I told the psychologist about my constant daily challenges with adult life. I also mentioned that I'd written a book of tips to help faculty use videos in their teaching.

"Huh," he said, "Very interesting. A book of tips? Short chapters? The perfect book for someone with ADHD to write."

Our conversation alone was enough for the psychologist to tell me that I probably had ADHD, but he wanted to do some testing. He sent me home with a pile of tests, most with lots of tiny bubbles in which to fill in responses and some with space for short answers where I described my life and learning experiences as far back as I could remember. I spent the next week wondering whether my world was ending and penciling in my responses to questions about my time management skills and attention span. My husband completed a questionnaire as well, to provide an outside perspective.

A few days later, I got a call from the doctor to discuss my results. He rattled off a lot of percentages: 95%, 98%, 99%, 99% . . . a lot of 99%.

"The results indicate that you have ADHD," he said.

I asked about the percentiles he'd mentioned. "What does it mean when you say that I'm in the ninety-ninth percentile for these things?" (if there was an ADHD award or prize, I didn't want to miss out).

"Well, on those questions, you scored higher than 99% of other people who took this test." (Yay! My inner overachiever celebrated.)

"And what does that mean?" I asked again.

"It could be indicative of severe ADHD, but again, all we can say for sure is that you scored higher than the majority of people." (Oh . . . maybe not a "yay" situation after all.)

He told me that I could take meds, which I would need to access from my primary care doctor or a psychiatrist (which would necessitate another referral, another round of calls to doctors, and more co-pays despite having excellent insurance—something many of our students don't have). He sent me back out into a raging pandemic with my new diagnosis.

Forty years old. ADHD. Locked down. Terrified. Anxious. Quite literally, at times, on the floor.

But, despite all of that, I finally had a name. Some of you know the exquisite relief of a diagnosis. A part of you does not want this thing. A part of you wishes you could ignore it. But a name. For me and many others, a name is better than an abyss. People without disabilities or chronic illnesses often say, "I'm so sorry" when you share a diagnosis. Those of us who've been down this road know we can say, "That's amazing. Congratulations. I'm so happy for you," when a recently diagnosed friend shares their news.

I finally had words to explain the wrongness, the weirdness, the lifetime of struggle hidden behind a public mask. There was no longer a sense that I was the only one who felt this way and lived like this, that this was my personal curse.

When used well, a name is a map—most importantly, a map to other people like you. I hope this book can serve as a map for all of us, a map through and toward a world where ADHDers not only survive but thrive. Where our strengths are celebrated and our challenges mitigated. Where our unique and beautiful open minds can invite all of humanity into new ways of thinking, learning, and imagining for the good of all humankind.

After over twenty years of studying, working, and teaching in higher education, with varied expertise in learning experience design, accessible online pedagogy, and faculty development, I have written this book by combining my educational expertise with my lived experience as a person with ADHD. I hope to use the strengths and challenges of these decades of lived experience to help us all rethink how we understand ADHD. Further, I hope this new comprehension of a complex condition will compel us to make simple and sustainable shifts in our design and teaching to improve learning experiences for students who have ADHD.

The Path Forward

This book is divided into two parts. I know you're primarily here for practical tips and strategies to weave into your work and teaching. Before we get to that, we've got some work to do. Society has taught us to view ADHD through a deficit-oriented lens. We'll talk more about that soon, but for now, I present as proof that the word "deficit" is literally in the name. Before I can offer you teaching strategies, we've got to (a) unlearn what we know about ADHD and (b) relearn a way to envision the open minds of ADHDers, their strengths, and their challenges.

In Part I, we'll redefine ADHD through that new lens, explore the many strengths and challenges of this neurotype, and propose new models to helps us understand what ADHD actually is—models that are more humanizing and holistic. I'm reminded of the words of one of my favorite artists, Corita Kent, about one of her own teachers, the designer Charles Eames (of the famous Eames chair). Of Eames, Kent said, "He always started fresh at the beginning. He showed us how to develop principles rather than follow formulas."[16] Part I will help you practice the principle of a strengths-based, challenge-aware approach to working with ADHDers and all students.

With that new foundation in place, we'll turn to practical design and teaching strategies in Part II. I will offer you specific tips for how you can bring these strategies into your classroom in a sustainable way that honors your needs as well as those of your students.

I expect many of you will start with chapter 1 and proceed in order. However, we are here to celebrate open minds, so feel free to start at the end and read backward; that could be quite fun. Or perhaps you want to close your eyes and point at a chapter. Who says you can't? Again, proceeding in order is probably most helpful, but do what works best for you.

While this book focuses on supporting you in your classroom teaching, I know that many of you come to this book as fellow ADHDers and neurodivergent friends, whether you're self-diagnosed, clinically diagnosed, or simply curious about the possibilities of your own neurodivergence. You are so welcome here. I expect that much of what I share with you, both in Part I, where we explore a new path forward for understanding ADHD, and in Part II, where we discuss specific teaching and learning strategies, will feel relevant to you personally. Stay open to the opportunity to learn more about yourself as you also learn how to best support your students.

I use plain, relatable language in my writing because I like to have fun when I write and connect emotionally with my readers. Plain language is also an accessibility choice. In the words of Jay Timothy Dolmage in *Academic Ableism*,[17] "The process of making academic writing more and more academic can be a process of ableism and it can reproduce ableism, creating steep steps." I use plain language to make my writing clear to as many people as possible. I use plain language to make my words more easily digestible and understood by ADHDers, other people with neurodivergence, and anyone whose memory and attention span is challenged. I use plain language as an invitation that reads: All are welcome here.

I also want to be clear that I prefer what is called identity-first language over people-first language. In other words, I usually say "ADHDers" instead of "people with ADHD." I am an ADHDer and I'm proud to be a part of this community, so I want people to honor that identity. Not all folks feel that way, and that's okay, because we're not a monolith. When in doubt, ask folks what type of language they prefer, and honor those preferences.

I just made use of the term *"ableism."* This concept is a vital part of this book in that I argue that the biggest challenge faced by ADHDers is not some deficit in our brains, but rather people's and society's ableism. Let's take a minute to define that term. I define ableism as the idea that disabled people are simultaneously weak and threatening and therefore less than fully human and undeserving of resources. Ableism and ableists make two key moves. First, everything they do and say conveys the idea that disabled folks are weak (i.e, deficient and disordered). Yet somehow, inexplicably, at the very same time, disabled folks are threatening (i.e., we're gonna get all you non-disabled folks, take all your stuff, and ruin your lives). If we're so weak, why are we such a threat? The second move is to use that weak and threatening characterization to downgrade our humanity in order to deny us access to society's most fundamental promises (e.g., life, liberty, and the pursuit of happiness). This framework is part in capitalism, which operates by creating in-groups and out-groups, with the in-groups getting too many resources and the out-groups lacking resources. Capitalism has to characterize various groups in society as both weak and threatening and therefore less than human in order to keep resources in the hands of the few rather than the many. You'll know you're dealing with ableism if you see words, tones, allusions, behaviors, and direct statements that make use of this frame.

Finally, as I always say in my workshops, I offer you two final invitations: First, take what you need from this book and leave the rest. I don't want an army of educators teaching like I teach. How boring. How ineffective. I want to inspire you to become your own best teacher, so please adapt my recommendations to your needs and the needs of your learners. Second, remember to celebrate the power of small. In a recent podcast interview, the host asked me what I most wanted listeners to know. "That's easy," I said. "Do small things in loving community."[18] When I get lost, that touchstone brings me back to discovering my next, best step forward.

Now, let's throw open the windows and enter the minds of our ADHDers.

Part One

Redefining ADHD

Chapter One

What Is ADHD?

Too often people with disabilities are only seen as the beneficiaries
and not seen as the leaders, the creators, the agents of change.
—Margaux Joffe, Founder/CEO, Minds of All Kinds

ADHD is the reason that I just had to get up three times in a row to get
my reading glasses. Each time I stood up to grab my glasses off the din-
ing room table, within full view of where I was seated at my computer,
something else drew my attention. First, I wanted to put my favorite
writing show, *Fireplace for the Home: Classic Edition*, on the TV. I sat back
down without my glasses. On the second try, on the way to get my
glasses (the ones that are about twenty feet away), I realized my lips felt
chapped, so I went to my purse to get some Aquaphor. I sat back down
again. Dammit. Glasses! The third time was finally the charm.

A lot of different definitions of ADHD exist, but I wanted to start with
this simple example to give you a taste of my daily reality. ADHD is living
your life having to do everything three times instead of once. Three tries
to get your glasses. Three tries to finish your laundry. Three tries to get
dinner started. As you can imagine, this is exhausting at best and demor-
alizing at worst. Occasionally, if I'm not too tired or stressed, I can get
things done on the first or second try. Most of the time, though, it takes

me multiple tries to accomplish the simplest tasks. I've rarely entered a room to get or do something and remembered what I was there to get or do on the first try. Take a moment to let that sink in and imagine how that constant backtracking would impact your own life and energy. The flip side of this challenge is that these constant "side quests" are where I often discover the serendipitous joys in life, make connections to new and surprising ideas, and find unexpected creative solutions to life's challenges. In a mind thrown wide open to the world, anything is possible.

With this lived experience in mind, let's now consider three definitions of ADHD: the first from the *DSM,* the second my own, and the third from my favorite TikTok star and doctor, Ned Hallowell.

The *DSM* Definition

According to the *DSM,* the *Diagnostic and Statistical Manual of Mental Disorders*, ADHD stands for Attention Deficit Hyperactivity Disorder. Worst name ever. Hard to say ten times fast. Zero out of five stars. But alas, this is the diagnostic title in the manual relied upon by most doctors and other clinicians in the United States. I use the acronym "ADHD" throughout this book for simplicity's sake. It's the term that most of us know and use. That said, I avoid using the full *DSM* diagnostic title whenever possible because, as you'll learn in this book, it's both inaccurate and harmful. When you know better, you do better, and I think we're absolutely at the point where we can do better than what the *DSM* has to say about ADHD.

The *DSM* is a diagnostic tool doctors and clinicians use. They currently work with the fifth edition. Fun fact about the *DSM:* it contained the diagnosis of "hysteria" for women until as recently as 1980.[1] (A full critique of the *DSM* is beyond the scope of this book and has been well-covered elsewhere.[2]) I was diagnosed with ADHD by a psychologist using the *DSM*. This diagnosis brought me greater self-awareness, improved well-being, appropriate care, and a sense of community. At best, the *DSM* is a double-edged sword. At worst, I call to mind the words of Jerry Garcia: the lesser of two evils is still evil. I invite you to think critically about the existence of the *DSM,* who benefits from it, and who is harmed by it. Think creatively about alternatives to the *DSM* that we might imagine into existence in the future.

Briefly, the *DSM* defines ADHD as "A persistent pattern of inattention and/or hyperactivity-impulsivity that interferes with functioning or development."[3] The *DSM* includes a lengthy list of diagnostic criteria that clinicians use to decide whether ADHD is at play. Without going too far off track here by detailing all those criteria, in the list of a couple dozen "symptoms," not one positive aspect of ADHD is mentioned. The *DSM* uses a purely deficit-based approach, which is true of all diagnostic criteria in the manual. This does not mean that individual clinicians won't use strengths-based approaches with their ADHD clients. However, the fact that the diagnostic criteria are deficit based is not up for debate. Well-intentioned *DSM* fans have argued with me that the *DSM*'s diagnosis and criteria are not deficit based, even though the word "deficit" is part of the name of the diagnosis. In this book, we reject any purely deficit-based models and instead opt for a strengths-based, challenge-aware approach.

But First, Attention

It occurred to me recently that before I define ADHD in more detail for you, including my own lived experience and alternative definitions, it's worth defining "attention" first. It's a word we throw around quite a bit, particularly in education, and as I always say to my students, "What you mean by that word and what I mean by it might be two completely different things." We are told and tell our students to "pay attention." What does that actually mean? If we're going to label someone as deficient in attention (I'm not going to do that, but you'll learn that many are doing that), we sure as heck better know what we mean by the word "attention."

The current definition of attention from the *APA (American Psychological Association) Dictionary of Psychology* is:

> *n.* a state in which cognitive resources are focused on certain aspects of the environment rather than on others and the central nervous system is in a state of readiness to respond to

stimuli. Because it has been presumed that human beings do not have an infinite capacity to attend to everything—focusing on certain items at the expense of others—much of the research in this field has been devoted to discerning which factors influence attention and to understanding the neural mechanisms that are involved in the selective processing of information. For example, past experience affects perceptual experience (we notice things that have meaning for us), and some activities (e.g., reading) require conscious participation (i.e., voluntary attention). However, attention can also be captured (i.e., directed involuntarily) by qualities of stimuli in the environment, such as intensity, movement, repetition, contrast, and novelty.[4]

Well, that's a mouthful! Let's translate this into plain language. One of the main jobs of your nervous system is to respond to stimuli (internal or external events or circumstances), and various factors affect its ability to do so. An obvious example is when you're asleep, it's difficult to direct your attention to your professor's lecture. If you've had a difficult day at work and come home with a snarky attitude and a headache, your nervous system is less likely to gather the cognitive resources to help you listen to your spouse's story about his day at work. If you're in a burning building, that external stimuli would take precedence over less threatening concerns like making a dentist appointment. In short, we all have cognitive resources, and various factors influence how well we can direct those resources.

I love to complement traditional dictionary definitions with the *Online Etymology Dictionary (OED)*, which details word origins. Here's a peek at their definition of "attention": "late 14c., *attencioun*, 'a giving heed, active direction of the mind upon some object or topic,' from Old French *attencion* and directly from Latin *attentionem* (nominative *attentio*) 'attention, attentiveness,' noun of action from past-participle stem of *attendere* 'give heed to,' literally 'to stretch toward,' from *ad* 'to, toward' (see ad-) + *tendere* 'stretch' (from PIE root *ten- 'to stretch')."[5]

Someone in the late fourteenth century would actively direct their mind, perhaps, to tending oxen, gathering wood for the fire, or possibly worrying over whether they'd fall victim to the plague. This idea of giving heed to something, specifically to stretch or reach out toward it, is quite interesting. It "embodies" the concept of attention, shifting the home base of attention from mind to body. Through this lens, we can recognize that the idea that attention is purely mental is not something written in stone but rather an idea that has evolved and shifted over time. That realization can remind us to be flexible and open as we continue to explore attention and ADHD.

What both the APA and OED definitions have in common is a distinct element of "this, not that" in the work of attention. There is also an agreement that choosing to "give heed" to one thing over another thing is both possible and valuable. This idea that one thing is more valuable than another is not a fact but a belief. In the book *The Open-Focus Brain: Harnessing the Power of Attention to Heal Mind and Body,* authors Les Fehmi and Jim Robbins challenge long-accepted beliefs about attention. They argue that Western, modern culture has elevated a single-pointed type of attention as the only way to navigate the world. The idea that this way is necessary is not only incorrect but has also done immense physical and mental harm to those who adhere to that philosophy.[6]

According to Fehmi and Robbins, "In our culture, we do not recognize or make full use of the full repertoire of attention styles. Few of us are consciously aware that there are different styles of attention, each with different qualities and each suited to different kinds of tasks."[7] Many folks I encounter see attention as a black and white switch that they either turn on and off, but it's much more nuanced and complex, and ADHDers are at the forefront of unique expressions of attention.

Authors like Cal Newport and Jenny Odell have previously critiqued the connection between attention and productivity culture within capitalist systems.[8] I would argue that the single-pointed type of attention Fehmi and Robbins want us to expand beyond is rooted in capitalism, which treats a focused worker as a good, productive worker. Our brains are much bigger and better than that limited view, though.

There are many ways of knowing, being, and utilizing our cognitive resources. Throughout history and present times, many people cultivate more open states of attention where they simultaneously take in all aspects of what they see in their environments as well as how their bodies and spirits feel. In other words, they are paying attention not to a single point, but to the entirety of their experience. Fehmi and Robbins argue that the single-pointed type of paying attention communicates to our nervous systems that we are in battle or under threat. Therefore, that perspective drains our resources and exhausts us when used as our only perspective. They conclude that practicing open awareness (open attention) instead signals to our nervous systems a state of safety and equanimity.

In short, the idea that attention is ideally single-pointed and that ADHD is a deficit of that single-pointed attention is, again, just an idea. Someone thought it up, told a friend, they bought into it, told another friend, and so on. Other ideas and options exist for directing, guiding, or expanding our attention toward the worlds in and around us. Perhaps ADHD is, at least in part, a more egalitarian approach to attention, and its so-called symptoms are pushback from the system—capitalism—that demands single-pointed attention on the job/production at hand.

This is not to say that single-pointed attention is worthless. That type of attention would allow someone to make a dental cleaning appointment, attend that dental cleaning appointment, and then make another dental cleaning appointment in six months. This sort of "adulting" task is a very typical challenge for ADHDers, and it's also true that taking care of ourselves obviously has value. That said, it's a stretch to say this is the only way to express one's attention. It's not. I am living proof of that. Millions of ADHDers are living proof of that. Billions of humans throughout history who practiced more open and fluid ways of being in relationship with the cognitive resources in their minds were living proof of that.

Attention speaks to how we direct our cognitive resources, and at least two possible guiding paradigms exist for that direction—one more fixed and one more open—with a seemingly infinite number of options in between. Keep these ideas in mind as we further refine and explore what it means to walk through this world with what is called "ADHD." Question your belief that a single-pointed attention style is the only type and is always beneficial. Remember, ideas are just something someone thought up and told someone else. We can think up new ideas when the old ones no longer serve us (if they ever served us at all.)

My ADHD Definition

The *DSM* defines ADHD as a disorder and a deficit. I define ADHD as a neurotype. By this, I mean that some human beings share certain neurological traits such as high levels of creativity, a strong orientation for justice, impulsivity, executive function constraints, a very limited working memory capacity, time blindness, or infectious joy for their favorite subject of hyperfocus.

ADHD is also a name. We could call the folks with these shared traits "The Fantastics." We could call them "Beautiful Brainy Besties." ADHD is a name that some people (some of the creators of the *DSM*) decided to call other people who share a bunch of neurological traits. I've heard people use the names "tornado person," "neurospicy," and "squiggly brain" as well. These are examples of names born not from the *DSM* but from our lived experiences. The best use of names is to connect us to our kin.

Finally, ADHD is a community; some folks with the traits I mentioned like to connect with other similar people for support and camaraderie. The community of ADHDers that I've found since diagnosis has been part of my healing, and you'll hear from several members of that community in this book.

The traits that people with the ADHD neurotype hold in common are a combination of strengths and challenges. If you view us only through the lens of our strengths (the "ADHD is a superpower!" crowd), you dehumanize us and miss half of our story. If you view us only through the lens of our challenges (the deficit-based crowd who wants to fix and save us), you miss the other half of our story. We are complex human beings, just like everyone else.

In summary, I currently define ADHD as the name we use to describe a neurotype that joins together a community of people who share certain traits, which you'll learn more about in the coming chapters. These traits present people with a combination of strengths and challenges.

A Unique Kind of Mind

Let's now turn to one final definition of ADHD. This definition is from one of my all-time favorite ADHD experts: Edward Hallowell, a medical doctor who also happens to have ADHD. I first encountered Dr. Hallowell in the year after my ADHD diagnosis, when I was confused, lonely, and searching for answers. I started watching his "Ned Talks" on TikTok, where he'd offer short videos with advice on living with ADHD.

Do you want to know the best part of his videos? It wasn't his expert advice on living with ADHD or how he translated neuroscientific principles into simple language. Instead, it was how he always started his videos by saying, "People with ADHD, people like me . . ." Whenever I heard this well-respected doctor and author say, "people like me," broken pieces of me would mend themselves back together. We'll talk later in the book about how important it is to center ADHDers' voices in conversations about us (i.e., nothing about us without us[9]) and how shame is one of the most prominent symptoms of ADHD (and not mentioned at all in the *DSM*!). I didn't name it as such at the time, but Dr. Hallowell's public declarations about ADHD helped bring my shame to the surface, into the light, where it could not survive for long.

Dr. Hallowell, along with his frequent co-author John Ratey (another MD with ADHD), has written one of my favorite books on ADHD, *ADHD 2.0: New Science and Essential Strategies for Thriving with Distraction from Childhood through Adulthood*. When people ask me what book they should read first to educate themselves or their kids about ADHD, this is the book I recommend. Let's add Hallowell and Ratey's definition of ADHD to our definition toolbox: "'ADHD' is a term that describes a way of being in the world. It is neither entirely a disorder nor entirely an asset. It is an array of traits specific to a unique kind of mind."[10] These doctors have also created an analogy for ADHD that resonates with many who live with this unique kind of mind: "A person with ADHD has the power of a Ferrari engine but with bicycle-strength brakes. The mismatch of engine power to braking capability causes problems. Strengthening one's brakes is the name of the game."[11]

I invite you to take a moment and read over these three definitions again: the *DSM*'s, mine, and Hallowell and Ratey's. How does each feel? How does each feel to explain to a child or a newly diagnosed adult? Which of these definitions would be most helpful in empowering ADHDers to acknowledge their challenges while celebrating their strengths? Your job is to hold these three definitions in mind and heart while recognizing that our knowledge of ADHD is rapidly evolving, due in large part to the work of ADHDers to make our voices heard. Keep learning. Keep listening. Seek out a diverse array of voices and ADHDers. How do they define their ADHD? How can you support them using a strengths-based, challenge-aware approach to teaching and learning?

Variable Attention Stimulus Trait (VAST)

Not only is Attention Deficit Hyperactivity Disorder a terrible name for our neurotype because it's blatantly deficit based, but it's also a terrible name because ADHDers do not have a deficit of attention. I repeat, we do *not* have a deficit of attention. If we define attention as directing our minds, bodies, and spirits toward something that compels our interest, ADHDers actually have an abundance of attention, not a deficit at all.

Hallowell and Ratey advise that we think beyond the *DSM* name of ADHD into the possibility of a new name for this neurotype that more accurately depicts its realities. If ADHD isn't accurate, what might we use instead? One option is VAST, the alternative name and model they propose, which stands for Variable Attention Stimulus Trait.[12]

VAST, they argue, more accurately captures the fact that ADHDers actually have an abundance of attention, not a shortage. "This is why the word 'deficit' in the name of our condition is such a misnomer," they write. "In fact, we do not suffer from a deficit of attention. Just the opposite. We've got an overabundance of attention, more attention than we can cope with; our constant challenge is to control it."[13] It's as if our brains are directing our attention to everything we're experiencing. Fun fact: The writers of the multiple Oscar-winning movie *Everything Everywhere All at Once* revealed that they wrote the film with the idea that Michelle Yeoh's character, Evelyn, was living with undiagnosed ADHD.[14]

Our attention is on everything. It's everywhere. It's all happening in our brains all at once.

The VAST model is important because it helps to attack the inaccurate and harmful stereotype that ADHDers are attention deficient. Not only is that idea used to shame and belittle us, but it also ignores one of our greatest strengths—the vastness of our interests and attention—which you can capitalize on in your teaching to better support your students.

Last year, I attended an online conference on second brains (we'll learn more about this fascinating concept later). The conference was a great example of neurodiversity. Lots of neurodivergent people of all types engaged and had fun with our neurotypical friends. While the conference itself wasn't geared toward ADHD specifically, a couple of sessions focused on this topic. I sought those out and had a grand old time hanging with a ton of my fellow ADHDers. I rarely get to participate in a learning experience with a lot of ADHDers openly identifying as ADHD.

At the end of one of these sessions, the conference moderator came on camera and told us that she'd never attended such an engaged online session. The ADHDers had brought an exceptionally high amount of engagement to this learning experience. This is one of our greatest strengths. Most faculty I work with tell me they are eager to boost student engagement in their courses. ADHDers, if celebrated and supported, can help you do just that.

Do you know those little "Grow a Giant Dinosaur from This Tiny Egg" toys you can get at dollar stores? The ones where you put the little egg in water, and it expands to ten times its size? ADHD students are a lot like that. Given the right conditions, our engagement can turn your classroom into a giant dinosaur. Okay, not exactly. But the more I seek out spaces built for and by ADHDers, the more I realize that one of ADHDers' many strengths is our ability to transform the energy of learning spaces with curiosity, excitement, and engagement.

With specific design and teaching choices that celebrate both the strengths and challenges of the VAST ADHD brain, these students can infuse your classrooms with engagement, joie de vivre, and creativity. It's time we stop thinking of ADHDers as if they lack attention and start realizing that their abundance of attention is an asset to every learner in our classrooms. We'll dive into specific strategies later in the book, but the invitation here is to first work on dropping the idea that your ADHDers have a deficit of attention and start recognizing that they have an abundance of attention.

What challenges does that create for ADHDers? What strengths can we celebrate with them? How might this fundamental shift in how we think and feel about ADHD benefit our ADHD students, all students, and you, my fellow educators?

The Open Neurotype (ON)

Building upon the three existing definitions of ADHD I shared with you earlier and the VAST concept from Hallowell and Ratey, I've developed a proposal for a new name that more accurately captures the reality of ADHD. My entry into the "New ADHD Name Contest" is ON, or the Open Neurotype.

The Open Neurotype name and model would allow us to combine the most cutting-edge research and theories on ADHD with the lived reality of those actually experiencing it. For you as educators, approaching your learners with the more accurate, strengths-based ON in mind, rather than the inaccurate, deficit-based name ADHD, would set both you and your students up for success.

The poor fit of the ADHD misnomer has been increasingly challenging for me throughout this writing process. The more I researched the ADHD mind and talked to my fellow ADHDers, the more I realized that we absolutely need new words, terms, and visions to explain this complex experience of living with ADHD.

The breakthrough that got me through being stuck in the old deficit-based ADHD mindset came when I stumbled upon an article by Mads Dengsø, a doctoral student in philosophy with a focus on mind and cognitive science at the University of Wollongong in Australia, entitled "Wrong Brains at the Wrong Time? Understanding ADHD Through the Diachronic Constitution of Minds."[15] After underlining nearly the entire article and completely rethinking my understanding of ADHD and this book, I contacted Dengsø about his work. He identifies as neurotypical but has long been interested in temporal aspects of cognition and the interactions between technology and the mind as a unique aspect of the human species. He began to get curious about ADHD, not as a deficit, but as what he calls "an alternative form of developmental trajectory."

One reason Dengsø's work caught my attention is that I had been deeply engaged with the literature on ADHD, which primarily views it as a disorder of the executive function system of the brain. This body of literature is most commonly associated with Russell Barkley, whose work has faced heavy criticism for being oblivious and ableist. I agree with that criticism, and it's also true that I cannot deny that my executive functions (e.g., time management, decision-making, and organization) are a constant challenge in my professional, personal, and creative life.

Dengsø critiques this heavy focus on executive functions, acknowledging that to many, it has probably felt like "the surest stick" to explain the ADHD mind. Still, he sees this stick as incredibly reductionist, failing to capture "both the complexity and the nature of ADHD." Dengsø's article, the one that made me rethink my understanding of ADHD and this book, has instead focused on the nature and complexity of this condition. Dengsø is not alone in that concern, as the hyperfocus on ADHD as a dysfunction of the executive function system of the brain, rooted in the prefrontal cortex, is increasingly being called into question (as if we ADHDers could ever be confined to one system in the brain!).[16]

I will note that Dengsø's article is a theoretical analysis, not empirical research. That said, in the next section, we'll explore lots of empirical research on creativity and divergent thinking that meshes well with Dengsø's theory on ADHD. I hope many researchers will be inspired to use the Open Neurotype model to perform research in the future.

The most important part of Dengsø's theory is his approach to ADHD. He points out that lower cortical thickness or maturity is a foundational feature of ADHD that leads to our strengths and challenges. I asked him to put this idea into plain language.

> I think one way that I think about it is that if you have several creeks running down the side of a hill, and the banks are more or less pronounced, you might get more or less spillover. That

spillover would be conducive to some forms of interactions. For example, if we think about how neurons that fire together wire together, neural networks that fire together might create, for people with ADHD, a heightened tendency for certain streams to intersect with others, which from a neurological perspective could be conducive to things like thinking outside of the box, getting new ideas, and heightened imagination. But it might also be less conducive to things like keeping a very linear focus over long times.[17]

Dengsø's explanation of ADHD suggests that we have a unique cognitive openness that results in predictable strengths and challenges. His theory gains support from consistent findings showing that the brains of people with ADHD differ in many ways from those of non-ADHD individuals, particularly in terms of lower cortical thickness and maturity.[18]

Another example to help folks understand the possible implications of cortical thickness, maturity, and rigidity as it relates to ADHD is to imagine the adults' table and the kids' table at your recent family holiday dinner. One could imagine the adults following the rules (maturity) and eating in a proper or more constrained manner. Meanwhile, at the kids' table, they're making faces at each other, hiding food under the table, and giggling hysterically (what we define as immaturity). The working theory here is that cortical thickness equals cortical maturity equals greater rigidity in thinking, feeling, and behavior in neurotypical brains and people with higher levels of cortical thickness. In ADHDers, perhaps one aspect of the ADHD nervous system is that our brains, for whatever reason (possibly childhood trauma), our brains have less cortical thickness. This allows less rigidity in thinking, feeling, and behavior, as well as heightened connectivity between various brain systems and ADHDers' signature creativity. Neither of these brain styles are right or wrong, just as neither the adults' table or kids' table is right or wrong. That said, when given the choice, even in midlife, I always opt to sit at the kids' table at parties. It's way more fun.

The coin of this more open and flexible neurotype has two sides. Open hearts allow us to feel love and joy, but they also mean we're vulnerable to heartache. Open minds are no different. Cognitive flexibility protects us from rigid thinking that blocks us from new ideas and experiences. It is likely the source of ADHDers' creative talents (much more on creativity later), but that openness is also why it took me three tries to successfully direct my brain to pick up my reading glasses, as I mentioned at the start of the chapter. My open mind was taking in elements of the environment that a more closed or neurotypical brain would've filtered out.

Neither an open nor closed neurotype is good or bad. Both open and closed neurotypes hold inherent human dignity and are valuable ways of experiencing the world. Further, while I used the terms "open" and "closed" neurotype and "neurodivergent" or "neurotypical" for simplicity's sake, it's likely that these concepts are not hard binaries. Rather, they represent a fluctuating field of possibility of what our brains can do really well and what they don't do so well without necessary support. In truth, the more I do this work, the less sure I am about whether a neurotypical brain style actually exists, though I am certain that there are people who align themselves with society's neurotypical expectations. Use the open and closed neurotype model as another way to think, feel, and talk about neurodiversity, that is, the vast variety of neurotypes existing across the human species.

Our job as educators is to design and teach for all neurotypes. I hope that someday in the future, perhaps when my son's generation is writing books about ADHD, this concept of ON will help to open more minds to the realities of ADHD.

ADHD as a Disability

Now that you have three definitions of ADHD, let's answer another critical question: Is ADHD a disability? This question often goes unspoken or whispered in many discussions about ADHD, so let's bring it to the surface together.

The first answer is that it depends on whom you ask. If you ask me whether I consider my ADHD a disability, the answer is, "LOL. Yes. Obviously." I loosely define a disability as a physical or mental condition that limits and challenges our activities of daily living (ADLs). In the example I provided at the start of this chapter, you can see how simple tasks take me three times as long as someone without ADHD. That is one of many ways that ADHD affects my ADLs. Full disclosure, though: It took me a year in therapy and in community with my ADHD peers to start accepting and recognizing my ADHD as a disability. Ableism is real, and all of us internalize it, including those with disabilities. It's only after four years of exploration, four years of digging at that internalized ableism around ADHD, that I'm able to laugh at the idea that I'm not disabled by it because it feels so obvious that I am.

I once asked a friend who has an ADHD diagnosis if she sees herself as disabled. She responded, "Oh no. I don't think I'd qualify, and I want to work." In her view, the government decides someone's disability status. If you qualify to receive disability benefits, you are disabled. If not, you aren't. I disagree with this, but I share this story because I think this is a common view of how disability should be defined.

As I mentioned earlier, ADHD is not only a condition but also a community. That, too, is part of my personal definition of disability. Identifying as disabled connects me to other people who are facing the same challenges without adequate support, and in that community, there is immense power. In chapter 4, we'll learn a bit more about the model of disability justice, but for now, the answer to whether ADHD is a disability is that it's not a yes or no question. Like beauty, it is in the eye of the beholder. Don't assume that students with ADHD identify as disabled, but also make sure an opening exists for people to name and claim that valuable identity. In the meantime, I think it's important for all of us to continue to create space for people to understand disability as much more than whether or not the government deems us worthy of access to disability benefits. In chapter 4, we'll discuss the social model of disability in more detail. For now, keep in mind that disability is perhaps not what you've been taught it is, not a deficit at all, but a community and a way of being in the world.

The Many Faces of ADHD

Which part of me is my ADHD, and which part is my chronic physical illness, a disorder of the autonomic nervous system called POTS (postural orthostatic tachycardia syndrome)? I can't tell you. No one can. But both are a part of me. Both come with a combination of strengths and challenges. They're all mixed up inside of me, along with other aspects of my identity, including my race, class, gender, and sexual identity. They combine to influence how others perceive and treat me and how I perceive and treat myself. It makes sense, doesn't it, to say that we aren't one thing or another, but a combination of our experiences and identities? And since people built all the systems in which we study, work, and live, doesn't it also make sense that these complex identities will interact with our power structures and systems in specific ways? It makes perfect sense to me. What I just wrote is also known as intersectionality,[19] a concept I was lucky to have learned in my undergraduate women's studies courses that helps me more accurately engage with reality.

Defining ADHD is tricky for a lot of reasons. By nature, we ADHDers love defying explanation. Another reason it's hard to define ADHD is that it's always mixed up with other aspects of our identities. Three interviewees I spoke to for this book identified as Black women and Asian American women. All three told me that race was incredibly salient for them in relation to their ADHD.

Kat Stephens-Peace is an assistant professor of higher education at Oakland University in Rochester, Michigan, where she received her formal ADHD diagnosis during her doctoral studies. Her dissertation looked at the experiences of Black women with ADHD, a group with which she identifies, combining her research with her lived experience.[20]

"Who is the face of ADHD?" she asked me in our interview. "ADHD shouldn't be divorced from other markers of identity. Race, gender, class, migration status—all of those things make it more complicated."

I invite you to ask yourself Kat's question. Who is the face of ADHD for you? Close your eyes. Whose face do you picture when you hear the words ADHD? How old are they? What race and gender? And from there, I invite you to notice, behind that vision, a sea of faces from every walk of life, people whose identities are also all mixed up with their ADHD. Some identities protect them from ADHD's greatest challenges, while others make access to support for ADHD much harder. Intersectionality reminds us to see all the faces, to make space for all the stories, and to work to provide everyone with the support they need to thrive. As you read this book, written by a middle-class, cisgender white woman, remember that I am only one face and only one story of many.

Courtney Sobers is an associate professor of chemistry at Rutgers University. She spoke to me about her experiences, like Kat's and mine, of living with ADHD for most of her life and receiving a later-in-life diagnosis. "I come into it as a Black woman," she said. "We don't get to be ditzy or disruptive. It's just like there's something wrong with you."[21]

It is also vitally important, now more than ever, that we recognize and support the experience of trans ADHDers. As I write this, the trans community in the United States is under attack from our government. Their human rights to life, liberty, and the pursuit of happiness are under attack. Trans ADHDers are experiencing these world events while also trying to manage the daily challenges of life with ADHD. My words fail me. There are no words for how deeply unacceptable this is in a supposedly free society. As we work to do better for all ADHDers, I ask you, my readers, to continue to seek out the voices of trans ADHDers and support our fellow human beings in the fight for justice. Additionally, a recent systematic review of the literature on ADHD found a shocking (though unfortunately not surprising) dearth of attention to trans ADHDers. "Since 2014, 17 articles have been published on the TGD/ADHD nexus."[22] For those of you who invest some of your time and energy in empirical research, this is a call to action.

Now that ADHDers are bringing our experiences into the mainstream, and as more of us access a diagnosis or self-diagnosis so that we can get correct care and join in community, we must remember that the ADHD experience is not the same for all of us. Throughout the writing of this book, I've felt in my bones that we ADHDers and other neurodivergent folks are creating a pivotal shift, a shift where our voices, not the voices of non-ADHDers who want to degrade and/or "fix" us, will lead this movement. I feel just as deeply that we must ensure that *all* of our stories are told and represented. We didn't come this far to do this halfway. If you raise your hand to ask for the inclusion of ADHDers, make sure you also ask for that group of ADHDers to be diverse in terms of other identities, including but not limited to race, class, and gender. We must have working definitions of ADHD to help us understand it and provide appropriate support in and out of the classroom. It's equally important that those definitions don't close us off to viewing the many faces of ADHD.

AuDHD

As we continue to dismantle the stigma of ADHD with our brave voices, awareness of ADHD is growing exponentially. I would argue that the past three years have seen more development in ADHD awareness than the previous thirty. One of those rapid developments is the connection between ADHD and autism, another neurotype and identity that has long been misunderstood and poorly supported. People with autism have been harmed and abused. Autistic folks are speaking up, researching and supporting their own community, and dismantling the legacy of centuries of abuse. As with ADHD, our knowledge of autism is rapidly evolving.

One of the discoveries emerging from this process is the overlap between ADHD and autism, with many people now receiving or claiming a dual diagnosis known as AuDHD. Before 2013, according to the *DSM*, one could not be diagnosed with both autism and ADHD at the same time.[23] Clinicians told us that these two diagnoses could not coexist. Today, just about a decade later, researchers and clinicians tell us that perhaps up to 70% of folks with autism also have ADHD.[24] First, this is yet another reason to take the *DSM* with a healthy grain of salt. Second, people are exploring the idea that ADHD and autism might actually be different manifestations of the same neurotype. That's a big, exciting, scary conversation we can expect to hear more about in the future.

My favorite description of AuDHD is that it's like trying to drive your car with the brake and the gas pedal pressed to the floor. Fun times! The autistic part of the nervous system acts as the brake, managing sensory overwhelm through robust routines. The ADHD part of the nervous system is the gas pedal, throwing people with vigor into the great variety of life. As you might imagine, AuDHDers experience inner turmoil as they face these competing needs and desires.

Most importantly, we can marvel at the tenacity of folks with AuDHD and their different kind of minds. What lessons do AuDHDers hold for our world? How can we best support them in living their best lives? How can we design systems that release AuDHD learners from constantly having to be quite so tenacious? While this book focuses solely on ADHD, please keep AuDHD on your radar. I predict the next twenty years will be momentous for AuDHD as our definitions and understanding evolve, led by ADHDers, autistics, and AuDHDers.

You, too, have evolved, having arrived at the end of this chapter on ADHD definitions. Take a minute to take stock of what you've just read and learned. Has your understanding of ADHD shifted since you began reading? Did you root out any stubborn and unhelpful ableism that let you view ADHD through a deficit-based lens? I hope you feel excited and curious about all the possibilities for teaching and learning in partnership with our amazing ADHD learners.

Summary

Let's recap chapter 1. You'll find these brief summaries at the end of each chapter. In this chapter, we learned about:

- How the *DSM* definition of ADHD is deficit based and why it is worthy of critique
- Types of attention, including open awareness and single-pointed attention
- My definition of ADHD: a neurotype, name, and community
- Drs. Hallowell and Ratey's description of ADHD as a unique kind of mind like a racecar brain with bicycle brakes
- The VAST (variable attention stimulus trait) alternative definition of ADHD

- My Open Neurotype (ON) alternative definition of ADHD
- Thoughts on whether or not to consider ADHD a disability
- Using intersectionality to consider how all our identities co-exist with ADHD
- Growing awareness of AuDHD, a combination of autism and ADHD

We've been busy. Now that you have considered several ways we might define ADHD, I hope you are open and committed to letting your definition evolve. In chapter 2, let's get more granular about the types of strengths and challenges that inform the ADHD experience. Understanding these strengths and challenges is critical for your later work designing and teaching for ADHD learners' success.

Chapter Two

ADHDers' Strengths

It is not our differences that divide us. It is our inability to recognize, accept, and celebrate those differences.

—Audre Lorde

The other day, I was walking around the house, mumbling to myself about having a chapter of this book to edit. My husband overheard me. "I can't believe you've written another book. I don't understand *when* you wrote another book."

My explanation: "ADHD."

Remember Hallowell and Ratey's description of a race car engine with bicycle brakes? That's how I wrote this book. My ADHD powers me to create in many different ways on many different topics. While ADHD challenges me most minutes of every day, its strengths are undeniable, and it is from this position of strength that this chapter begins and that your work with ADHD learners must begin.

Starting with strengths should never ignore challenges. In other words, the answer to an ADHD learner struggling to meet a deadline should never be, "But you're so creative! Why don't you create a solution to meet that deadline?" That's not strengths based; it's toxic positivity. A strengths-based approach acknowledges that in each of us, including

ADHDers, immense strength, capability, and intelligence exists that we can draw upon to face life's challenges. Those strengths naturally blossom under the light of correct care and supportive conditions. What that might look like in the above example would be reassuring the learner that their experience is common, first and foremost, humanizing their frustrations. I often tell my students, "That's very human of you." Sometimes, we forget that our struggles are human struggles and that in naming them, we aren't separating ourselves from the human species but more intentionally connecting to them. Rather than, "But you're so creative," which can discount the challenge, try "And I know you can figure this out. We can figure it out together." Using "and" holds space for strengths and challenges, and "but" discounts those challenges.

From this place of balance, we can offer resources. The support resource is you, who can sit down with the student and "backward design" a plan to complete the assignment before the deadline. Depending on your institution's resources, this might mean connecting them to a peer tutor, academic advisor, or academic coach. If this is an issue your students repeatedly face, perhaps you'll want to create a video with some support resources that you can easily reuse with multiple students.

Our job as educators is to co-create these successful conditions with our students. You are not attempting to diagnose, treat, or cure anyone's ADHD or other mental or physical illness. That's not your job; you're not qualified to do it, and your students have not agreed to have you take on that role. Again, our job is to co-create learning conditions where all our learners can learn, grow, and succeed. This chapter will help motivate you to create those conditions by exploring common ADHD strengths.

Neuroplasticity

Neuroplasticity is one of my favorite things in the world, and it's where we'll start as we consider the strengths of our ADHD learners. Neuroplasticity sits at the intersection of spirituality and science. It answers the question, "Can people change?" with a resounding "Yes!" We can learn new things. We can unlearn old habits or ideas that no longer serve us and the world. In short, neuroplasticity means that our brains are not fixed entities. Instead, they are plastic. Not plastic as in synthetic, cheap, or poisonous. The good kind of plastic: flexible, adaptable, and strong.

For a long time, the prevailing belief was that our brains were fixed. You got this type of brain or that type of brain, and you were stuck with it till death did you part. You were born "smart" or "dumb," and that was that. We now know that this couldn't be further from the truth.

Tracey Tokuhama-Espinosa defines neuroplasticity as "the brain's ability to change—for better or worse—throughout life. Plasticity—the reorganization of connections in the brain—is perhaps the most fascinating aspect of the human brain to teachers because it is the epitome of learning."[1] The epitome of learning!

Most people recognize that our behaviors can shape every part of our bodies. If I exercise five days per week for a year, my body will change in predictable ways. If I were to become sedentary for the following year, my body would change in other predictable ways again. Certainly, as I move through my mid-forties, I can see all sorts of changes to my face and body on a nearly constant basis, many of which lead me to dramatically exclaim, "What in the heck is happening to me?" In short, we accept that our bodies are in a state of constant flux, some of which is within our control, but the brain still appears to many folks to be a closed system, fixed forever and inaccessible to our manipulation. It's not. Our brain, in many ways, is a lot like a muscle. The parts of it that we "exercise" will quite predictably change. That malleability is true for every human, including folks with ADHD.

Even if folks are willing to recognize that brains and people can change, many still believe that the same scientific rule does not apply to ADHDers and other folks with mental illnesses and disabilities. "We can change, but they're stuck like that," they mutter. Wrong. Scientifically, morally, and personally wrong. Some would argue that neuroplasticity is one of our greatest strengths as a species and our reason for existence. That strength exists in ADHDers and all neurodivergent people. We can learn. We can unlearn. Period.

A recent study considered the effect of faculty's view on intelligence on their adoption of active learning strategies in the classroom.[2] Active learning strategies provide students with opportunities for action and agency. They are generally considered far more effective than passive learning alternatives such as sitting and listening to lectures. Active learning includes but is not limited to small group collaboration, discussion, problem-based learning, gamification, and peer teaching. This study found that when faculty held incorrect beliefs about intelligence (that it is fixed instead of fluid), they were less likely to adopt active learning strategies in their pedagogy. Faculty who viewed intelligence as fluid were more likely to use effective active learning strategies in their classrooms.

Many people, and many educators, hold fixed views of intelligence about students, but I suspect this view is even more likely in their beliefs about learners with ADHD. Too many believe that if you have ADHD, you're just stuck with this so-called terrible thing, and there's nothing that you or your teachers can do about it. But I have good news for you: ADHDers' brains do not operate outside of the fundamental laws of neuroscience. Yes, our brains are different from our neurotypical peers', but the fundamental principle of neuroplasticity still applies. Our brains, like every other human brain, learn and change.

When I was first diagnosed with ADHD, the psychologist said to me, "ADHD is knowing what needs to be done but not being able to do it." That feeling is widespread among those living with ADHD (sometimes referred to as ADHD paralysis by both ADHDers and clinicians). Still, it shows an inherently flawed understanding of how brains—all brains—work. Neuroplasticity reminds us that every brain, every person, is capable of learning and change. With practice, correct care (which may or may not include medication), support, and environmental/classroom conditions that celebrate our strengths, neuroplasticity means that we have the power to learn new habits and unlearn old ones.

An example of neuroplasticity in action would be a student who doesn't use a planner and struggles to meet class deadlines. Keeping in mind that the ability to meet deadlines is not a moral good, we can also recognize that failure to meet deadlines stands in the way of this student's goals. The fixed view of ADHD says: "Well, she knows she needs to meet deadlines, but she just can't do it." Period. Done. Oh well. Good luck out there. Recognizing that this ADHD student's brain is plastic, just like everyone else's, reminds us that with a combination of challenge and support, perhaps through working with an academic coach, this student could learn how to meet her deadlines better. She could work with caring faculty who celebrate her as a whole person, cheer on her progress, and give her grace when she makes mistakes. Things like finding a planner that's a good fit for our ADHD brains, stickers or other fun tactile elements that give us hits of a pleasure neurotransmitter, other fun rewards, positive praise, and doing things in community can all help ADHDers do the things we want and need to do.

No student or brain is fixed. We are all capable of growing and learning. I would argue that learning is our birthright, the "why" of our existence on this planet. Neuroplasticity is the neuroscientific representation of this birthright and is a strength of all humans, including our ADHD learners.

Variety

We ADHDers love to start things, especially a new creative hobby.

In the past few years, I've started the following hobbies: watercolor painting, mixed media art, gel plate prints, outdoor gardening, building terrariums, indoor plants, sculpture, wheel-thrown pottery, and handbuilt pottery. Between the first and second drafts of this book, I decided to take up French for the first time since my senior year of high school, and also proudly consider being a fan of the TV program *Big Brother* an additional new hobby. There is so much joy and excitement in starting something new, and we ADHDers are a living celebration of the motto, "Variety is the spice of life."

Look at the world around you, around us. Is our world working? Is it really working for the vast majority of people? Is it working for other life forms on this planet? It would seem to me that when scientists are warning that many species have gone extinct or are on the verge of extinction, that's a pretty good sign that things aren't working.

We need new ideas. We need to start and try a variety of new things: new approaches, new schools, new unschools, new higher education pathways, new poetry, new ways to give care, and new relationships with the other life forms on this planet. The old ways have brought us here. I want to try some new ways. I want more than two choices when I vote for president. I want variety.

Your ADHD students are natural champions of variety. Let's celebrate this energy in our courses. Create space for idea generation. Create space for students to think critically (breaking down concepts) and creatively (generating new concepts). Ask your ADHDers to solve problems. Give them space to explore a variety of issues and questions. Let them play outside the often-rigid boxes that education and society create for them. The answers to our world's problems, I suspect, won't be found in those boxes anyway. Educators constantly tell me they want more student engagement. Here you go. Our zest for life and desire for variety can energize your classroom to benefit ADHDers and all learners.

Curiosity

ADHDers are deeply curious about the world around them. Sometimes, we hyperfocus our curiosity on a specific topic; sometimes, it manifests as curiosity about anything that crosses our path.

Recently, my son and I have been watching season 26 of *Big Brother* together. For those not familiar with this reality TV show and game, at a certain point in the season, the "houseguests" who get "evicted" from the show go to what's called "The Jury House." They're sequestered until the end of the game, at which point they'll vote on the winner. This morning, I asked my son what happens when someone wants to leave the jury house. They're obviously not held captive, so what happens if they want to see their family or get a hankering for a late-night Big Mac?

My son said, "You notice some interesting things." I'll choose to take that as a compliment!

I have always been naturally curious, and I'm not alone in that. A recent paper[3] posits that the heightened curiosity among ADHDers might be an evolutionary benefit (i.e., hunters and gatherers who were curious enough to explore their environment would've had an advantage) that is perhaps less advantageous in today's modern society, where we don't need curiosity to head to the grocery store and get our food for the week. In this modern world, the gift and talent of curiosity can get pathologized as distractibility. The good news is that we have also evolved to a point where we can choose to reject pathology paradigms and instead think more critically and creatively about respecting people's inherent differences using the neurodiversity paradigm.

You can help your ADHDers express their natural curiosity by giving them chances to ask questions, jot down the interesting things they observe in their environments, and marvel at all the textures of life that constantly surround them. Again, educators want engagement, and ADHDers have plenty to share. Some of us ADHDers are ready to shine our creativity into your classrooms and the world. Others will benefit from your repeated invitations to help them trust their creative talents. In chapter 8, you'll find an entire chapter dedicated to celebrating creativity, a close cousin of our naturally curious minds.

Divergence

In addition to our plastic brains, spicy variety, and high levels of curiosity, we ADHDers often take chances. We are willing to accept the risk of going against the status quo. We don't think, act, or feel within the box that society prescribes. For a long time, particularly with the rise of the *DSM*, that divergence has been used against us, and certainly, when we use it carelessly, it can cause us trouble. But for now, I want you to begin (or continue) thinking about divergence as one of ADHDers' greatest strengths, perhaps a strength that you, too, would like to cultivate or practice.

Mads Dengsø, the philosophy doctoral student and researcher we met earlier in the book, talked to me about the strength of diversity as one of the lenses through which we can consider ADHD. "One of the most important questions of life, and especially of science," Dengsø told me, "is not to do with how we best optimize within preset parameters, but precisely in questioning and thinking outside of preexisting parameters."[4] This is why I hang around people smarter than me: They drop knowledge like this.

Take a minute to think about your teaching. Are you here to get students to work within preset parameters or to think outside those preexisting parameters? In other words, is your work in education dedicated to upholding the status quo or expanding beyond it? I, for one, am here for the latter. I'm here to imagine, design, and create better, more humane, more colorful worlds that are in right relationship with all life on this planet. I'm here, teaching, writing, parenting, and living toward a future where our species learns to respect the laws of life on Earth. I'm here for a higher education that lives up to its name. This obviously requires us to think outside of preexisting parameters.

"Let's say I'm a social system," Dengsø told me, "and I have a problem I need to figure out. I'm much better served with a wider toolbox, even if I don't necessarily use all the tools available. Just having a wider array of resources is inherently strengthening at the ecological level." "When we analyze things at the ecological level," Dengsø continued, "we find that having a wider berth of diversity is actually a performance enhancer."[5]

We're learning this in both beautiful and challenging ways as humans destroy biodiversity in our planet's ecosystems and attack programs that support other types of diversity in our education system. Scientifically speaking, diversity is a strength. Divergence from the norms that led to the frightening possibility of species collapse? Strength. It is time to recognize and listen to the guidance of ADHDers, with our uniquely divergent perspectives.

Take a moment to reflect on how you invite divergence into your classroom. Do students know they can choose the road less traveled? Contradict you? Build something new? How do they know that? We'll get into specific teaching strategies in part II, but for now, take some time to reflect on your mindset about divergence as a starting point.

Creativity

You, like all of us, have learned that ADHD is a deficit. You have learned that people with ADHD are both weak and threatening. You have learned that we need to be fixed and saved.

What if all of that is a lie?

What if ADHDers are the creative experts of our species? What if, instead of being ignored, shamed, fixed, or assimilated, we were meant to lead the human species into a new era, using our creative skills to imagine and create new worlds? Of course, this doesn't negate the challenges we face. It doesn't mean we have superpowers. It is simply choosing to view the reality and totality of our humanity, which includes both strengths and challenges, for the good of us as individuals and for the greater good of our communities and our species.

Anecdotally, most folks I encounter are familiar with the idea that ADHDers often hold creative strengths. Few are aware of the nuances behind these strengths and the research to support them. What we pay attention to grows. This research is compelling, and on a personal level, after months spent in the muck of deficit-based research, when I turned to the research on ADHD and creativity in my writing process, I felt a profound internal shift.

On one hand, I was straight-up mad. Why was I just finding out about this research? Why did I have to root it out myself? Why didn't any of my education training mention it? My psychologist or therapists? Why is this research hidden, and who benefits from that? On the other hand, I felt a deep sense of comfort reading the positive research. Hearing people tell the truth about you after being bombarded with lies is a vindication. And that is our goal here: to tell the truth about the ADHD experience so that we can do a better job teaching and supporting our ADHD learners.

Numerous studies have found that ADHDers, when compared with non-ADHDers, demonstrate higher levels of creativity. Let's look at a breakdown of some of the most important research on this topic:

- Holly White and Priti Shah found that ADHDers scored higher on the "Unusual Uses Test."[6] Participants were asked to list all possible uses for common items (in this case, a bucket and a brick). ADHDers scored higher across the board on fluency, flexibility, and originality. They demonstrated higher divergent thinking (thinking differently) skills and lower convergent thinking (keeping it the same) skills than their non-ADHD counterparts.

- Adolescents with ADHD demonstrate greater creativity than non-ADHD peers. Anna Abraham and colleagues' 2006 study attributed this to a greater attentional focus.[7] You read that right. (Remember, ADHD, or the Open Neurotype, is not a deficit of attention but an abundance of attention). ADHD subjects were better able to think outside the box and demonstrated a greater ability to overcome the constraints of examples provided in the experiment than their non-ADHD peers.

- White and Shah also found that ADHDers have higher overall real-life creative achievements across ten different domains of creativity.[8] This research is important because it shows that ADHDers outperform non-ADHDers in creativity not only in lab settings but also in the real world.

- In Nienke Boot and colleagues' 2017 study, ADHD symptoms, regardless of clinical diagnosis, were associated with higher self-reported creative behavior and publicly recognized creative achievements.[9]

- In a "cell phone task" that asked subjects to come up with ideas for a new type of cell phone marketed to college students, ADHDers scored higher than non-ADHDers on originality, flexibility, and novelty. Researchers attributed the higher flexibility of ADHDers to the "semantic distance" demonstrated on this task. Semantic distance was measured when subjects were given a word and asked to respond with the first word that came to mind. ADHDers tended to provide words that diverged further from the given word. Here, we see more evidence that ADHDers have a greater ability to think beyond constraints than neurotypicals.[10]

- Christa Taylor and team explored the implications of ADHD for college engineering students. They found that employers highly value creativity demonstrated through divergent thinking skills in engineering jobs. However, a significant mismatch exists between the skills taught in engineering courses in higher education and the skills demanded by employers.[11] Engineering students with ADHD demonstrated those sought-after divergent thinking skills at higher rates than their non-ADHD peers but also showed lower levels of academic achievement in engineering courses. The authors concluded that post-secondary engineering programs are missing out on an opportunity to serve ADHD engineering students, the field of engineering, and a society that could benefit from engineers with exceptional levels of divergent thinking.

- ADHD is associated with higher levels of "entrepreneurial mindset" and "entrepreneurial alertness."[12] ADHDers utilize more intuitive and less analytic approaches than their non-ADHD peers. An interesting finding of this study is related to what researchers in the business field call RICH: resource-induced coping heuristic. In short, we could say that RICH represents scrappiness, or the ability to do a lot with a little and to adapt in the face of lack. ADHDers demonstrated higher levels of RICH than their ADHD peers. They creatively figure out a way through any block.

- Finally, in a recent piece for *Scientific American* summarizing her ADHD and creativity research and highlighting her most recent study, White writes:

    ADHD may create difficulties for individuals in many contexts that require focused, sustained attention, such as school, where students are expected to sit still and pay attention. On the other hand, the same distractibility and chaotic mind can give people with ADHD an edge when it comes to creative, original thinking. This new study suggests that ADHD may be especially beneficial when the goal is to create or invent something new without being locked into and constrained by old models or conventions. The innovative, original thinking style of people with ADHD may be a great fit for innovative fields where it's an advantage to be on the cutting edge.[13]

The list above summarizes some of the most compelling research on the connection between ADHD and creativity, and for the sake of brevity, it is only a sample of these findings. In addition to anecdotal reports from both inside and outside the ADHD community, we now have strong evidence that ADHDers do, in fact, possess significantly greater creative skills than non-ADHD counterparts.

Recognition Sensitive Euphoria (RSE)

In *ADHD 2.0*, Hallowell and Ratey describe the intense and sometimes debilitating effects of Rejection Sensitive Dysphoria (RSD), a strong sensitivity to rejection and critical feedback, which we'll learn more about in chapter 3. Since, like me, they use a strengths-based approach, they also flip RSD on its head to consider how providing their ADHDers with appropriate support through recognizing their strengths can powerfully affect our learning and well-being. They describe RSE as ADHDers' "enhanced ability to make constructive use of praise, affirmation, and encouragement. As much as we can get down in the dumps over minute criticism, we can fly high and make good use of even small bits of encouragement and recognition."[14]

In other words, the rejection sensitivity descriptor is only partially accurate, and once again, only half the story. Perhaps it's better to say that ADHDers have increased sensitivity (or, again, responsiveness), period, and that our environment and teaching choices can help or harm our highly responsive learners. Whereas a neurotypical student might operate closer to the center, experiencing mild disappointment from criticism and a small amount of motivation from encouragement, ADHDers are vast and open, remember? Our brains open out toward the extremes, toward agony and ecstasy and the entirety of the human experience. A strengths-based, challenge-aware approach honors the gifts of this sensitivity and makes intentional choices to reduce shame resulting from it.

In a 2009 study of kids and adolescents with ADHD, Gregor Kohls and team explored whether ADHDers experienced both social and nonsocial (monetary) rewards differently than their non-ADHD peers.[15] The ADHDers demonstrated hyperresponsiveness to social rewards. How do you make use of social rewards in your classes? Smiling, nodding, heck, even a good ol' fist pump, are great ways to provide your students with social rewards, and evidence is pointing to ADHDers being particularly ready and willing to receive those rewards.

As an educator, by capitalizing on RSE, you have the option to help your ADHD students relate to their sensitivity in ways that result in a greater sense of agency, a boost to creativity, and a brain left free to focus on learning instead of recovering from shame. Catch your ADHD learners doing something well. Celebrate their strengths. Provide them with evidence that you see them in their totality. This praise will be worth its weight in gold to them.

Self-Reported Strengths of ADHDers

A lot of the information we have on ADHD strengths comes from outside observations or anecdotal reports. Both have value, but it's also important that we center the voices of ADHDers in this conversation. L. M. Schippers and colleagues addressed this problem in a recent study, reported in the article "Associations Between ADHD Traits and Self-Reported Strengths in the General Population."[16]

These researchers found three self-reported strengths that were statistically significantly associated with ADHD traits: hyperfocus, cognitive flexibility, and sensory processing sensitivity. We'll discuss hyperfocus in more detail in chapter 7. Still, in general, hyperfocus is a commonly reported ADHD ability to "lock in" to a task, become deeply engaged, and block out the rest of the world, often for hours at a time. In my early days of writing this manuscript, I sometimes wrote six thousand words a day, and time ceased to exist during those writing days. Cognitive flexibility aligns closely with the Open Neurotype model I presented in chapter 1. ADHDers are more open to possibilities and often make interesting connections between seemingly disparate ideas.

Sensory processing sensitivity as a strength is particularly interesting, and I want to take a moment to note some details on this finding. People often present sensory processing sensitivity as a challenge rather than a strength. Schippers and team distinguished this trait's negative and positive aspects using different subscales. They found that folks in their study with ADHD traits rated themselves high for both: the negative captured "ease of excitation and low sensory threshold," and the positive frame reflected "aesthetic sensitivity."[17]

I relate to this idea of sensory processing sensitivity as both a strength and a challenge. I am extremely sensitive to my environment in too many ways to mention within the constraints of this book. A few things come to mind: I cannot wear anything made of wool or linen. Even writing and reading those words makes my skin crawl. I must always position the seam on the toe of my socks on the top of my foot, never on the bottom. If it's not in the right spot, I can only tolerate it for a second before I rip the socks off my feet. I cannot stand chemical odors and can smell them a mile away. My husband is a cleaner, so we've had our fair share of arguments that start with my asking, "What is that smell?" My husband will say, "I cleaned with bleach, but I had the fan on and windows open, and it was four hours ago." It doesn't matter, I can still smell it.

But again, there are two sides to every ADHD coin. The bad news is that I notice and feel everything. The good news is that I notice and feel everything. I was telling my therapist about something that had recently overwhelmed me, and I commented, "Because, you know . . . I'm so sensitive to everything." I didn't say it with the most positive connotation. She said, "You're very responsive to the world around you." That hit me differently.

The term "sensitive" has been weaponized against many neurodivergent and ADHD folks. Lately, I've been using "responsive" in its place, and I feel that has helped me to see my sensory processing as an actual strength. I'm a very responsive person. That's also why I notice slight shifts in people's behavior that allow me to say, "Hey, I just wanted to tell you I love you today, and I'm really glad you're in my life." My responsiveness to my students helps me to create caring, effective, engaging learning environments. My responsiveness motivates me to finish this book to make the world a better place for all my fellow ADHDers.

These three self-reported strengths of people with ADHD are based on one small, strengths-based study in a sea of deficit-based studies. We need more research like this to help us understand how people with ADHD see themselves, what their strengths are, and how we can design a world that best supports those many strengths.

Summary

Here's a recap of chapter 2, where we explored the strengths of ADHDers.

- Neuroplasticity is a fundamental strength of all humans; our brains constantly change, and we have immense power to shape those changes. That is true for ADHDers as well. ADHDers are capable of learning and growing just like everyone else.
- ADHDers bring the spice to life. We love variety.
- Curiosity is a common ADHD strength. Your ADHDers have lots of questions, so do your best to hold space for those questions, even if you don't have time to answer them.
- Divergence is a paradigmatic, rule-breaking space in which ADHDers excel. People with ADHD have open minds that allow them to see less obvious possibilities.
- ADHDers are tremendously creative individuals with unique minds that can learn, grow, and ideate in interesting and novel ways. They consistently outperform non-ADHD counterparts in both real-world and lab tests of creative ability.
- RSE, or rejection-sensitive euphoria, describes ADHDers' strong response to praise, encouragement, and recognition.
- As always, it's important to center lived experiences. ADHDers self-report strengths that include hyperfocus, cognitive flexibility, and sensory processing sensitivity.

As educators, we can view our ADHD learners as valuable assets to the classroom community and as students who can help fuel engagement in the classroom. The medical model and the accommodations model of education often operate from a space of deficits, so it's up to us to use a strengths-based, challenge-aware approach. Always make sure that you are approaching the question of ADHD from a place that acknowledges the inherent strengths of all ADHDers.

Chapter Three

ADHDers' Challenges

To be human is to be beautifully flawed.

—Eric Wilson

This was a difficult chapter to write, and I want to give you a heads up that it might be a difficult chapter to read, especially if you have ADHD or love someone who does. In particular, I discuss some data on life expectancy for ADHDers, and it's not pretty. However, do note that the worst parts of this data are outcomes for *untreated* ADHD. As I state throughout this book, correct care, support, and community can make all the difference. Please use this data as a loving nudge toward providing that kind of care, advocating for others to receive that care, or seeking it for yourself.

As you read about the challenges people with ADHD face, ask yourself what it would look like to try to fix that challenge not through focusing on individuals but instead through designing and adapting society to meet the needs of ADHDers. Within the social model of disability, we focus first on fixing society to meet the needs of individuals rather than trying to fix individuals to fit into society. By challenging ableism and designing and teaching with the needs of our ADHD learners in mind, we can mitigate the challenges you're about to explore. The biggest challenge that ADHDers face is ableism. Period. By reading this book, you are committing to doing your part to address that.

As I write this, at the age of forty-four, I have just been accepted to my first two juried art shows. It has taken me four and a half decades to claim my identity as an artist and to step joyfully into the art community. I feel different when I'm surrounded by artists, designers, fellow weirdos, and other neurodivergent people than when I'm in rooms full of non-artists, non-weirdos, neurotypical people. I still have ADHD, of course, but it doesn't feel like a curse. Rather, in these "weird" spaces, my ADHD feels like one part of me, a part of me that fuels creativity and a part of me that might just need a hug before it carries on to the next creation. Spaces exist that affirm the experiences of ADHDers and neurodivergent folks. They exist, they are possible, and we can continue to design and redesign more.

In the remainder of this chapter, we will identify common challenges ADHDers face, and together, we will remember to prioritize redesigning systems and spaces over redesigning people.

Minority Stress

As I was editing this book, I had the opportunity to attend the 2024 City University of NY Neurodiversity Conference. The keynote speaker, Monique Botha, is a researcher and professor who studies (and has) autism. The data presented on the realities of the abuse and discrimination experienced by autistic folks are stark and unacceptable. Still, I simultaneously felt immense hope, along with my anger and despair. We are in an era when people researching neurodivergence bring their lived experiences with neurodivergence into their work. We are no longer objects of anyone else's savior fantasy; instead, we are subjects of our desires for a better world.

Botha's work focuses, in part, on applying Ilan Meyer's minority stress model to the experiences of autistic folks.[1] Botha and Frost found that among the autistic folks they studied, "Minority stressors including everyday discrimination, internalized stigma, and concealment significantly predicted poorer mental health, despite controlling for general stress exposure."[2] In other words, living as a minority, in this case someone with autism, is a tremendously stressful experience.

While researchers continue to explore the relationship between ADHD and autism, I believe it's fair to apply the minority stress model to ADHD, and I urge folks to perform more research on this application. Marginalization is stressful, not because of some inherent defect inside of marginalized folks, but because of the toxic environments that marginalization creates.

As you read about other challenges faced by ADHDers, remember that the greatest challenge of living with ADHD is navigating a world designed to misunderstand us at best and harm us at worst. This is not hyperbole, as you'll soon see when we examine the data on ADHD and life expectancy.

Life Expectancy

One of the biggest misconceptions I encounter about ADHD is that it's a minor annoyance. Many people hold the image of a young boy (often a young white boy) in elementary school speaking out of turn and having a tough time staying seated at his desk. The child pesters his teacher and distracts his classmates, but many view him as more of a punchline than a human being. This stereotype barely scratches the surface of ADHD's potential effects and the reality that ADHD impacts all ages, races, and genders in profound ways. "The overarching mistake too many people make about ADHD is to think of this mountain of a condition as a molehill of a problem for a rare few. *Big* mistake."[3]

When left untreated, ADHD can take thirteen years off our lives.[4] This is more than the other top four mortality risks combined. In the most severe (and untreated) cases of ADHD, life expectancy might be cut short by as much as twenty-five years.[5] Reductions in life expectancy are linked to ADHDers' higher rates of substance misuse,[6] suicide,[7] increased likelihood of accidents,[8] and our tendency to struggle with access to basic preventative health care, such as dental hygiene.[9]

Most of these life expectancy studies, in fact, most studies on ADHD in general, look at boys and men. We don't know how this plays out for women. Does our socialization to be "good" mitigate some of these impacts by decreasing certain risk-taking behaviors? Or do the increased demands on women to perform emotional labor and care work for others actually lead to worse outcomes? We know shockingly little about the experiences of girls and women, particularly women of color, living with ADHD. We need to find out more. I know many of you reading this are skilled at empirical research. One practical action step to better the lives of ADHDers is to call for a more diverse and accurate body of research to support positive change on our behalf. I hope you'll lead the charge for that type of work.

This data, in my view, is one of the biggest challenges surrounding ADHD: we live with a neurotype that is not supported, is deeply misunderstood, and is often shamed into deadly submission. I am fighting, both for myself and for my community, to change this. That battle is one of the things that keeps me well. I invite you to join me in that fight. These numbers are shocking and unacceptable, but they're very much vulnerable to our shared efforts to change them.

The good news is that treatment works. Some folks don't like the word "treatment" because they see it as a tool of the medical model and of the *DSM* to try to fix ADHDers. I'm okay with it if it's used within a strengths-based, challenge-aware model that is critical of the medical model. Treatment can give ADHDers access to correct care, whether in the form of medication, psychotherapy, ADHD coaching, lifestyle adaptations, or educating oneself about the roots of ADHD and potential supports. Treatment can help us care for ourselves in the present and immediate future while we also do the slower, more gradual work of fixing society to be less ableist.

College Learning Effects

ADHDers also face challenges with college learning, persistence, and success. Based on a sadly limited amount of research, what we know so far is that students with ADHD have lower grades and are less likely to persist and graduate from college than their non-ADHD peers.[10] They also show lower levels of study skills, such as time management and test preparation. Other notable issues include higher rates of substance misuse in students exhibiting more symptoms of ADHD[11] and lower rates of self-esteem.[12]

Remember, though, that this data is based only on students with a formal ADHD diagnosis who have also disclosed that diagnosis to the researchers. Just as the rates of ADHD are probably much higher than 5%, I expect that the college-level data does not come close to capturing the totality of the challenges ADHD students are facing. As someone who started her career in higher education in enrollment management, I have long wondered how many of our students who leave college are students with unrecognized, undiagnosed, or undersupported ADHD. I expect that our undiagnosed ADHD population is a huge piece of the college completion puzzle, and it's a topic I rarely hear about from the higher education community. Again, the good news is that this is an area ripe for improvement. The strategies you're learning throughout this book, including shifting to a strengths-based, challenge-aware model, can address this problem by designing and teaching for our ADHD learners, regardless of their diagnosis status or disclosure of that diagnosis.

Executive Function Constraints

For a long time, most ADHD roads have led back to the idea that it is fundamentally a disorder of the executive function (EF) system of the brain. Let's take a moment now to define EF in more detail. ADHD impacts the EF system of the brain; you'll get no arguments from me about that contention. Within the neurodiversity paradigm though, we can reject the pathologization of our EF as a disorder and instead embrace the combination of strengths and challenges that our unique EF profiles provide.

The EF/self-regulatory system consists of self-awareness, inhibition, attentional management, verbal and nonverbal working memory, problem solving, and self-motivation.[13] Here's what that looks like in plain language, more specifically:

Self-awareness: To make decisions and take action beyond primal reflexes, a person needs to first hold a sense of self.

Inhibition: To pursue a chosen action, a person must first choose *not* to do something else.

Attentional management: A person needs to focus their cognitive resources on the chosen action.

Verbal and nonverbal working memory: This is the process of picturing chosen actions in the mind and then giving oneself verbal instructions as to how to pursue them.

Problem solving: This is the process of figuring out how to best go about taking the chosen action and adapting to any barriers that arise.

Self-motivation: This concept means the ability to see the chosen action through to the end and not give up.

In a popular TikTok video by creator Lisa LaCroix that I often share in my ADHD workshops, Lisa offers a peek into the daily life of an ADHDer. Her video is an excellent example of how the EF system of ADHD works, told through the lived experience of someone with ADHD. Here's the transcript of her video:

> All right, let's clarify something. ADHD is not, "I'm gonna write this email. Oh, look, a squirrel." It's more like, I'm gonna sit down to write this email. Wait, I should probably brush my teeth before I do this, but now that I'm in the bathroom I'm realizing that I forgot to take my medication, so now I'm gonna take my medications, so I get my little pill cutter out, but then I realize I don't have anything to take my medication with, so I have to go downstairs and get a cup. When I'm getting a cup I realize that I haven't made any coffee yet, so now I need to make coffee, and then I look over at the dishes, and I see that they're dirty, which somehow reminds me that I need to do a load of laundry, so I go downstairs and do a load of laundry, come back upstairs, completely forget what I'm doing, but don't worry, coffee has a smell, so I remember that I was making coffee. Finish making my coffee, realize we don't have creamer. Oh crap. I should make a note that we need to go get creamer at the grocery store. No. Wait. Focus. Gotta go upstairs. Take my

pill with my coffee but leave my coffee in the bathroom. Still haven't brushed my teeth. Get back to the office. Sit down to write that email. What the heck was that email about? I don't know. Oh, by the way, I'm still not wearing pants. And instead of doing anything, I'm gonna make a TikTok.[14]

At the time of this writing, Lisa's video has over four hundred thousand views. Lisa's strengths are evident in her TikTok. Clarity of explanation: she takes a complex concept and explains it in a relatable, fun, heartfelt way. She's a great teacher. Creativity: Lisa's a storyteller. She's not just telling us about the ADHD experience; she's showing us and living it out loud for us. And finally, her editing and tech savvy are apparent. She had to piece together the different scenes, the overlay text, transitions, and lighting. This is talent.

And Lisa's challenges are also evident. This is life with ADHD. This is every day, every moment, with ADHD, to varying extents.

I'm not sure I've ever walked into a room and immediately remembered why I was there. Instead, I arrive and notice whatever is right in front of me. *I should put that book back on the shelf. I should bring that glass back to the kitchen. I really need to charge that device.* The original goal? Gone, baby, gone. Or if my husband, son, or dog are in the room I've arrived in, I'll start chatting with them. I often leave that room and move through several others before remembering, "Oh yeah, I went to the office to get my earbuds." Yes, you did, Karen. Ten minutes ago.

This happens to everyone occasionally. It happens to people with ADHD constantly. Every room, every time; every goal is disrupted. What could take a minute takes ten. Multiply this by a hundred of these occurrences each day. I prefer not to think too much about the hours of my life lost to this constraint—the hours that could've been spent in rest, play, creativity, or work to make the world a better place.

Finishing our coffee. Brushing our teeth. My personal nemesis: flossing. Taking our medication or vitamins. Taking a shower. Putting lotion on our dry skin. Cleaning anything. Cooking anything. Scheduling the doctor's appointment. Putting gas in the car. We try and fail to do whatever simple action we have chosen for ourselves, our little microgoals that are the mundane, often boring, but very fundamentally important stuff of life.

The first strategy for addressing these constraints is to notice them. From there, understanding how and why my brain works this way due to ADHD has been a massive help. I'm not a lazy jerk; the functional, chemical, and structural makeup of my brain is not like neurotypical people's brains, and I have predictable EF constraints that I can plan for and mitigate with appropriate support. In Part II of the book, you'll design and teach to honor these EF differences in your ADHD students.

The Glitchy Switch

Current research points to significant differences between people with and without ADHD in two of the brain's networks: the default mode network (DMN) and the task-positive network (TPN). The relationship between these two systems is gaining attention, and we'll be learning a great deal more about it in the coming years. For now, here are some basics of how this challenges people with ADHD.

The DMN is the system in the brain that ruminates and reflects. It's where daydreaming and being "lost in thought" live. It's me, back at Central Park Elementary School in Pennsville, New Jersey, with a bowl haircut and purple corduroy pants, staring out the window during math class. It's also where we can imagine new ideas and reflect on how to support our loved ones and the causes that matter most to us.

The TPN is where the action happens. It allows us to direct actions toward our goals. It is the brain network that is allowing me to write this sentence. It's the part of my brain that will make the lunch my stomach is calling out for, hold a conversation with my husband after work today, and play a board game with my son. It's the part of the brain that drives cars and notices when they need a little thing called "gasoline."

In non-ADHD brains, when the TPN activates to focus on a task, the DMN deactivates, and vice versa. Makes sense, right? You're daydreaming, ruminating, and reflecting with your DMN. You're imagining what you want for lunch and what you want to do when you leave work. Now, it's time to take some action toward your goals. Your TPN activates, and your DMN deactivates. Your brain switches from reflection to action. Throughout the day, the non-ADHD brain switches back and forth between these two systems without conscious effort.

In the ADHD brain, things operate a bit differently. Research shows that when our TPN (action brain) turns on, our DMN (reflection brain) stays "on," too.[15] When our brain enters activity mode, our reflective mode persists. Tasks do not induce my reflective brain network to turn off. My DMN laughs in the face of tasks. *I'm not going anywhere (insert evil DMN laugh)*. This is what Hallowell and Ratey refer to as the "glitchy switch."[16]

Most people know that ADHDers are easily distracted by external stimuli, but what most people don't realize is that, like the old horror story trope, the call is also coming from inside the house. Yes, external stimuli distract us, but we are also distracted by our own brains. Our DMN, the reflective, ruminating brain network, distracts us from completing tasks, working, or acting toward our goals and desires.

You know when you get an important phone call and ask your kids to turn down the television so you can hear the person who called you? For ADHDers, the TPN is the person on the other end of the line, and the DMN is your kids, continuing to blare the TV. You're trying to listen to what your boss is saying (your TPN), but you can only hear some YouTube video about a video game (your DMN).

Think of this in the college classroom. We all regularly shift between brain networks, but for ADHDers, that reflective brain network stays active. This doesn't mean our TPN isn't working. It doesn't mean we can't complete tasks. It means that we need a bit more structure and stimulation to complete said tasks. One of the tricks I've learned is to doodle when listening to boring but necessary lectures. Doodling gives me enough stimulation to keep my DMN from overriding my TPN completely. Yet I've heard many educators lament that their students are doodling in class because they assume that means they aren't paying attention. For ADHDers, that might be exactly how they *do* pay attention.

Challenge your assumptions about attention in the human beings in your classroom. There is no one way to experience and express attention. Your ADHD learners are doing their best to work with their "glitchy switches." Can you meet them in that space of strength and challenge?

Object Impermanence

My husband is what some people might refer to as a "neat freak." He's one of those people who cleans up the counters and used dishes while he's cooking dinner. When he places dinner on the table, the kitchen looks almost entirely clean, unlike when I cook, and it looks like a food bomb went off.

Our shared bathroom has a small bathroom counter area and three drawers. My husband keeps all his items in his drawer. I use the other two drawers for items I don't use regularly. My daily needs, like my toothbrush and hairbrush, sit on the bathroom counter.

This has caused some friction in our relationship over the years. My husband used to have a tough time understanding why I didn't put everything in one of my two drawers to keep the counter clear. For most of our marriage, until I got my ADHD diagnosis, I would repeatedly tell him that's how I liked it. Now, with a stronger knowledge of ADHD, I'm able to explain that the reason I need to use the counter instead of drawers has a name: object impermanence.

Object impermanence means that it stops existing if I don't see it. Even if something is put away in a drawer, neurotypical folks are able to "hold" the concept of that item in their minds and call up that mental file as needed. For ADHDers, it doesn't work like that. Remember, our minds are more fluid and open. We don't have the same internal neural structures that support object permanence.

Here's another example of this: I have a couple of vitamins that I need to take daily. I put them on the kitchen counter to remind myself to take them each morning. When I first started taking them, my husband would tidy up, placing them in the cabinet just above that counter. The first time he did this, I forgot to take them for a week. I forgot to even ask him to stop doing that because, in my mind, there were no vitamins. They didn't exist and never existed.

About a week later, I opened the cabinet, looking for something else, and saw my vitamins. What? Who are you? Where did you go? It took a minute for me to get my vitamin bearings. I then processed that he had put them away, that I'd forgotten to take them, and that I needed them to be on the counter, where I could see them, if I was to have any chance of remembering to take them. I communicated ("communicated" is one word for it!) that to my husband and have since remembered to take my vitamins most days.

Another example of object impermanence relates to using a planner to remember appointments. Again, here's the rule: if ADHDers don't see it, it doesn't exist. Consider how that might apply to using a daily planner to remember assignments, study tasks, or other appointments. Imagine that a student with ADHD takes the initiative to write all their assignments into a paper academic planner. That's great, but once that planner is closed, those appointments cease to exist for that student.

Every ADHD planning system rests on the extent to which it can address object impermanence, typically through using additional external structures. Using external reminders like alarms can help. I have an open-format desktop paper planner that doesn't have a cover, so my tasks for the week are always right in front of me. We'll talk much more about designing around object impermanence in chapter 6, but for now, know that it's a constant challenge facing us ADHDers. Begin to consider what aspects of your teaching and course might be hidden from your students, often with the best intentions.

Time Blindness

Object impermanence has a cousin, and her name is Time Blindness.[17] Just as we have a hard time remembering items that aren't right in front of our faces, we also have a tough time tracking the passage of time. Set a timer for fifteen minutes. Ask a neurotypical person how much time has passed. Ask an ADHDer how much time has passed. The odds are that the neurotypical person's estimate will be more accurate.

There are a couple of possible reasons for our time blindness. First, again, our open minds are more fluid. We don't have those rigid internal neural structures that help us stay focused on the passage of time. Next, our glitchy switch causes us to remain in rumination when we're trying to focus on tasks, such as noticing the passage of time.

You can imagine how this plays out in the classroom. You tell students they must complete an assignment by the end of class. If not, they'll need to take it home for homework, or maybe you'll even tell them they have to hand it in without completing it. Without external reinforcements and support, ADHDers might lose track of their time, assuming they have much more time or too little time to complete the task. If they overestimate their remaining time, they won't finish the task and will have the added stress of homework or a poor grade. If they underestimate their remaining time, they might feel rushed and stressed about finishing the work. This also has major ramifications for assessments such as timed exams.

Time blindness is a major challenge for ADHDers. In the coming chapters, we'll learn more about designing and teaching to mitigate this challenge. Rest assured that while time blindness is a daily experience for ADHDers, it can be supported through some creative and kind classroom design choices. Begin to think about how you make time external (if at all) in your classroom in preparation for that later discussion.

Emotional Regulation

Before we discuss how emotional regulation challenges ADHDers, it seems worth a moment to define what emotions are. My non-psychologist definition of "emotion" starts with a hyphen: e-motion. An emotion is a feeling whose job is to create motion by either changing our path or keeping us moving along the same path. When I feel anger, I am meant to be moved toward action. When I feel sadness, I'm meant to reach out for comfort. When I feel gratitude, I am meant to sink more deeply into connection with the ground beneath me. I (we) get in trouble when we try to block our emotions because, again, their job is to move. When we don't let them, they get pissed and act out. The experience of repressed anger is often more destructive than anger itself. Like all of its emotional friends, anger is simply there to move us toward action. Our higher mind (what my therapist calls "the wise mind") then gets to decide what type of action would be best in response to that anger.

Another way I think about emotions is that they are clues, perhaps breadcrumbs, meant to move us forward on our path. The poet Rumi called them "unexpected visitors" and encouraged us to welcome them all. Learning to take this step back from my emotions, to name them as energy that wants to move me or clues that can guide me forward, is the result of a lot of therapy, some twelve-step groups, and some good old-fashioned human suffering.

Now, let's throw my unique kind of mind, a mind with ADHD, into the mix. Remember, one way we think about ADHD is using Hallowell and Ratey's description: a racecar brain with bicycle brakes. That applies to our emotions as well. Remember when you were a new driver, and you were still learning how much pressure to apply to the car's gas pedal? Sometimes, you'd push too hard, and your entire body would be pressed against the seat like an astronaut hurtling into space. But then you'd push too lightly and you wouldn't go anywhere.

On the one hand, emotions can hit us ADHDers hard and fast, completely overtaking us. On the other hand, sometimes our emotions are very "light," and we fail to notice them until they build and build. Emotional regulation speaks to someone's ability to feel and process an emotion before bringing in their trusted, wise mind to guide their course of action. It's something I'm working on right now in therapy, with my therapist teaching me "Emotions 101." It's incredibly helpful to walk through these fundamentals.

I suspect that the more open nature of the ADHD brain allows our emotions to bounce around more freely, and that can feel chaotic and unnerving when one isn't able to name what's happening inside of them. Personally, since my diagnosis, the ability to say to myself, "Hey, honey, you have ADHD. Emotions can hit you hard and fast, or you might not notice them when you need them. But it's okay. You're learning," has been life-changing. That recognition alone has helped.

Our friends Hallowell and Ratey share some research in *ADHD 2.0* about small but significant differences in "the central strip down the midline of the cerebellum called the vermis" between ADHDers and non-ADHDers.[18] That part of the brain appears to be part of the network that helps with emotional processing. In ADHDers, it's smaller. I suspect we'll know a lot more about that in the next couple of decades. I don't worry about the size of my vermis very much, to be honest, and you don't need to either. What's important to remember is that your ADHD learners might be moved more intensely by emotions, or they might not notice their emotions at all. Remember that we are all constantly influenced by our emotional messengers. Simply realizing that some emotional dysregulation could be playing out in a student might be enough to help *you* stay calm and defuse the situation. You don't need to match that student's emotional dysregulation. You don't need to dive into the pool with them. Stand on the side and direct them how to swim to safety.

Co-regulation is a promising model that you can apply in your classrooms to help support your ADHDers' self-regulatory strategies. Co-regulation speaks to this energy of not diving into the pool but standing on the side helping your learners.[19] We co-regulate with our learners when we spend time becoming more deeply attuned to our own emotions, noticing what sends us into a state of dysregulation, and taking steps in and out of the classroom to tend to our well-being. Ideally, from this grounded center, we can better hold space for our ADHD students to have emotional ups and downs. Our continued, consistent presence, with or without verbal reinforcement, can soothe our ADHDer learners experiencing dysregulation. If you have a student who is starting to become agitated, try to take at least a moment or two to check in with yourself before you react. This space of self-awareness sets the foundation for your and your students to partner in your shared well-being.

Next, recognize that the solution to a lot of emotional dysregulation is time. Emotions allowed to move will move right along when we let them. Ask an upset student if they want to take a break in the back of the room or take a quick walk to reset. In many years of teaching both faculty and students, I've learned that a five-minute break can cure about 90% of emotional overwhelm in classroom settings. In the other 10% of cases, you might encourage the learner (privately, if possible) to head home and follow up with them later, possibly with a connection to any of your institution's counseling resources. If you have even the slightest thought that the student is a danger to themself or others, follow your institution's crisis guidelines and get them immediate help.

Emotional regulation is a big challenge for ADHDers, but our ability to feel so quickly and deeply is also the reason that we might be the first ones to reach out to hug the person who is crying in public. It's why we create amazing art that moves other people to intense emotions. It's why we write books baring our souls to an often unkind world in order to make the world a bit less unkind. When we treat ADHDers with awareness and compassion,[20] we can mitigate the challenges of these racecar emotions in and out of the classroom.

Rejection Sensitive Dysphoria (RSD)

When I present workshops on ADHD to college educators, the vast majority are familiar with the basics of ADHD. There is one concept I teach, however, that surprises them: Few have heard of RSD, or Rejection Sensitive Dysphoria, a co-existing trait of the vast majority of folks with ADHD. Some estimates suggest that as many as 99% of folks with ADHD experience symptoms of RSD.[21]

RSD results in extreme emotional pain from an actual *or perceived* sense of criticism or rejection. As you can see from its name, the term "dysphoria" implies that the perception of rejection is often at odds with the situation. An example of this would be a professor suggesting to a student that they could benefit from utilizing the writing center to work on their transitions between paragraphs. From the professor's point of view, this is a neutral or even positive recommendation. The students' transitions feel murky, and the writing center can help them improve. The underlying desire is to help the student.

A student with ADHD and RSD could interpret this very differently. They might experience emotional pain of "unbearable intensity"[22] from what they perceive as extreme criticism of not only their writing skills but also their general abilities and very humanity. The professor's goal of helping the student goes unmet because, in the face of the tidal wave of shame resulting from RSD, the student shuts down, loses trust in their professor, and perhaps even attempts to avoid additional shaming by not turning in assignments or dropping the course.

RSD is commonly understood to be a neurobiological phenomenon common among ADHDers and other neurodivergent folks. Remember my suggested new name for ADHD is ON, or Open Neurotype. Another way to think about ON is that in having this cognitive openness to everything in our environment, we are also a bit like an unguarded castle in times of war. We take it all in, which offers us many gifts, but it also means we're more vulnerable. Yet these neurobiological underpinnings can be helped or harmed by the social and learning environments we design, and RSD is a social-neurobiological experience.

Sometimes, RSD can be so intense that it shows up in ways similar to major mood disorders with extreme symptoms, including suicidal ideation. However, RSD is typically shorter in duration and, again, depends on exposure to perceived or actual criticism. People who experience RSD often describe it with vivid sensory descriptions tied to experiences of severe pain.

Most faculty who learn about RSD feel empowered by this information. They say they feel like someone has opened a long-locked room in the house of their pedagogy. They get curious about how they can use this information about RSD to better communicate with their students, particularly in how they provide feedback in their classrooms. I hope you, too, are feeling empowered by this. To be clear, the message here is not that you are responsible for a student's RSD but that we are all accountable for mitigating the impacts of shame as we work to dismantle deficit-based cultures.

I love RSD. Let me rephrase that. I love that I know about RSD. I do not love RSD. RSD feels like catching on fire from the inside out. Or it did, at least, before I knew what it was. For me, RSD is an example of "knowledge is power." That can hold true for you and your students as well. The more openly we talk about RSD, the less of a hold it will have on all of us.

Be mindful of your word choices with your students. Instead of saying to a student, "I can see you're really sensitive about feedback," you might try saying, "I can see you're very responsive to the feedback I give you." That lands differently, doesn't it? We don't need to pretend this isn't happening. We can mindfully note our concerns (without ever trying to diagnose anyone). For example, a statement of fact: "I am noticing that you are responding to the feedback I have given you." From there, you can also hold space for your students to name that experience, and then together, you can find a path forward.

Masking

Masking is a tricky issue to discuss in this section of the book on ADHD challenges because while it's a challenge for ADHDers, it's also a solution. Masking is a common strategy of ADHDers and other neurodivergent folks to ease our discomfort and stress when faced with pressure from unsupportive and inflexible environments or people. We put on a mask of what seem like socially acceptable behaviors and hide our neurodivergence. It is very common for ADHDers to not even realize they've been masking at all until later in life, and then it can be quite overwhelming to realize how much they've been masking. The lines between our true selves and the masks we've worn to protect us from an unkind world can blur.

When I think of masking, I think about a meme of Big Bird from Sesame Street sitting in a business meeting. He's sitting at the conference table with a bunch of serious business types, his hands in front of him, preparing to take notes. You can see in his eyes that he's completely freaked out and he's fighting to hold in his gregarious, playful Big Bird energy. It's one of my favorite memes because it speaks to how I often feel in social settings.

In most meetings, I'd love to move my body, make big motions with my hands and arms, and have strong facial expressions. Intense energies move through me when I'm in a meeting setting with other people, and it would feel really good to express those energies. My brain also takes in everything, everywhere, all at once. Both my DPN and TPN are firing, which means I'm making random and rapid connections between ideas that I am eager to share with others.

Instead, I mask.

I try my hardest to sit still and behave. I don't want people to label me as disruptive.

I wonder where all that energy goes. Well, actually, I don't wonder. My hunch is that when we suppress energy like that, it gets stuck in our systems and shows up in other ways (for me, physical illness symptoms and anxiety). I often avoid certain social settings rather than deal with the consequences of feeling forced to mask. That, of course, results in isolation, which also leads to physical symptoms and anxiety. A lose-lose, right? I'm learning how to release some of those energies, show up as my authentic self, and choose spaces where I can be my whole self without sacrificing my well-being.

I was fortunate to have the chance to speak to Ying Deng, who goes by ADHD Asian Girl online. Ying is a fellow ADHDer and offers ADHD coaching services geared toward mindfulness to support other folks with ADHD. Ying told me about her experiences as a first-generation immigrant, born and raised in China, who came to the United States when she was seventeen to attend college: "Being an immigrant definitely influenced how I experienced ADHD, and being Asian, we already have a lot of masking that we do. I am very myself in front of my partner and close friends, but just being an immigrant, there are things you need to mask."[23]

Once again, the ADHD experience is not a monolith. Race, class, gender, and immigration status are all potential factors that might influence how and how often an ADHDer masks. Your job as a professor is to get curious about whether you are creating genuinely inclusive spaces where your ADHD students can show up as their whole selves or whether you're creating neuro-normative spaces where your students feel like they need to fall in line with the masses.

One example would be intentionally inviting students in onsite classrooms to choose standing, sitting on the floor, or alternative seating options over sitting in a typical classroom desk or chair. Modeling that for your learners can sweeten the invitation. Some classrooms have exercise balls that not only allow for movement but also encourage it. Some ADHDers might need to pace to focus. Could you create space in the back of your classroom for students to pace and release some of that caged-up energy?

Do I continue to mask? Absolutely. I'm okay with that. If I don't know and trust the people I'm around, I will mask as a starting point. Are there negative consequences to that? Absolutely. But for now, it feels like the safest option. But if I can establish a sense of safety and trust with people, I will begin to lower the mask. In the meantime, I will keep working to create a more inclusive world, actively hoping that more spaces will feel weird, free, and open in alignment with my authentic ADHD self.

Embracing My ADHD, Despite the Challenges

To close this chapter on the challenges of ADHD, I want to answer a question that gets tossed around every once in a while in the ADHD community and that I suspect some neurotypical folks wonder about as well.

If I were to wake up tomorrow and be offered a "cure" for my ADHD, would I take it? This is a question that came up for me quite a bit when I was first diagnosed. That period of time was overwhelming, not only because it coincided with the start of a global pandemic, but also because I was not given any accurate information about ADHD from my providers nor any direction about navigating ADHD in a disabling world. For months, I felt like I was standing on the edge of a precipice, and I can remember feeling very strongly that I wanted to scratch the ADHD out of my skin. And yet, at the same time, a trembling but hopeful voice inside of me whispered that the best path forward was not trying to cut the ADHD out of me but rather to accept and celebrate myself just as I was. That voice didn't know much at the time, but it knew enough to tell me that my ADHD was not the root of my pain during that tumultuous period. Rather, ableism and deficit-based thinking, both of which were as well rooted in me as they are in many of us, were the sources of my pain.

Today, I can tell you with complete assurance that the question of whether I'd take a cure for ADHD is the wrong question. ADHD is not the common cold. If there was something I could take, with few side effects, to cure a cold when I get one, I would take it. ADHD is not a sickness. It's not a disease. It is a neurotype. One of many. It is a way of being in the world. Like any other way of being in the world, it brings strengths and challenges.

My ADHD is integral to who I am. It's part of why I'm so silly and weird, two traits I've grown to not only accept but to love. My ADHD is a huge part of why I'm a talented learning experience designer and educator. I think of myself like a canary in a mine, singing out at the first sign of boring or dehumanizing learning experiences. My ADHD helps me see the world through a lens of childlike enthusiasm. I don't want to lose any of that. Instead, I want to work on designing a world that affirms neurodiversity in all its forms, alleviating the many challenges that co-exist with my ADHD strengths. Together, we can also ease these challenges for our students.

Summary

Let's review some common ADHD challenges we learned about in this chapter.

- Ableism and minority stress are the most significant challenges most ADHDers face.
- Data on ADHD shows that our life expectancy is shortened, compared to our non-ADHD peers. Our job is to ensure ADHDers receive access to correct care to mitigate these threats.
- ADHD, when untreated and unsupported, often results in negative effects on college learning and less success for college students.
- Executive function (EF) is the "little CEO" of the brain. ADHDers' EF constraints are often a major challenge.
- The glitchy switch means that the DMN (default mode network) in the ADHD brain remains active at the same time as the TPN (task-positive network), meaning that ADHDers are often both internally and externally distracted from active tasks.
- Object impermanence describes the concept that when ADHDers can't see something, it ceases to exist for them.

- Time blindness means that compared to neurotypical peers, ADHDers have less accurate perceptions of time, either over- or underestimating the passage of time.
- ADHD affects our emotional regulation and can result in overwhelming emotional experiences and expression.
- RSD, or rejection sensitive dysphoria, means that ADHDers are extremely sensitive to criticism.
- Masking is a self-protective habit used by ADHDers in noninclusive, poorly designed settings.

ADHDers are complex human beings with special kinds of minds. We experience a combination of strengths and challenges that can strongly influence our lives, well-being, and learning experiences. I invite you to keep a strengths-based, challenge-aware approach at the center of your teaching practice when working with ADHD students. Remember, the biggest challenge that ADHDers face is always ableism. Many other challenges impact our daily lives and learning, but remember that creating inclusive spaces is the best way to help us face and overcome the barriers of a disabling society.

Chapter Four

Transitioning from Old to New Models of ADHD

I wish for a world that views disability, mental or physical, not as a hindrance but as unique attributes that can be seen as powerful assets if given the right opportunities.

—Oliver Sacks

When I'm in the shower, pretending that Oprah is interviewing me in those Adirondack chairs in the trees behind her mansion, I imagine she asks me, while wearing her incredibly stylish reading glasses, "What was the biggest surprise when writing this book?" Well, Oprah and dear readers, the biggest surprise when writing this book was how much of my own ignorance and ableism I had to excavate to get closer to the truth of living and learning with ADHD.

My first draft virtually exploded in my lap one day when I came across an article discussing the open nature of the ADHD neurotype. This article led me to the Open Neurotype (ON) model I shared in chapter 1. I realized how infectious and crafty deficit-based models can be, and upon taking another look at my first draft, I saw how much I relied on those models. It was back to square one for me, but I wouldn't change that experience, because it brought me here to you to share these hard truths that we all need to face to varying degrees, and that's even better than talking to Oprah (well, almost).

In this chapter, we'll explore a multitude of models to guide your work designing and teaching for ADHD students' success. We will also more deeply analyze how deficit-based models work and why they harm us. I expect one or two of the strengths-based models I share will resonate strongly. Others, perhaps less so. Use these models not as a prescriptive recipe for how you should understand ADHD but as an open, flexible, adaptive lens through which to consider the ADHD experience. Again, the goal here is to help you realize that, like me, you were taught to believe in deficit-based models, but the good news is plenty of better alternatives exist. This chapter will conclude Part I of the book, where our work is to redefine ADHD, preparing us for Part II's simple and sustainable teaching strategies.

Person Fixing Versus Society Fixing

The first models we'll consider come from the disability studies field. They posit that there are two distinct models of disability through which we can view the world: the person-fixing and the society-fixing models. Since we've established that ADHD can be experienced as a disability, this is a great starting point to help us dismantle the deficit-based approach and begin anew. I love the simplicity of this model.

The person-fixing model views the disabled person as broken and in need of repair. The society-fixing model views society as broken and in need of repair. Simple enough? Let's apply this to ADHD as an example.

People with ADHD struggle with working memory, which means it's tough for us to hold things in our minds. I often use the saying "In one ear and out the other" to describe my working memory. If I don't write it down, it doesn't exist. This memory issue has countless consequences in my daily life, and one of those consequences is forgetting appointments.

Imagine you are an office manager in a doctor's office who helps schedule patient appointments. Patient X calls to make an appointment, and you schedule her for Monday, March 7, at 2:00 p.m. Patient X says to you, "I have ADHD and need help remembering appointments. Will I receive any automated reminders?"

You reply, "We don't have an automated reminder system. I suggest you write it down in your calendar if you need help remembering it."

March 7 at 2:00 p.m. rolls around, and Patient X is a no-show.

In the person-fixing model, we view this as Patient X's fault. She has ADHD. She has and is the problem. She's the one who needs to be fixed. She should've written down the appointment.

In the society-fixing model, we view the doctor's office system as the broken link in this chain of communication. Recognizing that they serve clients with ADHD who struggle with working memory, they could set up a system to send an email and text reminder to their patients a day before and an hour before their appointments.

Through which lens do you view the world?

This book relies primarily on the society-fixing model. Of course, as an ADHDer, I've learned not to assume the existence of just and supportive systems. I have to work with a doctor's office that is not accessible for people with ADHD. But at the same time, I will also imagine and create a world where that's no longer the case.

Asking the simple question, "Am I trying to fix the person when I could instead fix systems and society?" can be a powerful tool for change in our lives and our teaching. If you find you're in person fixing mode, that's okay. That's what most of us were taught, and we've been good students. But of course, we want to do better once we know better, and fixing systems instead of people is not only more just but a heck of a lot more efficient, if our goal is to create a better world for all life on this planet. In addition to no longer trying to fix people, another frame we can use to more accurately engage with the reality of the ADHD experience is to shift toward ADHDers' strengths. What if we don't need to be fixed at all? What if, instead, we have immense unnoticed strengths?

Strengths-Based, Challenge-Aware

When I was first diagnosed with ADHD, one of the things that helped me through the trauma of a later-in-life diagnosis (coupled with COVID lockdowns, remember) was to think about how I could help others. I read a lot, listened a lot, and reflected a lot. I asked myself what model we might lean on, instead of deficit-based approaches, to best understand, support, teach, and celebrate ADHDers.

What I've arrived at is this: strengths-based, challenge-aware. Within this model, we center people's strengths and humanity, and at the very same time, we hold space for complexity, for the recognition that strengths coexist with challenges. That the student who just earned an A on the test might be losing sleep over the less structured project that's making her feel worthless and stupid. That the talented learner who carries around a binder full of their amazing artwork has not turned in an assignment on time once this term. That the caring undergraduate who volunteers for your peer mentoring program hasn't seen a dentist in four years, and the fear and shame he carries with him about his teeth is nearly constant. That the superstar student who just wrote a killer essay in your class self-medicates daily with drugs and alcohol just so that they can feel human.

Hallowell and Ratey use a gorgeous term for the complexity of the ADHD experience: a "condition of paradoxical pairs."[1] This concept has served as an essential foundation in the development of my model and in the teaching methods I will recommend that rely on it. In other words, on one side of the ADHD coin is a strength. Flipped, we see its complementary challenge.

For example, my brain is an idea factory. If you need an idea, look no further. The flip side of that strength is that I often struggle to finish projects as the next great idea pulls me in. Both are true. The name of the game for us ADHDers is to find the middle path—to design rich, fulfilling, meaningful lives within our inherent paradox.

Hallowell and Ratey describe ADHD as "neither entirely a disorder nor entirely an asset. It is an array of traits specific to a unique kind of mind." Here is a brief taste of our paradox, as described by Hallowell and Ratey: "A lack of focus combined with an ability to superfocus; a lack of direction combined with highly directed entrepreneurialism; a tendency to procrastinate combined with a knack for getting a week's worth of work done in two hours; impulsive, wrongheaded decision making combined with inventive, out-of-the blue problem solving; interpersonal cluelessness combined with uncanny intuition and empathy; the list goes on."[2]

We ADHDers are the living both/and.

When educators ask me about how they should approach any given challenge related to ADHD (I'm asked those kinds of questions daily), I start with: strengths-based, challenge-aware. If you stumble at any point while reading this book or translating this work in the world (and I expect that you will, because this is complex work), return here. View and support ADHD through a strengths-based, challenge-aware lens. With this frame in mind for how we can support individual learners, let's turn to a more communal lens for systems-level disruption of the status quo: disability justice.

Disability Justice

Care Work: Dreaming Disability Justice, by Leah Lakshmi Piepzna-Samarasinha, frames disability as "a political movement and many interlocking communities where disability is not defined in white terms, or male terms, or straight terms."[3] Disability justice gets disabled people organized to lead and participate in social movements. It prioritizes reflection on existing versus ideal systems and the actions required to bring those ideal systems to fruition. Most importantly, disability justice centers disabled communities. Disabled folks are the best leaders and the wisest guides to examine, elevate, and support disabled folks.

Compare the disability justice model with the *DSM* (the aforementioned *Diagnostic and Statistical Manual of Mental Disorders*), which could be considered the opposite of disability justice. A very particular group of people (primarily affluent, white, male doctors) created the *DSM* to describe and categorize people living with mental illness and other "mental disorders." The *DSM* centers that privileged perspective while marginalizing disabled voices. Isn't it wild to think that someone who has never lived a day in their life with ADHD would dare to consider themselves an expert on the ADHD experience and prioritize their knowledge over the lived experience of someone with ADHD? That is not to say that non-ADHDers cannot be valuable allies in this work. However, the point is whom is centered in the work and whose expertise is empowered and valued.

The disability justice model reminds us to pay close attention to who is at the proverbial table. Imagine, for example, your institution decides to establish a committee on the experiences of ADHD students. The committee consists of faculty and staff who've volunteered to do this work. Are any students on your committee? Are there any neurodivergent folks? If not, through the lens of disability justice, this committee has not only failed in its charge, but it has harmed those it's claiming to help. Finally, a disability justice lens would make sure that a diverse group of ADHDers were leading that committee, also ensuring representation across race, class, gender, and sexual identity. Black and Brown folks live with ADHD. Folks without access to health care live with ADHD. Trans folks live with ADHD. If justice is your goal, ensure that you do the necessary work to represent the breadth and depth of the ADHD community. Last but not least, compensate the committee members for their work. Wage theft by businesses and corporations harms disabled folks, and it is not aligned with disability justice or supporting ADHD learners.

Disability justice reminds us to always balance our work with individual students in our own classrooms with broader coalitions looking to disrupt the status quo. The work ahead is never personal or political; it's always both. With this in mind, let's continue our journey to root out the personal and political failures of deficit-based mindsets and models.

Deficit-Based Models and ADHD

To ensure we're all on the same page, let's discuss a solid definition of "deficit-based model." It has been most thoughtfully defined by Richard Valencia, who's dedicated his career to naming the harms and motivations of deficit-based thinking. He writes, "The deficit thinking model, at its core, is an endogenous theory—positing that the student who fails in school does so because of his/her internal deficits or deficiencies. Such deficits manifest, adherents allege, in limited abilities, linguistic shortcomings, lack of motivation to learn, and immoral behavior."[4] The six characteristics of deficit-based thinking as defined by Valencia are: victim blaming, oppression, pseudoscience, temporal changes, educability, and heterodoxy.

More recently, Lori Patton Davis and Samuel Museus explained their take, building on Valencia's work: "Deficit thinking holds students from historically oppressed populations responsible for the challenges and inequalities that they face. Overall, these perspectives serve as tools that maintain hegemonic systems and, in doing so, fail to place accountability with oppressive structures, policies, and practices within educational settings."[5]

Here's my version of that definition: Deficit-based models weaponize difference and diversity through a deadly combination of ignorance and intent to characterize human beings as deficient and, therefore, less than human and deserving of fewer resources than the supposedly non-deficient, supposedly more human people in positions of power.

The deficit-based approach to ADHD in our society is not very well hidden; it is written into the name "attention deficit hyperactivity disorder." Through this dominant lens, also known as the medical model and summarized with ruthless efficiency in the *DSM*, we ADHDers are deficient and disordered, weaker (but somehow also threatening), and only exist to demonstrate the generosity of the neurotypical people who line up to fix and save us.

This is the foundation on which the vast majority of ADHD research and practice rests: clinicians, educators, researchers, and graduate students begin with the idea that people like me, people with ADHD, have "attention deficit hyperactivity disorder," a definition that ignores all potential strengths and gifts, and therefore skews any research and practices grounded on this faulty foundation. Remember, the latest research on ADHD led by researchers and experts with ADHD recognizes it not as a deficit of attention but rather an abundance of attention.[6]

Specific to our work in education, deficit-based approaches aren't grounded in the science of how people learn, a science that recognizes the innate power of human potential when given the right circumstances to flourish. Instead, they are grounded in the desire to hoard power in the hands of a chosen few. Since we, as educators, are committed to the science of learning, we are in a unique position to take the lead in weeding out these approaches in education, in service of not only our ADHD students but of the world, which is missing out on their many gifts and strengths. We are in a unique position to address and ultimately end the lies told about ADHD and the harm done to this community through deficit-based approaches.

Deficit-Based Models as Harmful

I'm exposed to deficit-based thinking about ADHD daily, but one experience stands above the rest as a time when I felt the smallest, the most ashamed, and the most exhausted. Can you guess where this experience took place? In a college course I took a couple of years ago, a course offered by an institution claiming it was geared toward helping educators support neurodivergent students, a course filled with K–12 teachers (note: teachers are not the problem, but training teachers in deficit-based models is a problem[7]). I was one of the only folks working in higher education in this course and the only student in the class who openly identified as neurodivergent.

The things I heard and read there are hard to put into words. The entire energy of the course was infused with a savior mentality: that "those" students were broken, disruptive, and defective and that "we" educators could use the course strategies to fix and save them from themselves. It was as if neurodivergent students were another species altogether.

In the first couple weeks of the course, I raised my hand in live sessions and participated in the asynchronous discussion, gently and firmly reminding my fellow educators how inappropriate, ineffective, and dehumanizing their words were. Eventually, I ran out of steam. It was like a twisted game of dehumanizing Whack-A-Mole without any fun prizes at the end.

Again, teachers are not the problem. Every one of those teachers had been exposed to ableist viewpoints since they were in the womb. Every one of those teachers went through a K–12 experience grounded in the deficit-based model of ADHD born out of the *DSM*'s faulty foundation. They then studied higher education, where those deficit-based approaches were rarely questioned. The vast majority of us need to work to unlearn our ableism before we can get to the work of best designing for and teaching our ADHD learners.

Zaretta Hammond, in *Culturally Responsive Teaching and the Brain*, writes, "Teachers' deficit-oriented attributions of student performance influence their instructional decision making, resulting in giving students less opportunity for engaging curricula, interesting tasks, and culturally congruent ways of learning."[8] Seeing students as walking deficits eliminates classroom learning opportunities and engagement opportunities. It hurts them. It hurts you.

Hallowell and Ratey describe the effects of deficit-based approaches specific to ADHDers: "ADHD was totally misunderstood for so very, very long. Tragically, terribly misunderstood. This led to the sadistic and systematic betrayal of innocent children, punishing them for what they could not control, and the wholesale wasting of the talent of generations of adults."[9]

I agree with Hallowell and Ratey. Where I disagree with them is that they're using the past tense. If only.

As a human, as an ADHDer, and as a faculty development professional trained in the learning sciences, here's my quick take on deficit-based approaches: they well and truly stink. They hurt ADHD learners. They hurt all neurodivergent learners. They hurt our neurotypical peers by teaching them that a massive swath of society is less human than they are. They hurt the human species by blocking the power of neurodivergent minds to imagine new, better, more just worlds. They impede learning.

Strengths-based models are caring, humanizing, and effective.[10] They also tell the truth about our learners. One of the core values of higher education, at least one of my core values, is the pursuit of the truths of human existence. No deficit-based approach will ever lead us to greater truths in or beyond our classrooms.

The Shame of Deficit-Based Labels

Many folks might have a sense of the academic meaning of shame, thanks to the work of Brené Brown, a researcher and Oprah-anointed author who has studied shame, vulnerability, and what she refers to as "whole-hearted living." Brown defines shame as "the intensely painful feeling or experience of believing that we are flawed and therefore unworthy of love and belonging—something we've experienced, done, or failed to do makes us unworthy of connection."[11] I have also heard the difference between guilt and shame described in this way: guilt means you've done something bad (a potentially adaptive feeling to motivate positive change) while shame means you *are* bad (a maladaptive feeling that blocks the motivation to make positive change).

Shame is no joke. We are social animals who deem exclusion from our groups or communities as one of the greatest threats we can face.[12] The experience of believing we are not worthy of being part of a group is not only emotionally devastating; it can also feel life-threatening to our nervous systems. For most of human history, to be excluded from our tribes meant almost certain death. While we could argue that this is no longer the case, shame remains psychologically and physiologically threatening and damaging.

What impact does shame have on learning? In the classroom learning environment, how does a student's sense of not belonging in that environment influence their ability to learn? What happens if a student believes they haven't just made a mistake in your classroom, for example, but are fundamentally unsuited for your classroom?

Kathleen Cushman, co-author of *Belonging and Becoming: The Power of Social and Emotional Learning in High Schools*, describes shame as having the ability to "stop learning in its tracks."[13] When the brain is focused on the threat of shame, "not much else gets through."[14] Research has shown that shame reduces the sense of self-efficacy (a belief in one's ability to accomplish a task) in college students.[15] It is also important to keep in mind that women and other marginalized groups, especially those with histories of trauma, report higher rates of shameful feelings.[16]

Shame is a barrier to learning. This does not for one second imply that we should wipe our classrooms clean of challenges or healthy stressors that are balanced by robust support. High expectations and challenges balanced with personalized, caring support are one of the foundations of effective pedagogy.[17] That's not shame. Remember, shame is not about making a mistake but about believing you *are* a mistake. There is a world of difference between recognizing that you made a mistake on an assignment and believing that you don't belong in a class, or perhaps even in college, because of that mistake. Professors are a key factor in determining whether students will view their inevitable mistakes as either lessons to carry forward or as evidence that they simply don't belong. You can use your reading of this book to recommit to eliminating shame from your courses and teaching. Feeling curious about more ways to design and teach against shame? Not to worry. The entirety of chapter 5 focuses on shame.

Now that we're exceptionally clear about how ineffective and dehumanizing deficit-based models are, I wish I could tell you that the system on which higher education bases its support of disabled students relies on strengths-based approaches. Sadly, I cannot. Let's take a look now at the primary model of higher education, grounded, unfortunately, on deficits, barriers, and a student-fixing model.

The Accommodations Model of Higher Education

The current model of supporting ADHD students in American higher education is called the accommodations model. An accommodation is a specific support designed to meet the needs of disabled students, like those with ADHD, as deemed appropriate by a disabilities counselor at the institution and based on a documented diagnosis granted by a clinician or doctor. The accommodations model's foundation is the same faulty foundation on which the "attention deficit hyperactivity disorder" idea is built: the *DSM*.

How does this play out for a typical ADHD student?

Let's imagine that a student who has struggled with symptoms of ADHD her entire life (but has never been formally diagnosed) believes she could benefit from taking her upcoming history exam in a separate room, away from her peers, to lessen the distractions that have caused her problems on past exams. Here's a typical list of what she would need to do under the accommodations model to access a low-distraction testing environment.

1. Have a documented disability diagnosis from a licensed clinician
2. Have a documented disability diagnosis that was received during a specific time frame, such as within the past three years
3. If she wasn't diagnosed in K-12, get a referral to a psychologist who offers specialized testing for adults (this testing typically includes long wait times and can cost thousands of dollars in fees)
4. Contact her health insurance company to see whether this testing is covered
5. Secure the necessary referral to a psychologist from her primary care physician
6. Make an appointment with the psychologist
7. Attend appointments (testing might require multiple appointments) at the psychologist's office
8. Find transportation and childcare, as needed, in order to attend the appointment(s)
9. Wait for the psychologist's test results
10. Find and review the procedures required by her institution's disability services offices
11. Make a copy of her diagnosis for delivery by hand or scan and email it to the disability services office
12. Make an appointment with a disabilities counselor to review the accommodations they are willing to offer her
13. Attend the appointment to discuss accommodations granted (which may or may not feel sufficient for her learning needs)
14. Advocate for herself for additional accommodations as needed
15. Figure out the procedure for telling her professor about these accommodations (which varies by institution and is often

perceived and enacted differently by various professors within the same institution)

16. Bring the hard-copy accommodations letter to her instructor or email it to them
17. Remind the professor before the exam (probably repeatedly) about her accommodations
18. Process the emotional elements of having to complete this months-long (perhaps years-long) process just to be able to sit in a room to take her exam with fewer distractions

At what point would any reasonable person give up and take the exam in the main testing room? When I read through this list, I say, "This cannot be real. This cannot be the method that the industry that dares to call itself higher education has decided on to meet the needs of its learners. It cannot be real."

It's real.

Reading this over makes me feel embarrassed to call myself a higher educator. I hope you feel equally disturbed by the obstacle course that we place in front of our ADHD and other disabled students. I hope you feel rage at those who dare to accuse students of malingering. I hope your heart breaks for the students who make it to the end of this obstacle course, as they might still encounter professors who refuse to meet their accommodations or treat them with disdain for needing them. I encourage you to make a similar list of the steps required to access accommodations at your institution. Then, use any subsequent feelings of embarrassment or rage as a call to action. Discuss this list with your peers. Share it in faculty meetings. Use it as fuel for positive change.

Kat Stephens-Peace, who we heard from in chapter 1, is an assistant professor of higher education at Oakland University in Rochester, Michigan. She earned her MEd from Columbia University and her PhD from the University of Massachusetts, Amherst. She, like me, has ADHD. Stephens-Peace told me the story of her diagnosis, describing how, during her undergraduate experiences, "There was something different. Something didn't feel right, and I didn't know what it was."[18] This nebulous sense of something different and wrong, you'll remember, closely mirrors my own diagnostic journey. Stephens-Peace told me she went to the accommodations office at her institution, and the person there handed her "a long list of providers, most of whom I could not afford to go to because they were all private pay and exorbitantly priced. That was pretty much the end of the conversation. I never went back to it."[19] She was later diagnosed with ADHD during her doctoral program.

This is an Ivy League–educated higher education professor telling us that she had years-long difficulties navigating the accommodation maze on which higher education relies. ADHD students should not have to survive a gauntlet in order to learn.

When I asked Courtney Sobers, associate professor of chemistry, whom we met in chapter 1, about her undergraduate experience when she lived with ADHD but did not have a formal diagnosis, she told me, "I was one of two Black chem majors. That was the more pressing concern. The biggest stressor was being one of two Black people."[20] For many of our ADHD students, racial, sexual, or gender identities and the daily lived experiences of those identities might present as more obvious or stressful than their ADHD. That doesn't mean these folks aren't suffering because of ADHD. That doesn't mean that noticing their ADHD strengths couldn't be a benefit. That doesn't mean that access to correct care for ADHD wouldn't dramatically improve their lives. It means that they have additional barriers that complicate their ability to engage with the accommodations model of higher education and that we have a lot of work to do in dismantling interconnected webs of bias and oppression.

Do you feel the shakiness of this faulty foundation, on which we have built the house of higher education and the teaching of our ADHD students? Would you rather join me in building a solid foundation, one grounded in the reality of ADHDers' strengths and challenges? Fantastic. Let's leave this deficit-based nonsense behind us and move forward to models that empower us as educators and our ADHDers as learners. Should we, however, leave it behind by swinging to the other side of things and proclaiming ADHD as a superpower? Let's consider that concept now.

The Superpower Model

I can still remember the giant pendulum at the Smithsonian Museum swinging back and forth, back and forth.[21] Washington, DC was one of our favorite places to visit as a family when I was a kid. The pendulum would swing all the way in one direction, then all the way in another, never stopping in the middle. Whenever I hear someone describe ADHD as a superpower, I think about that pendulum.

It makes a ton of sense that after centuries of being dehumanized, degraded, and abused, the ADHD pendulum would swing in the opposite direction, and we'd declare ADHD a superpower. It also makes sense to me that folks would understand some of the ways in which our ADHD minds do work as a superpower. Sometimes, people look at the variety of interests and projects I'm pursuing and say, "How do you do *all that*?" I always answer honestly: "ADHD." Remember: racecar brain, bicycle brakes. That said, I'm very hesitant to embrace, either personally or collectively, the idea of ADHD as a superpower.

Have you ever seen a superhero movie? Superheroes are the most miserable people on the planet. They're tortured and lonely. I'm not going to spoil it, but the ending of the most recent Spiderman movie, *No Way Home*, well, it continues to haunt me. Superheroes are treated as a means to an end rather than as complex humans with unique needs, just like everyone else. They're expected to sacrifice themselves to save humanity. It makes for a great story, but in the real world, it's dehumanizing and dangerous.

Generally speaking, I avoid superpower and superhero lingo when talking about ADHD; I encourage you to do so as well. I much prefer a strengths-based, challenge-aware approach. I don't want a superpower. I want to stay alive, be as healthy as I can be, live a fulfilling life, and when possible, contribute to the greater good.

If you are someone with ADHD for whom the superpower model is empowering, do what works for you. But regardless of your ADHD status, I invite you to consider that this model might actually be disempowering for a lot of people. Instead of a huge swinging pendulum, let's instead consider the value of settling into a more balanced, middle-path approach to ADHD. An approach I love that feels very middle-path is UDL, or universal design for learning. It empowers both students and educators from a place of strengths and balance. Many of you are probably already using UDL, but let's look at it more deeply through the lens of ADHD.

Universal Design for Learning

At various points in my educational career, I remember hearing that a teacher's job was to teach to "the middle." You'd have some exceptional learners who'd be bored if you did this, but oh well. You'd have some learners who'd be left behind, but oh well. You were only human, after all, so teach to the middle you must, as Yoda might say.

As the energy of social justice movements has combined with a growing body of knowledge related to what's generally called the learning sciences, it's rare for me to come across the idea that we should teach to the middle any longer. We now know it's entirely possible to create learning conditions that support and challenge all students to learn, grow, and thrive. Yes, I said *all* learners.[22]

There are many takes on the UDL model, so let me once again encourage you to use my ideas as a springboard to learn from many different folks on this topic. For me, UDL is a philosophy of teaching that embraces this core idea: all my students have the potential to learn, grow, and thrive. My job is to optimize the conditions in which they can do so.

One of my concerns with UDL is that it can unintentionally reinforce ableism if not used carefully. Let me give you an example. Imagine you are a person with ADHD who identifies as disabled. You enter a learning experience that applies the principles of UDL to create an accessible learning environment for you and other students. The classroom is enriched with lots of choices, basic accessibility options like captions and transcripts, and the course content is drawn from a rich body of literature that includes disabled folks. Sounds good, right? But you, a disabled person, still don't find any space to share your disabled identity, an essential part of who you are and how you learn. Sometimes, UDL can be a sort of disability whitewashing. "Since we created an accessible course, we don't even need to talk about disability!" It doesn't sound so good anymore, does it?

While no one with a disability should ever be forced to disclose it, there should always be a space created in workplaces and learning experiences for those who wish to do so. The goal of UDL is not to ignore disability or banish it from the classroom. The goal of UDL is to create accessible learning experiences for all students. For me, if I can't bring my disability, a huge part of my identity, into the classroom, it's not accessible.

In Jay Dolmage's classic book, *Academic Ableism*, he shares his own both/and take on UDL. Dolmage writes: "Universal design offers a means of placing those with unconventional abilities, needs, and goals at the center of the design process. When disabled people lead the process, we can more specifically address power imbalances that lead to exclusive spaces, interfaces, and pedagogy. On the other hand, a critique of universal design would point out that there is no built-in process for collecting feedback from users, thus no way to ensure that those who inhabit the designed space have an active role in its reconstruction."[23]

I take all of this to mean that it's fantastic to use UDL to design the most accessible learning spaces possible, but that design approach must always make room for seeking out, celebrating, and using students' voices. UDL has the potential to become a bit of a self-congratulatory pat on the back. Our students' feedback can help us avoid that pitfall.

When applying UDL with ADHDers in mind, work on designing for their strengths and challenges. Reduce the need for folks to go through the absurd and often harmful accommodations process to get their needs met. Create rich learning experiences that all students can access. Finally, and perhaps most importantly, ensure that your learners always have a space to show up as their whole selves and to weave those selves together with their learning experiences in your courses.

Recently, I've noticed that when students come to me with their formal accommodations letters at the start of a new term, I'm increasingly able to tell them that I have already designed the course with their needs and the needs of all learners in mind. For example, a student with

ADHD doesn't need special permission from me for additional days to turn in assignments, because I run a classroom with flexible deadlines for all students. This can be a great test of how accessible your classroom is: To what extent are common student accommodations needs already built into your course? All that said, I treat accommodation letters as a bonus opportunity to affirm students' disability status and to welcome them, all of them, to our course.

I am able to do this sort of accessibility work within my unique context and in alignment with the bandwidth afforded to me through a combination of privileges and barriers. Some of you will be able to do the same. Some of you will be able to do even more than I've mentioned here. Others face constraints that will limit the extent to which they can design accessible learning experiences for their students. Do what you can. And in the meantime, we will all keep working to remove those barriers for you and for our students.

I also want to take a moment here to speak directly to those instructors teaching large classes. I have long been a proponent of strong faculty unions to help us advocate for smaller course loads and smaller class sizes. My belief in the power of smaller courses continues to grow with time, but higher education has made little progress here. Large course loads and class sizes seems to be perceived as a necessary evil in higher education. For those teaching large classes, I invite you to consider Tom Tobin's Plus-One framework for applying UDL.[24] This framework invites teachers to offer one additional way that students can engage with course content. For example, let's say you require students to write a final paper summarizing their learning experience in your course. Using Plus-One, you would also offer students the option to develop a slide deck presentation instead of writing a paper. Another example would be posting a Ted Talk with captions and having your students discuss that video in an online course discussion. To use Plus-One here, you could download and add a transcript of the video, so students could opt to read the video's content as well. Plus-One is a great model because it is simple and sustainable for both students and educators, particularly those with large class sizes.

Additional frames that can be paired well with UDL include neuro-diversity and neurodivergence. While our present era often feels chaotic and terrifying, progress is being made for inclusion in many spaces, and the neurodiversity and neurodivergence paradigms are a huge part of that progress. Let's move now to including them in our understanding of how to best support our ADHD learners.

Neurodiversity and Neurodivergence

A strengths-based model that has risen from within autistic, ADHD, and other marginalized neurotypes communities is that of neurodiversity. This model has saved lives and is paving the way for a new era in which all neurotypes are respected and supported. That said, we need more clarity about what neurodiversity means and how it is related to but distinct from a related term, neurodivergence.

One of the best ways to understand neurodiversity is to begin with the concept of biodiversity.[25] Do you know how many species of life exist on planet Earth? Go ahead and take a guess. How many unique ways has life found to express itself?

Humans are one species, one expression of life; we tend to forget we're not the only species. We aren't—not even close. While scientists have cataloged over a million different species, they estimate that well over eight million species live on our planet.[26]

Life is crafty, isn't it? It doesn't rely on just one species to ensure its continued existence. Instead, it hedges its bets across eight million options. This vast variety of life on our planet is known as biodiversity. Biodiversity is the ultimate version of "don't put all your eggs in one basket."

Similarly, neurodiversity speaks to the vast variety of neurotypes within the human species. Human beings think, feel, and express ourselves in countless ways. Neurodiversity, like biodiversity, captures this vast variety of ways of being in these human bodies we call home. There is no normal neurotype. There is no right kind of neurotype. This thing called being human has chosen not to put all its eggs in one basket. Instead, it expresses itself and moves through the world in as many ways as there are people. Do certain fundamental commonalities exist among brains, just as certain fundamental commonalities exist among life forms? Yes, absolutely. But beyond those fundamentals, there's immense variation.

The term "neurodiversity" was developed collectively by autistic folks and their allies.[27] Within the model of neurodiversity, there is a vast variety of neurotypes. The autistic neurotype is one of many ways to think, feel, and live. The term "neurodivergent" is a related but distinct term that speaks to the individual's relationship to social structures that privilege certain neurotypes over others. This term is typically credited to activist Kassiane Asasumasu.[28]

Through this lens, some folks are neurotypical, meaning they generally conform to and are privileged by mainstream structures and systems in society. Some folks are neurodivergent, meaning they don't conform to and are not privileged by mainstream structures and systems in society. Examples of neurodivergent neurotypes include but are certainly not limited to ADHD, autism, bipolar, PTSD, schizophrenia, depression, stroke survivor, dyslexia, and dyscalculia.

Neurodiversity, again, includes everyone—every single one of us. It speaks to the vast variety of neurotypes in our species, including neurotypical and neurodivergent folks, just like biodiversity includes humans, bugs, plants, fungi . . . you name it.

But just as many humans initially see themselves as operating outside of and often above the concept of biodiversity, many neurotypical people see themselves operating outside of and often above the concept of neurodiversity. It's incredibly important that we get this right, because if we fail to include neurotypical people inside the neurodiversity paradigm, it implies that they are the norm and the rest of us are different (and deficient). Instead, neurodiversity reminds us that while social structures privilege some people over others, in reality, there is no norm.

I often see folks using "neurodiversity" when they really mean "neurodivergence." The simple rule is that a person cannot be diverse. Diversity is a description of groups, not individuals. If I were describing someone's race, for example, I would say that they are white, or Black, or Asian, or Native American. I would not say that someone's race is "diverse." If I were looking at racial diversity, a group that is all the same race is not diverse. A group that contains people from more than one race is diverse. However, many folks, often white folks, would describe a group of white people as not diverse but a group of Black people as being diverse. That normalizes and privileges whiteness. Don't refer to individuals as diverse or neurodiverse, only groups. I am part of a neurodiverse species. I am a neurodivergent person.

Got it? There is no normal neurotype. There is only the vast variety.

Now that you have a strong understanding of neurodiversity and neurodivergence, let's turn to a concept that has gotten less attention, but that is no less important: neuronormativity.

Neuronormativity

Sonny Jane Wise is a trans, neurodivergent public speaker who has made significant contributions to the neurodiversity movement. One of Wise's most profound contributions is articulating the concept of neuronormativity. Wise invites us to consider how we frame experiences like living with ADHD through the lens of neuronormativity.[29]

You might find it helpful to consider neuronormativity as similar to white supremacy and white privilege. The idea that whiteness is the norm and anyone who deviates from whiteness is different (and therefore less than, and therefore less deserving of resources) is one of the foundations on which racism rests and operates. Neuronormativity is the idea that neurotypical people are the norm and that anyone who deviates from neurotypicality is different, less than, and less deserving of resources.

Here's a simple example of neuronormativity: good students sit still in class, normal students sit still in class, and smart students sit still in class. Anyone who doesn't sit still in class is different. They're disruptive and less intelligent. They're not paying attention. Something is wrong with them. They don't deserve to learn.

After several thousand years of *Homo sapiens* roaming the planet, the idea that a human being who is sitting still is somehow superior to one who needs and wants to move their body is truly outrageous, but that's how neuronormativity works. It leads us to believe outrageous things. Our job is to resist it so that we can see reality. Humans exist within bodies that were born to move, that need to move, and that enjoy moving. Movement is a part of life and learning. So is stillness. Students who want and need to move in a classroom setting are human beings expressing their natural needs. Students who want and need to be still in a classroom are human beings expressing their natural needs.

Can you see how neuronormativity can seep into your brain, though? A student in your classroom is fidgeting or getting up and down a lot to sharpen their pencil. Neuronormativity tells you there's something wrong with them, and you shift into deficit-based assumptions about them. Yes, ADHDers are prone to movement over stillness. No, that doesn't mean we're deficient. It's one of many ways to be in this world.

Wise's work has challenged me to root out my own reliance on neuronormativity, even as a person who's lived her whole life with ADHD. We're all taught to believe that neurotypicality is superior. We all have work to do to unlearn that lie. As you continue through this book and take its message out into the world, get in the habit of asking yourself, "Is that the truth, or is that neuronormativity talking?"

I love Wise's work for many reasons, but one is that they've very much influenced me to be more inclusive of lived experience. Listen, I work in academia! I am constantly told to respect the research and to honor the literature over all else. I held a lot of bias about the value of lived experience, but Wise presents its value in a very balanced, nuanced way. To ignore Wise's voice and teachings because they are not presented to us in a peer-reviewed journal would be a massive loss for progress and humanity. We must center the voices of those with lived experience. Refusing to prioritize spaces that leave ADHDers out of conversations is one of the best ways we can do this work, and luckily, an established movement in the disability space can remind us of the importance of true inclusion.

Nothing About Us Without Us

One of my least favorite feelings occurs when I read an article, get an email, or attend a workshop where a neurotypical and/or nondisabled person makes bold proclamations about the wants and needs of neurodivergent and/or disabled people. Typically, these missives are a combination of total ignorance, saviorism, and blatant ableism.

A solution: *nothing about us without us.*

This slogan has a long history in political and disability rights movements, and it's now something you'll hear often from neurodivergent folks.[30] When we center ADHDers in campus conversations about how to best design and teach for ADHD learners, when we refuse to make decisions about ADHDers' needs without their representation, we are ensuring that the truth of their lives will be told because they're the ones who are doing the telling. Too often, this is not the case.

Everyone and their mother has an opinion about ADHD. An op-ed is circulating this week as I write this chapter, claiming that most people getting diagnosed with ADHD don't have it and they're just looking at their phones too much. On top of the exhaustion of managing our ADHD, we are also constantly bombarded with ableism and ignorance such as exhibited in that op-ed.

If you are a neurotypical and/or nondisabled person, I invite you to consider that sometimes the best ally is the one who knows when to be quiet. This is work that I'm doing, too. For me, a good ally knows the difference between when to speak up and when to shut up. Which choice centers ADHDers, instead of you? Which choice honors ADHDers' voices and lived experiences? Which choice leads to actions grounded in the actual wants and needs of ADHDers?

"Nothing about us without us" can get a little tricky as we seek to balance representation with privacy. Not all folks with ADHD openly disclose their diagnosis. Many don't. My social media direct messages and emails are filled with communications from people working in academia who are desperate for connection, information, and support but feel it's not safe for them to disclose their ADHD publicly. Many do, however, and it's up to all of us to make sure that ADHDers, other neurodivergents, and disabled folks not only have a seat at the table but also have the time, energy, and resources to sit at that table. In addition, neurotypical and nondisabled friends should be ready to shut up and listen once we're at that table. Further, the more we all work to create truly inclusive spaces (not just performatively inclusive ones), the more ADHDers will feel safe publicly disclosing.

What does "nothing about us without us" mean for our students in our classrooms and on campus? You want to make sure that neurodivergent students, faculty, and staff are represented at all levels and, most specifically, in any conversations and decisions that affect their learning and lives, but you also want to respect their privacy. How can we navigate that situation?

First and foremost, always respect privacy. Never force a student or colleague to disclose a disability, health condition, or neurotype such as neurodivergent or ADHD. For example, if you suspect that a student has ADHD, it is completely inappropriate (and likely illegal) to ask them if that's the case, even if you think they'd make a great representative on a college committee.

Instead, you can focus on creating conditions and spaces where neurodivergent folks are invited to share, if that feels safe and useful for them to do. If you are neurodivergent and feel safe doing so, you can share this part of your identity on campus. I tell my students about my ADHD diagnosis, and I've noticed more students than ever before openly disclosing in my classroom. I never force their disclosure, even if I think our community and that individual would benefit from representation. Instead, my job is to use my skills, privilege, and experiences to create safe and welcoming conditions for ADHD learners and colleagues.

Allow your students the opportunity to represent themselves and their needs. In meetings and on committees, ask, "Do we have representation from the people we are making decisions about in this room? If not, why not? Before we proceed, that needs to be addressed." You can't control the outcome of asking that question, but you can control your decision to ask.

Finally, I long for the day when we fill our executive leadership ranks with openly neurodivergent folks. I'm not holding my breath for this, as the current expectations of most of these jobs completely contradict the needs of ADHDers. This conversation is beyond the scope of this book, but certainly, college presidents and provosts with ADHD would have significant power to shape change and invest resources in supporting ADHD learners (and faculty and staff).

That said, I'm also here to remind you that executive leadership in higher education is but one avenue for leadership. "Small is good, small is all,"[31] adrienne maree brown teaches in her work on emergent strategy. Small actions from students, teachers, and staff add up through the power of interdependence to powerful shifts that will lead to positive change in formal and informal education spaces for ADHD, neurodivergent, and disabled humans. Interdependence reminds us that we don't have to do everything; we just have to do our part. And in tandem with others doing their part, our small acts of creation and resistance can move mountains.

Speaking of creating new ways forward, let's conclude this chapter with a model that has informed my professional work and personal life for the past twenty years: using a design ethos to consider clearly what is needed in our world and to then create solutions with our existing affordances and limitations in mind.

Learning Experience Design

By now, most folks in education have heard of instructional design (ID). In my travels, I've found that fewer people know about learning experience design (LXD). ID focuses on alignment between learning objectives and teaching strategies. It speaks to what you want students to know or be able to do by the end of the learning experience. From there, you select teaching strategies and learning resources that best match those initial learning goals. The keyword for ID is "alignment."

The keyword of LXD is "empathy."

LX designers begin with empathy for their learners. "Who are my learners?" they ask. "What do they want? What do they need?" Sometimes, LX designers create personas to help them tap into the power of empathy. They imagine typical learners and give them names, families, desires, interests, and challenges. These personas help guide design decisions. For example, suppose you're deciding between an online scavenger hunt or a collaborative group project. In that case, you can imagine the pros and cons for the persona you call "Carmen," who could be a first-generation college student majoring in marketing who has social anxiety and loves drawing comics in her spare time.

Another tool commonly used by LX designers is an empathy map.[32] Empathy maps can be used in tandem with personas. Designers might graphically display Carmen's wants, needs, strengths, and challenges to help them ideate learning solutions and strategies. Of course, ableist mindsets bleed into every aspect of our lives, and that can include attempting to empathize with our learners' needs. Testing our empathetic assumptions and making sure to include opportunities to hear from our learners to confirm that our assumptions align with their realities is vital.

ID and LXD are different. That difference is evident to me when I consult on course and/or community design. I often review an instructionally sound course, a course that has bulletproof alignment between learning objectives and instructional strategies, that is also soulless and lacks awareness of the needs of its learners at this moment in time. Of course, I'm speaking generally here, and many instructional designers create engaging and excellent courses, but one of the reasons I prefer LXD to ID is that it feels less formulaic, less focused on lining up instructional details into neat rows, and more grounded in creativity, fun, and play.

ID feels more instruction centered. LXD feels more human centered. ID feels as though it's more about schooling and LXD more about learning. ID feels like work. LXD feels like play. ID prioritizes the mind whereas LXD prioritizes the whole person. Because LXD centers human needs through empathy, it is a perfect model to ground our design choices as we work to support ADHD students' success and design against shame in our classrooms.

There are a multitude of models we can use to better understand and support ADHD. You can see how relying solely on one model, especially a deficit-based model, really misses the breadth and depth of the ADHD experience. I hope that at this point in your reading, you have questioned any remaining reliance you have on deficit-based models of understanding ADHD and have instead embraced better, more open, more realistic models that center the lived experiences of ADHDers.

Summary

The key learning concepts from this chapter on models include:

- We can consider disability through a person-fixing or society-fixing lens. Pay attention to which lens is most prevalent to you throughout this book and in your work.
- Balance a recognition of strengths and challenges when working with ADHD learners.
- Disability justice is a model that centers women, people of color, and genderqueer folks in the quest for freedom for disabled people.
- The history of ADHD in this country and higher education is grounded in a deficit-based approach. Deficit-based models do harm in many ways, including increasing shame for ADHDers.
- The accommodations model of higher education is a clunky bureaucracy at best and an oppressive nightmare at worst.
- Declaring that ADHD is someone's "superpower" is often well intentioned but can also be dehumanizing. Recognize both our strengths and challenges.
- Universal design for learning (UDL) prioritizes accessibility in design choices, regardless of whether learners qualify for formal accommodations, but be careful that you do not use UDL to erase disability from your classroom. Disability is an important identity that many people hold.
- The word "neurodiversity" speaks to the diversity within groups of people. The word "neurodivergent" is used to refer to individuals who diverge from mainstream norms.

- Part of our work in creating better learning experiences for ADHD learners involves rejecting standards of neuronormativity.
- ADHDers should be centered in conversations about ADHD on campus. Our lived experiences matter. Make sure that you involve us in decisions about our lives, learning, and well-being. Nothing about us without us.
- Learning experience design (LXD) can support your work with ADHD learners by prioritizing empathy.

Part Two

Simple and Sustainable Design and Teaching Strategies

In Part I, we worked together at the level of mindset. That is the bigger picture, long-term work of unlearning much of what society has taught us about ADHD, most of it deficit-based. I hope you now have a much richer, more accurate vision of ADHD. You see our challenges, of course, but you are also incredibly moved and excited about all of our strengths. You feel excited about working with your ADHD learners, both for their benefit and because you see how our ADHDers are creative leaders with unique skills and strengths that are well-suited for our current highly volatile era.

The following five chapters include simple and sustainable design and teaching strategies grounded in evidence-based practices and ADHDers' lived experiences. I want you to take a moment before you begin Part II to really feel the words "simple" and "sustainable" in your bones. The goal here is not to try to understand every strategy deeply or implement them all next term. That would be complex and unsustainable. That approach would sacrifice your well-being as an educator and harm you and your students.

Instead, play the game of small. What are one or two things you can do next term to create more inclusive classrooms? After you test out those strategies, reflect and refine them. Then, add one or two more strategies in the term after that. Small actions matter; when done in loving community, they can have powerful ripple effects. Doing one thing differently this term is a big deal. Your well-being matters here, too, reader. Please treat this book as a resource for the long-term work of inclusivity, rather than a checklist to fulfill at your own detriment.

In chapter 5, you'll learn how to design and teach against shame, one of the most debilitating aspects of ADHD. From there, chapter 6 will cover the power of making everything external and visible to overcome ADHDers' challenges with object impermanence and working memory. Next, we'll scale the mountain of metalearning to help your students learn about learning.

Do you recall that ADHDers regularly outperform neurotypical folks in both lab and real-world tests of creativity? You'll get to learn all about our creative strengths and how to amplify those in the classroom in chapter 8. In chapter 9, we'll wrap up the strategies section by reflecting on my "Be Like a Tree" model for flexible structure to support student learning and success (and, of course, your teaching and success!).

Which of those chapters feels most compelling for you at this moment in time? I encourage you to note that feeling and set that chapter as a priority. Remember, play the game of small and know that intentional, small actions are at the heart of every big change.

Chapter Five

Design and Teach Against Shame

————————

Have no fear of perfection—you'll never reach it.

—Salvador Dalí

Yesterday, I drove forty-five minutes to take an art class in Concord, Massachusetts, home of all things Revolutionary War. I had my own revolutionary experience.

I entered the building a few minutes before the 1:00 p.m. class.

"I'm looking for the printmaking class," I told the receptionist.

"You'll see the door right around the corner," she answered.

I entered the next room and saw a closed door.

That's strange, I thought. Why would they close the door before the class starts?

I tiptoed closer to where I could hear voices and heard what sounded like a teacher mentioning inks, color value, and paper.

Wait a minute . . . Crap. Crap. Crap.

I grabbed my phone and texted my husband.

"I think I screwed up the time of my class."

I frantically read through my emails, feeling a building sense of anxiety. I'd received two emails about the course in the prior two days. The first came from the art center. It was a reminder for the class, and while it listed the correct date, they did not include a start time. The second email came from the teacher. It was again a reminder that the class was coming up, suggesting we wear an apron to avoid making a mess of our clothes, but no specific date or time was listed.

I gave up on the emails and looked at the art center's website. I could've asked the receptionist in the next room, but I did not want to face her. I saw that the class had actually started at 12:00 p.m., and I was an hour late.

I stood there frozen for a few minutes. To go inside or leave? What would you have done?

I opted to head home and read on the couch with my dog.

Here's the thing: this was a victory for me. There was a time before I understood how shame and ADHD are linked when I would've been sent into a spiral by this mistake. Instead, I chose to nurture myself with kind words and actions while also acknowledging that the system had failed me. All these things were true. I was not and am not fundamentally incapable or stupid. I'm not a loser because I screwed up the time of the class.

I have ADHD. We experience and understand time and details differently. In a carefully designed world, I would've received multiple reminders that included the class time. I didn't. Both reminders I received did not include the time. I can note this failure, do what I can to address it (writing this book), and remind myself to double-check the times of things as best I can in the future. I can then curl up on the couch with my dog, who didn't see this as a mistake at all. In fact, he told me that my messing up the time and having to come home early was the best part of his day.[1]

Much of this progress in being kind to myself after this mistake came from strategies that go beyond the scope of the classroom, such as psychotherapy, medication, ADHD coaching, personal reflection, and supportive friendships with other neurodivergent folks. But remember, I would have avoided making a mistake at all if the learning environment had been designed differently.

Hallowell and Ratey consider shame to be "the most debilitating learning disability."[2] In this chapter, we'll explore how you can design and teach against shame.

Let Empathy Be Your Guide

A student falls asleep in class. Their instructor wonders, "What could be going on here? What might they be feeling?" Fatigue, physical illness, a hangover, mental illness, boredom, fear, resistance, and sensitivity are all possibilities. From this menu of possibilities, the empathetic professor can choose their actions regarding this student.

You sit down over the summer to plan your fall syllabi. You reflect on recent attacks on human rights in our country, gun violence, and the climate emergency. You recognize that your students are carrying trauma and anxiety into the classroom. Some could be experiencing trauma on campus, too. You create opportunities for students to take action through their coursework as an antidote for despair, clearly connecting their course learning outcomes to this volatile moment in human history.

A student with ADHD emails you in the middle of the night, frantic over the C grade you've given them on a recent paper. They tell you they've been up half the night, upset about their grade, and feel like they want to drop the class. They implore you to reconsider their grade. Some professors might say, "None of that emotional nonsense is any of my business. My business is teaching this student in this course, not caring about their feelings." An empathetic professor teaching against shame will encourage the student, perhaps share a brief story of their own grade challenges, and then nudge the student toward the next assignment. Many empathetic professors are removing grades almost entirely from their courses. Regardless of whether or not you use grades, an opportunity always exists in grading or feedback conversations to teach against shame.

Through the lens of learning experience design, empathy is not "touchy-feely stuff." It is the foundation of our design decisions. It views the totality of the human experience, which always includes emotions, as necessary inputs for our later design outputs.[3] To cut ourselves off from this information is surrendering our design choices to ignorance and chaos. We limit ourselves as educators and designers when we refuse to practice empathy. An empathetic professor's thoughtfully designed response to the student mentioned above could be, "Remember, a C means you've done average work that met expectations. That is a solid foundation, and you now have great motivation to improve on the next assignment. I'm going to give you lots of resources to succeed. I know getting a lower grade than we wanted is hard, and I've been there."

Empathy is the foundation of designing and teaching against shame, not only because it honors the needs and dignity of our fellow humans but also because knowing who our learners really are will help us design the best possible learning experiences for and with them. Empathy is the best way that I know to design against shame for our ADHD learners. But of course, learners aren't the only part of a learning experience, are they? What about their teachers?

You can practice empathy by asking and answering two questions. First, what do my learners want and need within the context in which they're learning? Second, what do I want and need within the context in which I'm teaching? Empathy maps are fancy tools for doing this sort of design work, but I much prefer a simple Google Doc. Have at it. Jot down your answers to those two questions with one of your courses in mind.

I recently answered these questions by removing all of the academic, peer-reviewed journal articles as assigned reading from a course I'd inherited. They don't fit the context in which I'm teaching or meet my students' needs. Most of my students are seniors planning on entering the workforce immediately after graduation. I switched out twenty-page journal articles for much more engaging, timely (and still evidence-based) shorter readings. Are you preparing students to teach and work in academia? In that context, assigning some peer-reviewed journal articles might make sense. If you aren't, take a closer look at the types of readings you're assigning. I'm hearing a lot of conversations lamenting how "students aren't doing the reading." Far fewer conversations question whether our hyper-reliance on peer-reviewed journal articles makes any sense.

Unnecessarily complex and dense reading has the potential to be a huge barrier to your ADHD learners. There's tremendous potential for ADHD students who struggle to get through a course with inappropriately assigned readings to misinterpret their struggle as evidence that they don't belong rather than evidence that the design of their course doesn't match their needs or this moment in history. That can result in a sense of shame that inhibits, rather than supports, their learning. Design against shame by using empathy to meet the needs of all learners and your needs as a teacher and person.

Find, Protect, and Create Spaces of Mutualism

I first learned about mutualism when I was helping my son, who was in third grade at the time, study for an upcoming science test. Many of us are familiar with parasitism, where one organism is helped and the other is harmed. Far fewer of us learn about another type of symbiotic relationship: mutualism. As my son and I moved through the flashcards we'd prepared for his science test, a lightbulb went off that fundamentally changed how I view our work as educators.

How many conversations about teaching, learning, and design are grounded in a model of scarcity and competition? Too often, students and educators are pitted against each other: It's them or us. Through the lens of mutualism, we can challenge ourselves to notice spaces in our classrooms that benefit us and our students. We find the existing win-wins and build on them.

Educator working conditions are student learning conditions. Educator working conditions are ADHD student learning conditions. One of the most frustrating symptoms of educator burnout is a disdain for the people we serve: our students. Educator burnout can turn a caring, passionate educator into someone who disdains their students. While the root of burnout is not our students and their needs, our students and their needs are what we see daily, so our brains often fight back against what appears to be the most apparent enemy. They're not. Quite the opposite. Our students and relationships with them can give us a sense of purpose, meaning, and motivation. Our real enemies are inequitable, unsustainable working conditions.

I once worked with an educator who was so excited to tell me about an online trivia game she'd designed for a class she taught in Zoom. The good news? The students loved it. The bad news? It took her eight hours to prepare. She fretted over how to continue to make these trivia games each week and fit that prep into her already packed schedule. I was happy to give her permission not to make another trivia game for her students that term, and she was visibly relieved to receive that permission. If teaching that course was her sole responsibility, then sure, make another trivia game. She was teaching four courses on top of advising and committee responsibilities. And, of course, this professor had also taken the time to sign up for my online course design boot camp. Her schedule was full. To take on that additional design responsibility would've put her at risk for burnout, harming her and her students. To draw a line and say, "I've done enough," was a powerful action to protect her and her students' well-being.

On the other hand, I recently made some fresh videos for a new course I'm teaching. As I made them, I almost caught myself making a rookie move: naming specific dates in the video. If I had done that, the video would've been dead that term, and I wouldn't have been able to use it in any future courses. I caught myself quickly. "Practice mutualism," I reminded myself. Making a video with specific dates is probably best for the students in my current course section, but it would not be good for me or future students in the long term. Instead, I found the win-win. I created evergreen videos with no specific dates.[4] That is the ideal solution for me and my students. In this space of mutual benefit, we'll often find our best way forward as educators.

Find the Right Kind of Difficult

We ADHDers are prone to going to extremes. For a long time, my professional life was either in a state of burned-out overload or total shutdown to recover from said overload. I'd vacillate between these two extremes. First I'd get totally jazzed on every idea that entered my head, say yes to every opportunity, and head down every rabbit hole without a second thought. Then boom—my body would slam on the brakes in ways I couldn't ignore. I'd be forced to shut it all down. Cancel engagements. Say no to everything but the absolute necessities.

Log out of social media. Stare out the window, pet my dog, and read Louise Penny novels.

Though my crisis would begin to resolve with rest, I'd be out of my mind with boredom within a week or two, at which point the cycle would start all over again.

I am learning to live in the middle. I am best protected against shame in the middle, and so are our students.

In *ADHD 2.0*, Hallowell and Ratey devote an entire chapter to how ADHDers might "Find Your Right Difficult." In it, they quote one of their clients, Jon, who says, "Either I'm doing what drives me, which is intense problem solving every second I am awake, or I'm bored/anxious/don't know what to do with myself."[5] Next to this quote is my handwritten annotation: "it me UGH! Yes!"

ADHDers are drawn to problems and challenges. We are bombarded with ideas daily and feel a need to bring these ideas to fruition. In the words of Hallowell and Ratey, "It's like an omnipresent itch to *make something*. If that itch goes unscratched, we tend to feel listless and depressed, unmotivated and out to sea."[6]

Much of the ADHD journey is learning to live in the middle—to visit those extremes, perhaps, but to then return to a healthy balance that sustains us for the long haul. I use the word "journey" very intentionally. I suspect this will be a lifetime of work. Like any journey, it will also involve barriers, expected and unexpected. Shame is one of the barriers we can anticipate, which means we can design around it to mitigate its effects. One of the design choices that can decrease shame in our classrooms is working with this concept of the right kind of difficult.

A starting point for this work is to talk to your students about it. "What's your right kind of difficult?" would make a great discussion, especially in the early days of a new course. What sorts of challenges inspire and attract your learners? What kind of challenges repel them or shut them down? How can their right kind of difficult protect them against shame? Share your own right kind of difficult with your students.

Once students have identified their right kind of difficult, they can treat it like a compass to guide them in current and future learning experiences. They can adapt learning experiences to align with their difficulty preferences more closely and to seek more support when faced with barriers. In that sweet spot of challenge, they can remember that too much or too little challenge, or a challenge that doesn't match their unique kind of mind, can often result in shame.

Here's an example of how this might play out in the classroom. Idea generation is the right kind of difficult for me. I love to take a situation, product, or experience and analyze it to improve it. Imagine that I'm a student in your psychology course, and you assign the class the task of designing a new app that would support college students' mental health, using the principles we had learned about in class. That would be a tough challenge, and my idea-generating strengths would kick in to motivate me. This is the right kind of difficult for me.

If, however, you assigned me hundreds of pages of reading from peer-reviewed academic journals each week, along with dull, cookie-cutter textbook quizzes to assess my learning, that would be the wrong kind of difficult for me. There's no space in that assignment to imagine and create new worlds, to bring my many ideas to fruition. It's dry, cold, and formulaic.

For another student, the reverse might be true. They might not get many ideas and prefer to rely on more logical, rote types of learning. They might prefer the heavy reading and quiz approach because they find it comforting to stay in the realm of the now instead of future possibilities. For them, the app design challenge is the wrong kind of difficult.

These are just a couple of examples for you to consider among infinite possibilities of how you might teach your students, but you get the idea. The solution to designing against shame by helping your students find their right kind of difficult is first to open a space to talk about this with them and to allow them time to self-reflect. Then, you can help students lean into their challenges by providing choice on assignments wherever possible. In the previous example, students could choose between a design challenge and an exam: two choices, not seven. Too much choice can overwhelm the best of us. Two choices are good for students and manageable for faculty.

Weaving choices into your courses is smart, compassionate, and effective design that will meet the needs of your ADHDers and all students.

ADHDers love a good challenge, and we will pour our hearts and souls into things that allow us to express our weird and wonderful views of the world. Your design choices give ADHDers a chance to face those challenges in your classroom. When challenges are presented as a threat or without careful consideration of the variety of neurotypes in your class, they will often show up as shame among ADHDers. But challenge is not the enemy. Let's work with our students to find the right kind of challenge.

Mind the Cognitive Load

As an ADHDer, I have a hunch that I've blown more fuses than the average neurotypical person. I've learned the hard way, more than once, that I can't blow dry my hair when someone's using a space heater on the same circuit. Lights out.

When I think about cognitive load, I often think about the electrical circuits in our home. When the lights go out from overloading these circuits, it's not to inconvenience us. Rather, it's to protect us from a fire. The circuit breaker is the electrical protection system in our homes. It shuts that circuit off if it senses that we're overusing energy beyond our limitations. No electricity, bad. But no fire, good. We then reset our circuit, pause to acknowledge our limitations, and move ahead.

Cognitive load theory speaks to both the capacities and limitations of our brains to process our worlds. The cognitive load of my brain is what I can process in any given period. People's cognitive loads, capacities, and limitations to process their worlds differ. First off, different folks have different cognitive loads. It's also true that our cognitive loads are constantly in flux, particularly for neurodivergent folks. What we can process on one day we might not be able to process the next day. This may seem obvious, but it's worth emphasizing. What I can process in this moment, the next hour, or this day differs from what you can process, readers. Depending on the topic, some of you have greater processing capacity than I do, and some have greater limitations.

Things like how much sleep you got last night affect your cognitive load. A sick child or an injured pet can reduce it. If you're exhausted and stressed, you'll have less cognitive load available to you. Certain foods, movements, and medications can increase or decrease it. For example, for many people, myself included, mindful movement can increase available cognitive load, which is why you can almost always catch me on my walking pad at my computer these days. Having a headache and taking pain medication for it would decrease my cognitive load. Cognitive load is not static, not at all.

When we perceive our cognitive load limitations as deficits, it can lead to a sense of shame. For example, I recently attended a conference billed as feminist. It was anything but. The conference model was panel discussions, so four experts were on a stage having a conversation. Since my working memory is limited, and these scholars were using very complex academic language, my cognitive load at this conference was overwhelmed. As I was holding one of their complex sentences in my brain, trying to translate it into plain language, they were already moving on to the next complex sentence. I left that conference feeling pretty awful about myself, wondering for the millionth time whether I'm not smart enough to work in higher education.

It was only the next day, when a friend who was also attending reported a similar feeling, that I could release my shame and reframe this as a "them" problem, not a "me" problem. Sadly, this feminist conference was not designed to promote inclusive learning. It was designed for exclusive learning. If the creators had designed from a place aware of cognitive load differences, they would've made many different choices to ensure all learners in attendance could both find and add value to the learning experience.

As a comparison, I recently attended a climate education conference that was fully online and used what's called an "open" conference model. What that means is a speaker would present for about an hour, and then those of us in the room would suggest subtopics related to their talk that we wanted to discuss in small groups after that main session. All those speaking sessions were recorded, and all the discussion groups took copious notes that could be viewed later. This model supported my cognitive load abilities and limitations. I was stimulated but also able to take breaks when I felt overstimulated. For example, one of the talks

I watched argued that we're in the middle of the collapse of modernity. I was able to pause the session to reach out to trusted climate activist friends to process the intensity of that concept; then, when I felt settled, I returned to the video recording. These were two valuable and challenging conferences with two very different design choices that had very different effects on my cognitive load.

Another important consideration around cognitive load is that ADHD "flares" for a lot of people.[7] Flares are when a condition we live with ramps up in intensity at both expected and unexpected times. An ADHD flare affects our cognitive load. Many women and folks who menstruate, for example, report that their ADHD is much more pronounced during certain parts of their cycle.[8] Keeping in mind that ADHD (along with many disabilities and health conditions) can flare and subside in intensity should be part of cognitive load and design conversations. What a student can process easily one day might take more time and energy the next. Many times, teachers can unintentionally shame a student by expecting them to be able to perform the same today as they did last week. But brains don't work that way, especially ADHD brains.

We can also shame our students by teaching them to ignore their physical, mental, and emotional needs to complete a task in our classes. If your students have reached their limit for the moment or hour, that doesn't mean they're done completely. It means they need a break. Many of us were trained in an academic setting where we were taught to push past our limitations because, in many parts of American culture, limitations are seen as a terrible thing. What's so bad about limitations? What if we taught students that instead of quitting or ignoring their needs, a third option exists? To rest. To take a break. To try again tomorrow.

Of course, the entire model of mainstream American higher education is based on everyone learning at the same pace, cognitive load and limitations be damned. That is something we can work on changing gradually, and it's a much broader conversation beyond the scope of this book. In the meantime, where do you have the power to adapt to your students' (and your own) varied cognitive load capacity? How can you design so that students with or without ADHD are empowered to take breaks when they need to, not because they're quitting, but so they can continue to do their best work in the long run? If a student gets overloaded due to inappropriate design choices, odds are they will blame themselves, leading to a sense of shame. Learn to challenge your students without overloading them to avoid shame by building regular breaks into your classes. For example, I know some faculty are moving toward a model of placing the final assessment a couple of weeks before the final day of class. That allows for ample time for reflection in the final class sessions and has the added benefit of giving students with missing work time to catch up.

Learn Cognitive Load Basics

Now that you have a basic understanding of how a lack of awareness of cognitive load can shame our ADHD learners, let's dive even deeper into the different types of cognitive load so you can apply this information to your design and teaching. I'm always shocked at how few educators have learned about cognitive load theory. Since it's critical to understanding ADHD, educating yourselves will help you create more inclusive classrooms.

The three types of cognitive load are: intrinsic, germane, and extraneous. Understanding the basics of each can help us think about reducing unnecessary cognitive load demands in our courses. Keep in mind that cognitive load is a theory about how our brains work and learn. If they x-ray your brain, there's not a big sign in there that says "germane cognitive load section." That said, this is a well-respected and useful theory that I'm confident you can hang your teaching and design hat on to work with your ADHD learners.

"Intrinsic cognitive load" refers to the amount of mental energy, or working memory, that is inherent to a learning experience or task. Generally speaking, we would argue that teaching someone to draw a circle requires less intrinsic load than solving an algebraic equation. The former is simpler by its very nature, and the latter is more complex. Learning experiences and tasks vary in their inherent level of complexity and challenge.

Now, let's throw ADHD into the mix and turn this theory on its head. It's sometimes said that ADHD makes the easy things hard and the hard things easy. For example, which task has greater intrinsic cognitive load, cooking a grilled cheese sandwich or presenting an hour-long workshop on cognitive load theory? Most folks would say that the workshop has greater cognitive load demands. Many ADHDers would disagree (me included). Sometimes, the boredom of mundane tasks makes them a greater burden on ADHDers' cognitive load than more interesting and complicated tasks. For ADHDers, we should avoid assumptions about the inherent challenges of any task and rely on asking them to define which tasks are most challenging, again helping them to discover their right kind of challenge.

As an example of this intrinsic cognitive load switch at play, remember Courtney Sobers, associate professor of chemistry? I can't even fathom how smart Courtney is to have achieved that career path. I'm a believer in growth mindsets and that we can learn anything we invest time in, but I don't think I could ever be a chemistry professor. Dr. Sobers spoke to me about struggling with the so-called easy stuff of life. "I'm in a mom group, and they get really offended if you don't remember kids' birthdays. It's so stressful." Dr. Sobers can understand and teach organic chemistry but is stressed out by trying to remember a child's birthday. Many people would categorize organic chemistry as having a greater intrinsic cognitive load than remembering a child's birthday, but that might not be true for an ADHDer.

"Germane cognitive load" is connected to the existing knowledge that we hold in our brains to which we can relate or "stick" a new learning experience or task. Think of germane cognitive load as a bulletin board to which we can pin the new concept we're learning. The bulletin board is our existing knowledge on a given topic. Our existing knowledge on a subject acts as a frame or foundation for new learning. These existing knowledge frames are also called "schemas," but I find it's more helpful to use metaphors: bulletin board, purse, velcro suit, or hangers in a closet. Germane cognitive load means that the more existing knowledge you have, the easier it will be to learn a new, related concept. If I already know how to draw a circle, then learning how to draw an oval will be easier. If I already understand addition and subtraction, multiplication will be easier for me to learn.

You've probably heard the term "scaffolding" as it relates to pedagogy. Scaffolding is the process of building toward more difficult concepts using simpler concepts as stepping stones. For example, I am learning to speak French right now. French is known for having complex and varied verb forms that often stump new learners. The subjunctive tense is infamous as being the most challenging. I'm in the A level, or beginner level, French classes right now. We are not learning the subjunctive tense! Instead, we are starting with the present tense. We will continue to add verb tenses in order of difficulty. In a year or so, I will have the foundation, frame, or schema of less challenging verb tenses active in my mind, making it easier to learn the most challenging tense.

We often talk about boosting, maximizing, or optimizing germane cognitive load, not lessening it. Since your ADHDers have a vast range of interests, calling upon those interests and their prior knowledge will help to boost their germane cognitive load. For example, one common approach to language learning is to encourage learners to listen to podcasts in their new language on topics that interest them. Since the learner likely already has a strong foundation in that interest, this will activate their germane cognitive load. I could listen to podcasts on ADHD in French, for example, to help me use my knowledge of ADHD, which is high, to support my learning of French, which is emerging. ADHDers cast a wide net on the world, taking in a wide variety of interests and ideas. Use our passion for learning and our plethora of interests as an asset in the classroom when working with germane cognitive load.

Finally, let's consider what's often known as the "bad guy" of the cognitive load crew, "extraneous cognitive load," which speaks to anything not central to the core learning outcomes of a task. Extraneous cognitive load includes things like reading and understanding instructions for an assignment. Another example is submitting a paper through an assignment link in a learning management system. Most professors in higher ed, regardless of their course's modality, require online assignment submissions. Figuring out how to submit an assignment online doesn't have anything to do with the core learning outcomes in your class (e.g., history, math, cybersecurity, whatever), so the submission process is considered a type of extraneous cognitive load. It's the extra stuff that's adjacent to the actual learning that still takes up time and energy. Many students perform poorly on assignments because of extraneous cognitive load demands. For example, a student might know the answer to the quiz but struggle to understand how to complete it online. Their poor quiz grade would reflect misunderstanding the quiz directions more than the student's actual content knowledge.

Reducing this "bad" type of cognitive load as much as possible will help your students focus on the true heart of their learning experiences. Don't write five-page assignment instructions (this might seem like hyperbole, but I've seen it!). Don't use a fifteen-point grading rubric. Again, it's not hyperbole. Simplify instructions. Be clear and concise. Teach students the how of being a student in your course along with your content. This might mean linking to a video with directions on how to take a quiz in your online course section, for example.

Here's a cognitive load shortcut for you, which is fitting for the topic of cognitive load, right? (1) Reduce extraneous; (2) Boost germane; (3) Don't make assumptions about intrinsic. If that resonates with you, you can even assign each of those suggestions a color and go through your course plan with a highlighter, noting any areas of opportunity for redesign. Remember, we want to challenge our students without overloading them, and in doing so, we will mitigate the negative effects of shame in our classrooms.

Be Intentional About Feedback

We've established that ADHDers experience both recognition sensitive euphoria (RSE) and rejection sensitive dysphoria (RSD), meaning that we're particularly responsive to both positive and negative feedback. In addition, our design choices of models like LXD, mutualism, and cognitive load theory can tremendously benefit our learners. Now, let's get a bit more granular about how to communicate with our ADHD students without instilling a sense of shame in them. That means it's time to turn to an interesting topic among educators: providing students with feedback.

Providing feedback to our learners is personal, political, and pedagogical. On an individual level, your words have immense power to influence a student's day, mood, sense of self-efficacy, and ability to achieve your course learning objectives and to meet their own learning and educational goals. You also bring your own wounds, fears, and stories to the feedback discussion. If you were brought up in academia via a culture of harsh criticism with very little praise, you might swing in the opposite direction and shower your students with positive feedback. You might also choose to continue to teach the way you were taught. You are a human being who brings the totality of your life, including your gifts and challenges, into every moment of feedback you provide to your students. In the moment you provide feedback, you hold immense power.

Do you view feedback as an opportunity for growth for both you and your learners? Do you ever weaponize that power against your students? To knock them down a notch? To put them in their place? Do you get a little dopamine boost in that moment of doing harm? Do you rationalize that choice by saying you're trying to prepare them for the real world? If so, that's very human of you, and I want you to notice and name that in the hope that you'll try a different approach. Notice what personal feelings come up when you work with students with disabilities such as ADHD. You are human, and we all carry bias.

Politically, you bring your own varied identities and relative privileges to feedback conversations, as do your students. Also inherent is the fundamental power dynamic of teacher and student, which historically grants the most power to the teacher. However, we are starting to experience shifts in the post-#MeToo, social media savvy, current higher education climate that have granted students increasing amounts of power, particularly when joined together in solidarity, to disrupt this traditional dynamic. Also, be aware that you live in an ableist world and that this political reality cannot help but affect your feedback and teaching.

Finally, your feedback is a pedagogical choice. Your teaching choices around feedback can act as either a springboard to learning or a barrier against it. Many of the faculty I work with tell me a great deal about what their students are or aren't doing with feedback (e.g., they aren't reading it, they aren't using it, etc.) When I respond by asking them to describe their own feedback pedagogy, I sense hesitation. Naming our teaching choices and pedagogies and focusing our energies where we have control can be a very empowering choice for educators.

Weave all of this into the reality that many ADHDers experience RSD, a heightened sensitivity to criticism, whether perceived or actual. Couple that with our RSE, which means that we thrive in environments where we receive regular positive encouragement. In short, feedback is important and complex, especially when working with our ADHD students. Let's aim to celebrate that importance while simplifying it a bit. How can you provide caring, useful feedback to your ADHD learners that alleviates shame, inspires growth, and helps your students meet their own learning goals and the objectives of your course?

To answer those questions, we've got to start facing some hard truths about feedback, such as the idea that feedback might not actually work in many cases. We spend a lot of time giving our students feedback. We then invest time and energy worrying over whether our students are reading and using that feedback. We are also often contractually obligated to receive feedback on our teaching and work from a supervisor or outside observer. In short, feedback is taking up a lot of real estate in our lives and brains, but do we have any evidence that it works?

In "The Feedback Fallacy," an article that has taken on cult status in some circles, Marcus Buckingham and Ashley Goodall take on the god of feedback, a god that many of us are mindlessly praying to on a daily, if not hourly, basis. "The first problem with feedback," they proactively start by saying, "is that humans are unreliable raters of other humans."[9]

Who? Me? An unreliable rater of other humans?

Yes. Me. And you.

Many of us are rightfully upset about the inaccuracy of students' ratings of us, but as the saying goes, when you're pointing a finger at someone else, you're pointing three back at yourself.[10] What we're getting in student evaluations of us are a bunch of flawed humans' personal opinions on a flawed human. Various social identities and influences, including race, class, gender, and sexuality, inform those evaluations. What we're giving when we provide students with feedback is the same: a deeply flawed human's take on another deeply flawed human. In short, feedback is subjective.

Buckingham and Goodall go on to say that feedback often does the opposite of our (stated) intentions. "Another of our collective theories is that feedback contains useful information, and that this information is the magic ingredient to accelerate someone's learning. Again, the research points in the opposite direction."[11] Basically, when we approach feedback from a deficit-based standpoint (e.g., you're doing this wrong), we trigger internal defense mechanisms in others that impair learning rather than promote it. In other words, we're better off building our feedback off someone's strengths, helping them to fine-tune their strengths to improve, rather than trying to fix what we believe to be wrong with them (which, again, is subjective in the first place).

A lot of feedback, not just in education, but in general, is often an ego play by the feedback giver. It's a way to position themselves into a place of power: "I'm the all-knowing one and you are the not-knowing one." It's a dopamine hit to make the giver feel better about themselves, unfortunately, at the expense of a fellow human being.

I want you to challenge yourself to recognize the inherent subjectivity in feedback. Even if you're pointing out that a student added 2 and 2 to get 5 and that their answer is incorrect, the tone and energy you convey in your feedback is still subjective, because you are two human beings, not two robots. That subjectivity is messy, but hey, that's what makes us human. With all that said, read on for six specific tips to help keep shame out of our learning environments.

Six Feedback Tips

1. Notice your own emotional experience when providing feedback.

Experiment: the next time you provide feedback to your learners, jot down three questions on a notepad beside you: (a) "What feelings show up when I'm giving students feedback? (b) How do I react emotionally to students who appear to have met the assignment's expectations? (c) How do I react emotionally to students who appear to not have met those expectations?"

See what shows up. For many of us, we might notice gratitude for or appreciation of the students who meet expectations and something less positive for the students who don't. Whether you use grades or practice ungrading, whether you are using a rubric or not, whether it's a high- or low-stakes assignment, let's stop pretending that teaching is not deeply relational and emotional work. Let's stop pretending that we're not human beings who bring all our own trauma, stress, and old habits to our interactions with students.

To begin, you don't need to do anything but notice. In my experience, the noticing takes on a life of its own. Awareness often leads to action.

I recently noticed an emotional reaction when a student I'd offered a lot of support and flexibility to throughout the term submitted an assignment that included the words "Chat GPT said:" at the start. It stung. It hurt! I felt that sting on a personal level but also at the broader level of wondering what the future of education holds for all of us. Naming that emotion and letting it move through me allowed me to take a breath, step back, and provide kind and direct feedback to that student. Engaging with our emotions as educators makes us stronger and sets us up to do a better job of supporting our students rather than trying to pretend that we don't have emotions at all.

2. Nonjudgmental feedback is not an oxymoron.

I know many kind, caring humans who struggle to give students positive and effective feedback. I used to be one of them. I wanted to focus on fixing the problem and often thought of positive feedback as too "touchy-feely" or a waste of time. It's not, particularly for ADHD students. If you struggle in this area, taking baby steps is okay. Instead of focusing on providing positive feedback, you might first become more aware of eliminating anything nasty, negative, or judgmental from your feedback.

Judgmental? You're wondering. But isn't it my job to judge them? No, it's not. Your job is to teach them. My therapist recently defined "judgmental" for me in the most succinct way: mistaking a preference for a fact.

Judgment: You really should've spent more time proofreading this assignment. It's riddled with errors. I don't know how you're going to pass this course. If you're not willing to put in the effort, you should probably consider dropping the course.

Teaching, kept neutral: I noticed a significant number of errors in your writing that could've been eliminated through more time spent on proofreading. Many students find success in using Grammarly.com or the college's tutoring services to help with proofreading. To make time for additional proofreading, it's important to plan ahead and build that time into your paper writing process.

Notice the difference? The second example doesn't utilize any positive feedback or demonstrate care, so it's still not aligned with the learning sciences on how to best provide feedback. However, I think it's important to meet people where they are, particularly educators who only received harsh feedback themselves after years in academia. Try starting out by sticking to the facts, not your story about the facts. Aiming for neutrality is a great first step to ease the harmful effects of shame in feedback.

3. Remember the value of a strengths-based approach.

Here's another experiment for the bravest of hearts. For one assignment, instead of providing critical feedback about what a student did wrong and how to fix it, try an entirely strengths-based approach instead. Find one thing each student did well and then treat that as a foundation for growth. This aligns with a model called appreciative inquiry (AI), which is a strengths-based leadership paradigm.

AI argues that it's more effective to strengthen what's working than to try to fix what is not. One of the ways I think about AI is through the lens of expansion and contraction. Critical feedback feels like a contraction; we are trying to shrink something. What often shrinks is the learners' self-esteem, especially with our ADHDers. Instead, ask your learners to identify something they did well that they could expand upon. Maybe they demonstrated creative and divergent thinking by presenting an argument you haven't considered. Maybe they related the course content to their own experiences. Maybe they turned the assignment in on time. Maybe they turned in the assignment late, but still, they turned it in. Try it, just once. Find the win and help the student envision how they can expand on it. The best feedback will motivate students to take action toward improvement,[12] and people who feel terrible about themselves after receiving feedback are not likely to do so.

4. Name the elephant in the room.

I hate critical feedback. It cuts me to the bone. For a long time, if you handed me ninety-nine kind words about my writing and one criticism, I would ruminate over the one criticism for three days. I share this because the adage of the feedback hamburger doesn't always help our ADHD-RSD students. The hamburger approach suggests that you start your feedback with a positive (top bun), then provide the critique (meat), and then wrap up with a final positive note (bottom bun). Again, for many years, when receiving feedback, I'd throw out those buns and gnaw on the meat, to my own detriment.

Though I've done a lot of personal work to detach from these reactions and to build new habits around how I receive feedback, it might always hurt to receive it. Someone can provide it to me with the utmost care, and I will still feel a sting. You know when you'd skin a knee as a kid? It hurts. When your parent or caregiver had to clean it off, it hurt worse. When it was healing, it hurt. Shame is a deep wound, and it hurts. Even if a skinned knee is handled with care, even if you get a kiss on your boo-boo after it is bandaged, it still hurts.

Let's talk about this with our students and name the feedback elephant in the room. Early in the class, spend significant time having a group conversation with them about how you will provide feedback. Talk to them about why it matters and how they can use it to meet their goals. Then, most importantly, ask questions about their experience with feedback and listen to their answers. How does feedback feel to them? Why do they seek it out or not? What strategies might you all use together as a learning community to make feedback useful? Will there be a pathway for them to provide feedback to you, perhaps by keeping a Google Forms survey open throughout the class to offer you feedback on your teaching? What would your classroom look like if feedback was brought out into the open and treated as a partnership and a conversation?

Too often, we dive right into the work, post the feedback in the learning management system, or write it on their papers without ever having discussed feedback. Feedback is personal, political, and pedagogical. I have found students to be incredibly receptive to this dialogue. Build on that excitement and start this conversation.

5. Circle back with feedback-sensitive learners.

As we've established, you have ADHD learners in your courses. Some of them have formal accommodations. Some don't. Some of them have disclosed their ADHD to you regardless of their accommodations status. Some have not. Whether or not you know that a student has ADHD, observe how your students process feedback.

When I was in tenth grade, my English teacher, Mrs. Bestwick, asked me to stay after class one day. This was a true RSD nightmare. I was a wreck all day waiting for our meeting. She sat down next to me at a student desk and asked me a question that I remember to this day. "Karen, do you know the first thing you do when I hand a graded paper back to you?"

"I look at my grade?"

"Yes. And do you know the second thing you do?"

"Ummm . . . no?"

"You look around at everyone else's papers to see their grades. I watch your face. If you get a 96, which is a great paper, but you see the person next to you get a 97, your face falls. It's going to be a very hard life if you're always comparing yourself to other people."

Mrs. Bestwick was not wrong.

If you notice that some students appear particularly sensitive to feedback, if you notice them frantically comparing themselves to other students, if you notice their faces falling when you hand back papers, follow up with them after class. This could be an in-person conversation: "Hey, I wanted to let you know that you did a good job on that assignment, and if you'd like to stop by during office hours, we can talk about it some more. We've talked before in class about how feedback can be tough, so I'm here to help you process this and move forward." The same can be said with a quick email.

Another option is to open up a survey or send a class email reminding students of what avenues are open to them to discuss your feedback. This is a great way to connect students to office hours (what some now call student hours) and to give them an actionable reason and motivation to attend those. In short, feedback should start conversations, not end them, especially for our ADHD and feedback-sensitive learners.

I want to take a moment here to recognize that the idea of starting conversations with your learners might induce anxiety in those of you who are feeling pressed for time and energy, now more than ever. I can remember when I was experiencing burnout in a particular job; I knew something was seriously wrong when one of my favorite students showed up to my office unexpectedly and I inwardly groaned. Working with students and developing supportive relationships with them was why I got into education, so wishing my students would leave me alone was a major red flag and a very typical symptom of burnout.[13] If the thought of inviting students into deeper and more insightful conversations about their learning is upsetting, that's very human of you, and I invite you to consider whether burnout might be a possibility. If not, as always, apply the strategies in this book to the extent that you're able, remembering that even the smallest shifts can have big, positive impacts.

6. Consider moving beyond written feedback.

Written feedback without other sensory cues can come off as harsher than intended. It's a bit of "Objects in the mirror are closer than they appear" energy. Feedback can feel bigger to ADHDers than it might feel or appear to others. Feedback in your learning management system (LMS) platform or on the paper may appear meaner than it is. Bringing our total selves to the feedback conversation can help relieve shame in our learning communities. Now, how do we do that in a way that honors our time and energy as faculty?

Carefully. And imperfectly.

As with many things, the extent to which you can provide caring, holistic feedback to your learners that is less likely to trigger feedback sensitivities is constrained by your course load and class sizes (more reason for us to continue advocating to our administrations to right-size those). Typically, those teaching smaller class sizes with smaller course loads have a great capacity to weave flexibility into their teaching and support their students' unique needs. During early COVID-19 lockdowns, I worked with an educator who had an emergency remote class of one thousand students. Even though she had a few teaching assistants to help her, she obviously had significant constraints. If you're teaching large classes, do your best and know that your best is good enough. Take everything here as an invitation and adapt it to the realities of your workload and bandwidth.

Could you use a tool like OtterAI voice transcription to provide feedback to your learners via a voice note with transcription? What about recording a quick video in Zoom or your LMS? These might take more time upfront when providing feedback, but they also have the potential to save time in the long run if students are more likely to apply your feedback, saving you from having to repeat yourself.

Other options include adding emojis, images, memes, or GIFs to your feedback to convey tone and emotions. These types of extra-verbal tools can soften the edges of criticism. Some learning management systems allow professors to add a quick voice memo. Create one with a kind word of encouragement and a reminder for the student to contact you with questions.

What about providing feedback via text? Remember, you don't have to give your students your private number to text them. I use a Google Voice number to text my students. Remind is another texting service many educators use to text students individually or in groups. Students are texting, and we want to meet them where they are. Text your class something like: "Just posted grades and feedback on the essay. Overall, you did good work. Check it out and let me know if you have any questions." This is a sixty-second intervention that can wrap your feedback in care and support.

Feedback is one of the main areas where I see many educators using the same old approaches that don't work for us or our students and getting stuck on a hamster wheel of frustration. Crafting caring and creative feedback to support our ADHD learners has the potential to help them, and as a bonus, transform the way we approach feedback with all our students.

Accept the Invitation from Access Friction

Perhaps, as you've read through this chapter on designing against shame, you've recalled previous teaching experiences where you designed what you thought would be a very engaging lesson or activity, and it imploded before your eyes. One way that can play out is when a lesson works really well for some of your students and is an epic fail for others. Group work is a great example. Group work is often fertile ground for ADHDers to share some of their creative strengths. What about students with social anxiety, though? What if being part of a group is too overwhelming for them? How do you balance these competing needs?

Carefully. Oh so carefully.

Access friction speaks to the wobble we feel when designing for the needs of all our learners rather than one subset. In meeting one student's needs, you create a learning barrier for another. We lean toward one, and it pulls us away from another, so we course correct and lean back toward the other. No matter what we do, we are pulling away from someone, wobbling in the middle of the scale.

Here's another example of access friction that I often encounter in my work: I facilitate workshops for faculty and staff, most often in Zoom, on topics such as trauma-aware pedagogy and supporting ADHD learners. I am a huge proponent of the chat in live, virtual sessions as both a learner and teacher. In *Crip Spacetime: Access, Failure, and Accountability in Academic Life,* Margaret Price cites the Zoom chat as a space of opportunity for learners. Students using a chat are presented with an alternative means of communication that is built into the Zoom platform, not an added "accommodation" that they have to identify themselves in order to receive.[14]

I start all my workshops by explicitly inviting learners into the chat, modeling chat engagement for them, and repeatedly asking questions they're invited to answer in the chat. One of my biggest frustrations as a learner is an online workshop where the chat feature is either turned off or discouraged. The chat is where learners can "learn out loud" together, process ideas, and share resources.

Occasionally, though, I hear from someone who tells me that they find the chat distracting. One woman's treasure is another one's trash. What is engaging and exciting for me is annoying for other people. Folks who use a screen reader that reads the Zoom chat when open might find that a distraction and a huge barrier to their learning. In all those cases, I invite folks to close the chat window in Zoom. I often take a breath there and use that as a teachable moment to remind folks that we all have different learning needs; we can do our best to meet those varied needs while simultaneously surrendering the illusion of perfection. Human needs are complicated and often in conflict, but the good news is that we are also problem solvers and can usually sort them out. As additional ways to balance the needs of all learners, I can summarize the chat activity verbally during the session and follow up afterward with a chat transcript.

Too often, people use access friction as an excuse to shut down accessibility. This is baloney. Access friction is an opportunity to discuss our wants, needs, and differences and to build better solutions. It is not an excuse to throw our hands in the air and give up on creating more accessible learning experiences.

A lot of access friction arises from conversations about stimulation and sensory needs. Many neurodivergent folks are overwhelmed by too much stimulation (e.g., noise, color, lights). One of my worst nightmares is a live concert, for example. Loud sounds, flashing lights, and so many people. I used to force myself to go to them because everyone else seemed to love them. No longer. I'm not a concert gal. I will happily listen to Taylor Swift in my house and car.

While I don't think most of you will be putting on a concert in your classrooms anytime soon, you get the idea here. Be mindful of lighting, noise, and sensory elements that overstimulate or understimulate your learners. What do you do, for example, if half your class wants the fluorescent lights in your classroom turned off and the other half wants them on because they struggle to see in the relative darkness? Of course, we want to prioritize fundamental safety first, but once everyone's basic needs are met, how can we, as a group of humans with contradictory needs, be creative about honoring one another's preferences and differences?

You'll talk about it with your learners. You could request a few floor lamps from your administration. You could make a deal with your students that the lights will be on for certain activities and off for others. Your light-sensitive students can be encouraged to wear a brimmed hat or sunglasses and celebrated in making that choice.

Designing learning environments that reduce shame and boost learning for ADHDers and all your students is a journey, not a destination. As with anything else, focus on progress, not perfection. Can you move your courses one step closer to greater access today? And can you do the same next month? And the month after that? All while cultivating spaces of mutualism that find and create benefit, both for you and your students? This is the charge and opportunity of designing and teaching against shame.

Summary

What are some key points from this chapter on designing communities that I want you to carry with you into your classrooms?

- Learning experience design (LXD) is a methodology grounded in empathy for our learners and ourselves. Start with empathy.
- Mutualism seeks to find, cultivate, and protect spaces of mutual benefit to students and educators. Design with mutualism in mind.
- ADHD learners love challenges but can become easily overwhelmed and burned out. Help them identify their ideal amount of challenge.

- There are three types of cognitive load: intrinsic, germane, and extraneous. Be mindful of unnecessary weight on your students' cognitive load.
- Consider the personal, political, and pedagogical influences on and effects of the feedback you provide to students. Most importantly, talk to your students (and listen to them) about the feedback experience.
- Access friction is an invitation to open to the complexities of the human spirit and our classrooms. What you do to create access for one student might impede another. You aren't failing if this happens. Name it, then return to that foundation of empathy. Seek creative solutions with your learners and your peers.

Shame is one of the deepest wounds for people with ADHD. Designing for shame free, engaging, supportive, inclusive classroom communities can help alleviate that shame. Remember, this is hard work, so let's also design with our own needs in mind and heart.

Chapter Six

Externalize Everything

I thrive in structure. I drown in chaos.

—Anna Kendrick, *Scrappy Little Nobody*

Baseball fans, you are probably familiar with the habit of players holding up their fingers to each other to indicate the number of outs in the inning. Luckily or not, depending on which team you're rooting for, players often forget to do this. Chaos ensues. You can watch a compilation video of the best examples of these mistakes on YouTube. My personal favorite is from the year 2000, when Mets left fielder Benny Agbayani catches a fly ball, assumes it's the third out, and runs over to the sidelines to hand the ball to a little kid in the stands, and the Giants player who'd been on third base scores. There were actually only two outs. The best part? When Agbayani realizes this, he takes the ball back from the kid.

Why do ball players hold up their hands with one or two fingers to indicate the number of outs? They're making that information external. They're tangibly, methodically, adding an external layer to what their brains already know because sometimes, our brains don't hold information as well as we would like.

I follow the adage that freedom comes from following self-formulated rules. One rule I've learned to obey since my own ADHD diagnosis is this: If it's not made external, it does not exist.

Take, for example, my 8:00 a.m. Zoom meeting this morning to interview one of the gracious subjects for this book. In addition to having this meeting scheduled in my Google Calendar, I set reminders on my Fitbit watch and Alexa device, wrote a meeting reminder on a Post-it note in the kitchen to greet me when I woke up, and told my husband and son about my meeting and asked them to remind me.

I have found out the hard way that one of these additional layers is not enough. If I were an MLB ball player (a girl can dream, okay?), holding up my fingers to my teammates wouldn't cut it. You better believe I'd have some additional reminders in place. Heck, since I'm a millionaire in this fantasy, I'd pay some tech genius to make me a glove that could automatically display the number of outs.

Neurotypical folks generally have "sticky" brains that can easily hold information, like the number of outs in a ball game. ADHDers are less able to hold onto information. Some call this a dysfunction or deficit in our working memory system. Because we don't do deficits around here, we're going to say that we ADHDers have a lot of challenges with working memory, that those challenges also connect to the strength of our open neurotype (ON), which allows us to see and interact with the world in beautiful ways, and that we can use many strategies to support our working memories.

Start thinking of providing external scaffolding, whether in the form of task lists, planners, or extrinsic rewards, as assistive devices for ADHDers. Just as a chair or stool is an assistive device for me, someone who can't stand for long time periods, so are external structures for people with ADHD. Now, let's get into the practical work of making all things external in our teaching and learning.

Offload Brain Space

Since ADHDers have limited working memory, making things external saves our precious cognitive resources. To do that, we can offload things from our brains to external spaces. We're going to talk about this offloading concept using two terms that I view as highly related: second brains and extended minds. Let's start with the former before proceeding to the latter.

The second brain concept was popularized very recently by author and creator Tiago Forte, who wrote about his model in *The New York Times* bestseller *Building a Second Brain: A Proven Method to Organize Your Digital Life and Unlock Your Creative Potential*.[1] Second brain building can be viewed through the larger lens of "personal knowledge management," though having a second brain sounds much cooler. Personal knowledge management, or PKM, began appearing in the literature in the late 1990s.[2] You can probably guess what else was rising in influence around the same time: the internet.

We were suddenly taking in more information than ever before, and PKM as a field was asking how we could manage and organize all that information. Forte has popularized these concepts with his Building a Second Brain course, conferences, and book. The important note here is that the second brain model falls into the bucket of PKMs.

A related concept is the idea of extended minds. Annie Murphy Paul most recently covered this concept in *The Extended Mind: The Power of Thinking Outside of the Brain*.[3] Paul argues that we can think with our bodies, surrounding environments, and relationships as an alternative to the mainstream "brainbound" thinking model that most of us rely upon. Extended mind theory is both personal and collective. It's also important to note that holistic approaches that honor the wisdom of bodies, environments, and the collective are as old as human history and woven into the fabric of tribal and Indigenous cultures. Paul is pointing anew to very old ideas.

Together, the second brain model from the field of PKM and the extended minds concept can help our ADHDers offload content from their brains, freeing up space and energy. I invite you to start noticing what you expect students to hold in their heads and to what extent you provide opportunities and support for them to offload content outside their heads. A quick example of this is providing students with a structured notes template at the start of the class or asking students to take notes in a collaborative Google Doc. Take a minute now and mentally scan your courses. What percent of content is brainbound and what percent is external? Now, let's look at each of these models in more detail and consider examples of how you can use them in your teaching to move toward more external supports.

Extend Your Minds

In one of my favorite TED Talks (and I'm not alone in this; it's had over 75 million views), Ken Robinson ponders the question, "Do schools kill creativity?" My favorite part of this TED Talk is when Robinson challenges the intelligence of university professors, who some argue are the smartest people on the planet.

Robinson says:

> And I like university professors, but, you know, we shouldn't hold them up as the high-water mark of all human achievement. They're just a form of life. Another form of life. But they're rather curious. And I say this out of affection for them: There's something curious about professors. In my experience—not all of them, but typically—they live in their heads. They live up there and slightly to one side. They're disembodied, you know, in a kind of literal way. They look upon their body as a form of transport for their heads.[4]

In the language of Annie Murphy Paul, professors are "brainbound." Brainbound is what Paul calls the idea that this organ inside of our heads makes up the entirety of our intelligence and is the captain of the ship of our lives. Paul argues that this is a uniquely American and Eurocentric idea that rests on "our society's emphasis on individualism"[5] and the expectation that "we operate as autonomous, self-contained beings."[6] Becoming brainbound is an idea that came from someone's imagination and that has been reborn in countless other imaginations throughout modern history. It has been reified, or made real, over time, and I would argue that American higher education is ground zero for the reification of brainbound thinking.

Paul presents an alternative model: our minds can and do extend beyond the organs inside our heads to three areas: our bodies, our environments, and our relationships. Put simply, each of those three areas can be a source of "mind": of learning, knowledge, information, emotions, and motivations to take actions to improve our lives and serve the greater good.

Copious evidence exists in support of these three types of extended minds. For example, our cognition improves with movement, so why is the model of K-16 education grounded in forcing students to sit still? Paul writes about a study on movement and cognition focused on ADHDers, which found that "more intense physical movement was associated with better cognitive performance."[7] All too often, I hear the casual ableism and unscientific belief that students who sit still are "paying attention" while students who are moving, fidgeting, or looking around the room are not. Aside from the fact that our bodies are designed to move in addition to being still, these types of movement can also be what's called "stimming," which is how many neurodivergent learners both activate and soothe their nervous systems to allow them to engage with learning. In another of the studies that Paul discusses, learners who doodled during a boring task were found to remember more than those who were not doodling. Doodling is a common stim of ADHDers and other neurodivergent learners. In short, reams of research show that all types of movement boost cognition, so again, why is education grounded on keeping students sitting still? Why do we view sitting still as an indicator of attention?

What types of movement do you encourage in your classroom? Can students stand, sit in a chair, or sit on the floor? Can students pace in the back of the room? I recently started using a walking pad while I'm working. It's been a game changer for me, and I don't just mean physically. It helps me focus and feel calmer when working, especially on mundane tasks. Where are the bodies in your classroom, and what expectations do you communicate to your students about those bodies? Encouraging movement can be as simple as taking regular breaks to invite students to move however they need.

The second type of extended mind is the mind of our environments. Environmental design influences cognition. Putting someone in a classroom with exercise balls, fidget spinners, and paper and crayons for doodling will have very different results, despite teaching the same content, than putting that same learner in a large, soulless, bare-walled lecture hall and expecting them to be still for fifty-five minutes. Paul notes the growth of a new field connecting environmental design (including virtual spaces) with learning and cognition. It's called "neuroarchitecture."[8] The spaces and classrooms we build, whether onsite or online, matter for our ADHDers. It's really amazing (and concerning) how classroom design often goes out the window after the K-12 years, with kindergarten and early education instructors taking the lead as experts in this area. Who on your campus oversees the critically important aspect of designing engaging and effective classroom environments in accordance with the science of learning? What is within your power to do, even if it's very small, to create a more engaging learning environment in your courses?

One example of neuroarchitecture that can improve cognition is what's called biophilic design, which connects us to the natural world. Paul cites evidence that in addition to time spent in nature, viewing pictures of natural spaces can improve cognition. We all struggle with demands on attention and focus, whether or not we live with ADHD, and Paul offers a solution for how we might boost our cognitive load: "We can do so by simply going outside."[9]

The learning environments we design with our students can connect and support or isolate and overwhelm. I think here of one of my favorite online courses that I completed in 2010 as part of my most recent graduate degree, which was 95% online. Each week, the professor posted a comic related to the course content as the banner at the top of the online course platform. It was the smallest touch, but I've never forgotten it. Not only was she taking the time to invest in the design of our learning environment, but she was also connecting course content to the power of creativity and humor by using comics. It's a simple strategy, but consider it next to a sterile online classroom with no novelty or humor. Environments matter a lot, and they can extend the reach and power of our minds.

For those teaching onsite, I expect you share a classroom with a lot of other professors and students and that you often teach in different classrooms each term. There's still room for growth here. Ask for colorful posters. Ask for flexible seating. Ask for windows and natural lighting. Ask them to get rid of harsh, fluorescent lights. Look for opportunities to invite students into this process. What would their ideally designed classroom look like? Student groups and clubs can work on classroom design as service projects at less-well-funded institutions. And if it's accessible to all students, for the love of all that is holy, take your students outside! I know there's no screen out there, but I promise you, a giant blue screen in the sky will more than make up for that.

The final type of extended mind that Paul covers is relationships, including thinking with experts, peers, and groups. In one powerful example, Paul writes about a professor at Northwestern University who redesigned his course using the model of apprenticeships instead of a lecture-based approach. Student failure rates dropped from 60% to 10%. The students spent less time in a large group passively receiving information and more time in small groups with an expert tutor to complement the hands-on apprenticeships. That tutor–student relationship allowed for a more personalized learning experience.

Group work is a touchy subject in education, but we avoid it at our peril. Paul makes a strong case for what she calls group mind, "in which factual knowledge, skilled expertise, and mental effort are distributed across multiple individuals."[10] The adage that two heads are better than one holds true. It can be messy, but according to Paul, research favors the cognitive benefits.

For ADHDers, group work can be particularly challenging. We do things differently from neurotypicals (not worse, just different), and without clear lines of communication and self-awareness, it's easy for differences to devolve into negative conflicts. I, for example, am very different from the stereotype of ADHD that claims we do things at the last minute. I'm what's called a precrastinator.[11] I try to do everything as early as possible.

When working in groups, my desire to get everything done as soon as possible to address the anxiety that grows as I creep closer to a deadline can be challenging. If something needs to be done by March 1, for example, I've found most people will begin work on it the week before or a few days before, with the bulk of their work clustered on the final day. No. No way. If I find out about that March 1 deadline on February 1, I want to start working on it right away, because as long as it's incomplete, it's a source of anxiety. I get annoyed at people who wait until the "last minute," which is often just people who are doing things in a very reasonable time frame. If you recall our last chapter about shame, I suspect my precrastination is a lifelong coping strategy to avoid shame for missing tasks or running late.

The key point here is to overcommunicate with your students about group work and to teach them to overcommunicate with each other. Teach students how to set group norms. Have students discuss and put in writing their working styles (precrastinator, middle of the road, procrastinator) for projects and other important logistics like contact information and how and when they will communicate about the project. Ask the group to discuss how they will handle it if someone doesn't contribute or if a team member has an emergency. These are skills that we all need to use in our lives and work, so these are skills we need to teach our students.

ADHDers are fabulous, supportive, creative teammates. Many choose career paths like becoming first responders or entrepreneurs, where solving problems and designing solutions in fast-paced environments are key success skills. Give them a chance to harness these strengths and develop these skills, along with your non-ADHD learners, and watch as the power and reach of their collective minds extend.

By considering bodies, environments, and relationships as ways of thinking, you have an opportunity to break out of the brainbound limitations of traditional ways of thinking and knowing and use a great deal of additional thought-power by way of extending minds, your own and those of your learners.

Use Second Brains

As I write this paragraph, a tiny pink Post-it note (because Post-it blesses us with various colors and sizes) is stuck to my desk next to my keyboard. It's labeled as follows:

S: 51240

G: 54240

A:

That **S** number represents my current word count on this book's first draft. The **G** is my writing goal for today. I'm working toward three thousand new words. When I'm done writing for the day, I'll write down my actual total next to the letter **A**. This is a very simple example of a second brain.

Alternatively, I could've looked at my word count when I sat down to write at 7:30 a.m. this morning. How long would I have remembered the number 51,240? Less than five seconds, if I had to guess. And the work of keeping that number in my head, along with my goal number, would've used precious cognitive resources. Why bother? Instead, I built a second brain that does the work for me. When I'm done, the tiny pink Post-it goes into a pile of tiny Post-its that I'm keeping on my writing desk as a sort of Post-it altar to the writing gods, and on my next writing day, I'll create a new second brain with new word counts.

Another example of a second brain is my Notion database. Notion is a database management tool popular in many spaces, particularly among PKM geeks like me. It's user friendly, intuitive, and has lots of easy ways to add visuals and fun creative touches. I have quite a large second brain built in Notion, with a bunch of pages, including interesting websites, personal and professional goals, and a gorgeous container of all my ideas called "Projects." Whenever I get an idea to make the world or higher ed a better place, I put it in my Notion Projects page. Projects include, but certainly aren't limited to: Teaching Strategy List, Faculty Development Consortium, and Design Your Days Workshop.

To be honest, I couldn't tell you exactly what's inside each of these idea lists within the Project database. But the thing is, I don't need to. Notion is taking care of them for me while I work on my current project:

this book. When the book is birthed into the world (knock on wood), and my personal bandwidth shifts, I will return to this database in Notion and go through each idea, determining which, if any, I want to invest my time in. But in the meantime, I don't need to use any cognitive resources to remember these ideas because, again, Notion does that for me. As we learned in the last chapter, cognitive load is a precious resource that must be protected, especially for ADHDers.

For those who don't love productivity-speak, think of a second brain as a caretaker. Whether a Post-it note, a Notion page, a Google Doc, or an old-fashioned analog list, these second brains care for our ideas while we go do something else, be it rest, work, or play. You can trust your second brain to hold and care for your ideas until you are ready to receive them back into your daily life.

Invite your students to create a second brain for your course. It doesn't matter so much what tool or tools you encourage them to use; what matters most is that you are clear and consistent in teaching them what a second brain is and how it might benefit them. ADHD students are particularly poised to benefit from a second brain, but all students can benefit from this PKM approach. By offloading information into a second brain whenever possible, you are helping your ADHDers build a system they can use in all their courses, in their careers, and in their activism and home lives. This system will free up cognitive resources for life, play, learning, service, and work.

One example of a second brain could be a Google Doc, where students keep a list of notes taken in each class or for each online module. Students could also design a Notion database to store everything related to your course or all of their courses. Some folks love Evernote, a popular note-taking app. I'm not a Microsoft Teams user, but I'm sure they've got a second brain solution that can work for you and your students. A $1.99 Mead notebook purchased at your local office supply shop could also work if that aligns best with a student's needs.

Talk to students about the why behind using a second brain. Let them know it will help them save their precious cognitive energy for learning. Answer their questions and listen to their ideas about how they can create the type of second brain that works for them. I'm sure there are other second brain apps that students know about that we've never heard of.

Get used to reminding students at the start and end of class (or the start and end of a learning module in an online course) to access and update their second brain. If you send out a link to a current event you want students to read about, add the following to the subject line: "Add this link to your second brain."

Along with your students' personal second brains, you might also wish to create a second brain for your course by designing and sharing a course website or other gathering of course information. This could live on something like Google Sites, but a Google Doc organized by dates would work just as well. At the end of each class or online unit, summarize what you did in class that week. If you're brave, you could even allow students access to edit this document. Since you can easily track changes in Docs, you would still maintain a certain level of control over the content of the Doc. Alternatively, you could allow students to comment on the Doc. Students could return to this course's second brain to review course content, consider upcoming tasks, ask questions, or catch up if they've missed class. And again, if you allow students some level of access to edit or comment on the document, you empower them with a sense of agency over the course and their learning.

The second brain concept is not new; we've been using analog lists, whether pictorial or written, for eons. But it is growing in popularity, largely thanks to Forte's book. I envision a future in which a first-year seminar course in higher education would be dedicated to students building a second brain system that they would carry with them throughout every course in their college career; this would allow them to not only keep track of notes and assignments but to more readily see the connections between ideas and courses. For ADHD students, this knowledge and skill, something I didn't learn until I was in my forties, through sheer force of will, could potentially be life changing. It's important not only for their well-being and learning but, from the standpoint of institutional efficacy, for student persistence, retention, and graduation.

Courtney Sobers, the chemistry professor with ADHD we met earlier in the book, shared one of my favorite examples of a second brain in our interview. Sobers uses what she refers to as her "giant notepad," an extra-large sketchbook marketed for drawing, as her second brain, or what she calls her "outside brain." She doodles, takes notes, and fills the pages with whatever she's thinking about or working on: "I'm taking ballroom dance classes right now, and I can't remember the choreography. I keep it in my notepad. It's turned into a lifeline."[12]

This is the power of second brains.

Create Checklists

I recently saw a higher educator on social media lamenting that folks wanted to boil some complex and nuanced concept down to a checklist. Higher ed loves its complexity, doesn't it? And there's a space and need for that, absolutely. But there's also space and a need for checklists that simplify complexity. Two seemingly contradictory ideas can be true, and I'm here to tell you I'm a proud champion of checklists.

Checklists save lives, folks. I'm not being dramatic, either. In *The Checklist Manifesto: How to Get Things Right*, Atul Gawande tells stories of architects, pilots, and doctors using checklists to *literally save lives*.[13] To keep buildings from collapsing, planes from falling from the sky, and infections from killing people during surgery. Let's not be snobby about checklists. Checklists and deep reflection can coexist.

What is the particular benefit of a checklist for ADHD learners? It simplifies complex information. It puts the concept in writing to reinforce verbal directions. It places a series of steps in a logical order. Students can reuse checklists and return to them multiple times. Students can engage with it more deeply and tangibly if you design the checklist to be interactive, such as one that's laminated or in Google Docs. I find that checklists are fun and motivating. On an emotional level, as someone who experiences anxiety along with ADHD, they can also be very reassuring. The pressure to hold things in my head is released. I can bookmark or hold onto a trusted checklist like a safety blanket.

Creating a checklist helps me to clarify my ideas. I created a trauma-aware teaching checklist in the earliest days of the COVID-19 pandemic, when there was an increased interest in my work around trauma-aware pedagogy. Over the past few years, nearly three thousand folks have engaged with that checklist. Putting the priorities of trauma-aware teaching into a three-page checklist forced me to get clear on those priorities. Is trauma-aware teaching much more complex than what can be contained in that checklist? Of course. Could it be an entire graduate degree program in and of itself? Definitely. It's also true that if an educator starts doing just one of the suggested tips on the checklist in their classroom, that's a step in the right direction.

How and where can you get started creating checklists for your students? As always, keep it simple and sustainable. My suggested tool is Google Docs. Use the checklist square for your bullet points. Give your checklist a title. If you want to create a short hyperlink, use Bitly, a website that creates easy-to-access short links.

A great time to start using a checklist is during the first week of class (or even the week before). What do students need to succeed on day one of your course? What work do students need to complete in the first week? If you're going to start with only one checklist, pre-week or week 1 are your best bets.

Ideally, you could offer students a weekly checklist to set them up for success. Of course, you don't have to implement these ideas at once, but rather, you could do them gradually over a few terms. Consider making "evergreen" checklists so you can reuse them from term to term because once you add dates, they need to be regularly updated. If possible, keep specific dates off your checklist to save yourself time and to practice mutualism.

Another great option for a checklist is for a specific assignment. Let's say you ask your students to create a concept map of their key learning experiences for a particular module. A checklist would break that task down into the smallest possible steps. They might begin by choosing a mind-mapping (also known as concept mapping) digital software or analog option. Next, they could complete the required readings and review course content. Third, they would identify the core concept at the center of their mind map. Finally, they would draw out supporting details from that center point to complete the mind map. This sequence of tasks might seem obvious to you, but for ADHDers, it's often tough to corral our vast minds into a confining set of steps. Checklists help.

Finally, some of you might consider creating checklists as a teaching activity. You could partner with students to design checklists for your course. Another option is to assign students the task of creating a checklist for a particular element in your course. This is a great skill for all students, especially ADHDers, to practice. During COVID-19 lockdowns, I designed a Trauma-Aware Teaching Checklist to respond to requests from the higher education community.[14] Please feel free to use this as a model as you design your own checklists with and for students.

Display Time Visually

ADHDers' brains operate on different time horizons than their neurotypical peers.[15] On one hand, time can get away from us, especially if we're hyperfocusing. We sit down to play a video game or read a compelling novel for fifteen minutes, and an hour passes in the blink of an eye. The opposite is true as well. For tasks that don't interest us, we tend to overestimate the amount of time that they will take, which can lead us to avoid the task completely (e.g., me and boring administrative forms).

External timers that display time visually can be an ADHDer's best friend. As I've mentioned, I like to layer my ADHD interventions and supports. I have a watch on my wrist with timers, various devices in my house that allow me to set timers, a program on my computer that lets me block certain tempting websites for a set amount of time, and finally, a small, purple cube with varying amounts of minutes on each side (five, ten, thirty minutes) that shows the passage of time and beeps when the time is up.

One of my favorite people on social media these days is Sarah Madoka Currie.[16] Sarah is a mad activist and recently anointed doctor of dis/ability and madness (i.e., mad studies) via the University of Waterloo, Canada. One of Sarah's scholarship practices is to post her lecture slides on social media. There's a lot to celebrate in what she shares, but my favorite thing is that she puts an agenda with time estimates on her introductory slides. Sarah has shared that she does this to provide students with a sense of safety and reassurance. They know what's coming. They know what to expect. They can plan. They can make choices about managing their attention and energy. This is really important for us ADHD folks.

Take stock of your approach to time in your teaching. Is there a clock in your class? Do you share an agenda with your learners that lists time estimates? Do you talk to students about how much time assignments might take? Do you encourage students to bring external timers into your class? If not, start displaying time in whatever ways possible. There's no time like the present to start this inclusive practice.

Teach Outlining

Fall 2011. Downtown Boston. I meet my doctoral advisor in a coffee shop. I've changed my dissertation topic at least ten times. Like many doctoral students, I am lost in the nebulous dissertation phase despite excelling in my coursework. I later dropped out of my doctoral program, but the advice my advisor gave me that day, while not enough to give me the full support I needed to succeed in the dissertation process, has stuck with me to this day.

"Write an outline," my advisor says. "Write a really good outline, and the paper will write itself."

God, how I hate writing outlines. Let me write freely. Let me rant. Let me wander, explore the scenic route, and see where it takes me.

That said, for certain writing projects, the structure of an outline, despite the frustration it will inevitably cause people like me, is often necessary to reach your writing goals. For complex writing projects that will weave together lots of big and little ideas, your own and other people's, outlines are a necessary evil for ADHDers.

Take this book, for example. To have the proposal approved, I needed to create a detailed outline along with a general overview describing the book and whom it would help. I hated doing that, but to take this particular route of publishing my book for an academic audience, it was a requirement. It's not an arbitrary requirement, either. I can't imagine sitting down to write a book like this without having an outline as a map. In the writing world, I've heard that there are pantsers (those who fly by the seat of their pants) and planners. I wonder if most pantsers are writing fiction, because I cannot imagine writing nonfiction by the seat of my pants.

I'm not a writing professor. I am a writer with ADHD. My two cents is that we should teach students to outline. We should teach them why they should outline. We should teach various outlining strategies. We should invite students to test these different strategies and reflect on what works for them and their writing and what doesn't. We should help students recognize that different writing projects necessitate different outlining approaches and help them prepare to adapt. We should be teaching outlining skills in all our courses that include writing, not just in our English courses.

A couple of basic, practical outlining tips that work for my brain and that might work for your students are a traditional outline and mind mapping. I'm sure most of you are pretty confident in teaching how to create a traditional outline. However, one additional note that you might find helpful is that the Outline View in Google Docs is really rad. Truth: I didn't figure out how to use this tool until about halfway through writing this book; it's been life changing. It allows me to always see my outline on the left side of my Doc screen. I can easily click to different sections. Finally, I can use Insert > Table of Contents (TOC) to create a gorgeous TOC based on the outline I created at the start of my document. An update button in the TOC will also bring in any changes I've made to the outline. Why aren't we all teaching our students this essential skill that will save them loads of time and energy?

A lot of folks might want to substitute or complement the traditional outline with a mind map. I typically start any new writing project with a pen and a yellow legal pad. I put the big idea in the middle of the page with a circle around it and then draw smaller circles and tentacles with supporting concepts outside the main circle. I let it be messy, and I don't edit myself. The visual aspect of the mind map pleases me, and since I'm really an analog gal at heart, the tactile nature of this approach motivates me. For less complex writing tasks, such as an 800-word op-ed, I often write directly from the mind map. For a book-long project like what you're reading now, the mind map alone wouldn't cut it for me. I started there, but then I put the concepts from the mind map into a traditional outline and added a slew of more detail.

Many folks with ADHD might prefer to fly by the seat of their pants when writing. Many of us will fight the routines and structures we need to succeed tooth and nail, at least at first. What I have found, however, is that those routines and structures allow me to bring my whole self and my ideas into the world. They are not about assimilation; they're about support. Ultimately, if a student wants to forgo outlines entirely, that's their choice. However, our job is to explain to them how that choice might work against their goals and to invite them to experiment with other options. The proof, as they say, will be in the pudding.

Get Into Google Calendar and Tasks

Another one of those "Why didn't anyone teach me this sooner?" skills is the ability to manage time and tasks in Google Calendar and Google Tasks. Granted, I'm of an age where these things probably didn't exist when I was in graduate school, but still, they've been around for a while, and some of you have been keeping them a secret. No longer. We shall tell the world of Google Calendar and Tasks, and all things will be well!

For most of my adult life, I have used random analog systems to keep track of my appointments and tasks. In college and graduate school, I would write down the major assignments for my courses on a sheet of paper and tape it to the wall next to my desk. As I completed each task, I'd cross off the assignment. How did I know when to work on these assignments or when they were due? I have no idea. My best guess is that since I was a full-time student as both an undergrad and grad student, attending my classes daily served as a reminder of the work to be done.

The life I live now, with multiple jobs, my own small business, and my personal/family life, would not be possible without the system I've created using my friends Google Calendar and Tasks. Every Friday, I spend about twenty minutes organizing the upcoming week in my virtual calendar. I drag items from Tasks into Calendar, review appointments, and make sure I've budgeted time for rest, family, wellness, and play. My calendar is connected to Alexa devices in my house that announce reminders before every meeting.

Is the system perfect? No. I have severe ADHD, y'all.

Just last week, I was supposed to meet with my friend and colleague Niya at 4:00 p.m. on a Friday (the one time she was free all week). I typically leave my desk around lunchtime on Fridays, so this meeting was outside my usual habits. I was happily folding laundry in my bedroom while watching *Friends* when I got a text from Niya at 4:15 p.m. "Hey, are we still meeting?" Because I wasn't at my desk, I totally missed our meeting. So, I still miss engagements sometimes, but it doesn't happen to me that often, now that I know how to externalize time.

I understand that there are different calendar systems, such as Apple iCal and Outlook, in addition to Google Calendar, and you might be questioning my recommendation for this one specific platform. To say that we should all be teaching students to use Google systems doesn't seem fair, but it also doesn't seem fair to throw our hands in the air and not teach them anything. Higher ed is funny. We teach students about quantum mechanics, differential equations, astronomy, and high-level anatomy, but we refuse to teach them basics like using a virtual calendar because it's too complicated.

I know we can do this. Your ADHD students need the support of a calendar and task system. Talk to them. Talk to your colleagues. Talk to your student affairs folks. Let's start teaching this essential skill of calendar management and task planning in all our courses, especially in our first-year courses to new students. Using productivity tools is a great way to make tasks and appointments external and more easily accessible to ADHD learners.

Articulate Do and Due Dates

One of the earliest time management lessons I learned for myself and then immediately started teaching to my students was the necessity of using both due dates and "do" dates. Typically, we're pretty familiar with due dates. An assignment is due on Thursday evening at 11:59 p.m., for example. That due date will be listed on a course syllabus and might be posted in the course calendar in an online course's LMS. Some students might even add that due date to a personal planner.

What about the do date, though? Let's assume this assignment is to write a one-page reflection on the course readings for that week. That means that students need to not only write the reflection but also complete the assigned readings before they write it, and if they really want to impress you, they might even make time to edit and revise after they write it. Of course, then there's the element of actually submitting the assignment, which typically happens in an online course's LMS these days. That's a lot of doing that's often completely ignored when we only talk about the due date, and it includes tasks that need to be started well before the actual due date and time.

Teach your students (and yourselves) to schedule time for do dates. Articulate the difference and help them develop this skill. This is a life-changing practice. Here's how you might begin: First, use an example of an assignment in your course that's coming up in the next few weeks. Ask students to identify the due date. You can lead this as a simple call and response exercise in an onsite class or post it as a video, announcement, or discussion in an online course. Once you have consensus on the due date, making sure everyone is clear on how to determine that, things get interesting. Ask students when their do date for that assignment is.

On what days and at what times will they complete that assignment? For this part of the discussion, you can expect a lot of variation, both in when they plan to do the work and how much time they anticipate needing to do the work. Aim for total participation here, whether verbal or written. Try to get every student to name days and times when they'll do that assignment and then share that with other students. Can you get some class consensus about the average amount of time students plan to devote to the assignment? Notice outliers, and investigate the decision-making process behind those outliers. If some students plan to devote twenty minutes to the assignment while others are estimating four hours, this large range is ripe for an interesting discussion. Then, particularly the first time you teach this topic, share an estimate of the steps you believe are part of writing a strong reflection (including how much time they'll need to complete the readings, to edit, and to submit) and how much time you think each step might take.

After this discussion, invite students to schedule time in a planner or Google Calendar for these do dates. Let them know that while they're obviously not required to stick to that plan, you will check in with them after they submit the assignment to see whether they stuck to their plan, giving them time to reflect on their process.

Then, follow through with that check-in. After the assignment's been submitted, ask students to share whether they followed the do dates they scheduled for themselves. Invite them to share with the class what worked and/or what didn't work. What do they plan to do differently next time? How clear are they on the difference between do dates and due dates? How might scheduling do dates improve their academic performance and decrease stress? This post-assignment reflection is a wonderful opportunity for metalearning (sometimes called metacognition), which is the process of learning how we learn (much more on metalearning in chapter 7, so stay tuned).

Consider running through this lesson at least once per term, ideally a few times per term. The pre- and post-assignment lessons on due dates versus do dates can be as quick as ten or fifteen minutes. Still, these lessons have immense power to help your ADHD learners get clarity on the practice of breaking down an assignment into distinct steps and scheduling ample time for each of those steps.

My calendar includes a combination of due dates and do dates. Each time I enter a due date for a task into my Google Tasks, I immediately take a minute to add any needed do dates. For example, this week I'm running a Climate Action Pedagogy (CAP) workshop on Wednesday at noon ET. That's the due date when my slides must be ready to share with my learners. However, as soon as I scheduled that workshop, I also added multiple tasks to my Google Tasks labeled "Create CAP slides" and "Revise CAP slides." I then dragged those tasks into my Google Calendar, assigning times to do the work that needed to be completed before the workshop.

A final word on due dates and do dates: When I interviewed Ying Deng, a fellow ADHDer, she mentioned something I hadn't thought of before about one of the ways she managed her coursework in college. "I started to realize," Deng told me, "that I couldn't sign up for courses that were too similar. I would try to balance out courses that had mid-term exams with ones that were more writing based."[17] Classes heavier on exams complemented writing-intensive courses, allowing Deng to make better choices about how to balance both do dates and due dates.

Deng wondered out loud whether courses could be labeled by the institution in course registration guides to help students make similar choices. We might start by labeling "exam based" or "writing intensive," but I imagine there might be other categories that would help students create a schedule. For example, I teach courses with many small assignments that build up toward a large, summative project. Students are doing the work little by little, so there's not a lot of work for them to do at the end (assuming they've stayed on top of revisions). That said, they have small assignments due each week. Perhaps this type of course could be labeled "formative assessments" or something similar. Students could then craft a schedule that considers content but also pedagogical approach. Let's start advising, designing, and teaching more intentionally about do dates and due dates to support students in their progress toward graduation and all of their learning goals.

Empower Decision-Making

My current hyperfocus is learning French. It's all I want to do. I am, of course, doing research and have a list of books I want to order and now want to take a Zoom class to learn French with others. Luckily, plenty of online language learning options exist now, more than ever before. That's good news. The bad news is, when I try to decide which one is best for me using only a brainbound approach, I get confused and stressed. No problem, though. I know that when I'm making a complex decision, it's time to put it in writing or into my Notion database.

If any aspect of your course involves asking your students to make a decision, teach them how to make that decision external. I like using Notion, but I could just as easily use Google Docs, Google Sheets,

Google Slides, or even an analog notebook. For example, imagine asking your students to choose a topic on which to write a research paper for your course. As part of that process, include a low- or no-stakes assignment where students make a list of all their potential choices, perhaps with columns for pros and cons of each choice. Then, have students label each choice from best to worst, perhaps using a different emoji to represent each level.

Another example of this is working as an academic advisor and helping your students decide on a course or program of study. Create a template that students can use for that decision-making process and then share it with them, teaching them how to make a copy they can edit using their own content.

Explain to students that trying to make decisions inside of our heads is difficult for many of us, and that pulling those decisions out of our heads and putting them on paper or on a screen can often provide us with immediate clarity. Then, remind students of the important step of ranking their decisions with a fun and simple system (again, I highly recommend emojis). Typically, through this process, most people can identify a clear winner quickly, helping them to not only make a good decision but also decrease the stress involved in agonizing over a decision without making progress toward a resolution. Teach your students (and yourself) how to make the decision-making process external. This will particularly benefit your ADHD learners.

Don't Turn Your Back on Artificial Intelligence

Since we're talking together in this chapter about the power of making things external, I'd be remiss if I left out AI, or artificial intelligence, a potentially helpful (and potentially harmful) tool. Whether AI will turn out to be a hammer, which helps more than it harms, or a gun, which harms more than it helps, will become increasingly clear in the coming decades. I am particularly wary of AI in light of the data we're getting on its climate impacts.[18] Even if AI is helpful, we don't need another fossil fuel guzzler.

I have worked in higher education since 2002, and in my entire career, I've never before seen a topic strike such a chord with faculty like AI has. Bad chords and good chords. You can offer a workshop promising people the secret to happiness, and ten will show up. Offer one on AI, and you'll exceed the fire department's recommended capacity for the room. I've had higher ed facilitators who do regular paid speaking gigs tell me that their work has dried up because they don't cover AI in their workshops.

One of my fun personality traits is that if I see everyone running in one direction, I'll drop to my knees and scratch and crawl in the opposite direction. I'm fun at parties, as you can imagine. In short, I'm contrary as hell and trust nothing popular.

I've played with ChatGPT a dozen times, but mostly I forget it exists. I notice its likely use in some of my students' and faculty learners' writing (yup, students aren't the only ones misusing AI), but I choose to always look at the big picture of learning and assume the good in people, so it doesn't derail me.

The most interesting and fruitful conversations I've had about the whole thing, to be honest, have not been with my fellow higher educators, who seem to insist on binary thinking on this topic, but with my fifteen-year-old son. We've talked about how to use AI mindfully, what the world might look like with more AI in the future, for better or worse, and how things like AI bans seem ill advised. My son has told me that the AI bubble will be bursting soon. Time will tell.

By the time you read this, my middle-path approach to AI might have been blown out of the water. It may have made a lot of people's lives profoundly better or worse by then. Maybe its novelty will have worn thin, and we'll be on to the next crisis. Maybe it will have taken over the world and threatened us with our own nukes like in the Melissa McCarthy film *Superintelligence*. If I had to guess, I'd imagine it will be a lot like it is now: a combination of help and harm surrounded by a lot of noise. I have no clue what's coming, but despite that, I feel a responsibility, based on the huge amount of interest in this topic, to say a word or two about what's here now and how it is affecting and might affect our learners with ADHD.

Let's start with the bad news. I worry about how AI will impact our ADHD learners and that higher ed's playbook on AI is straight out of Dr. Seuss's classic *The Butter Battle Book*, one of my favorites that my dad used to read to me as a kid.[19] The butter-side-up crew lives on one side of the wall, and their butter-side-down enemies live on the other. Their battle escalates from guns to very complicated Seussical weapons and machines. You build a bigger weapon, I match you. Repeat. In the final scene, one of the scientific "geniuses" has built an egg-shaped bomb that will blow all of them to smithereens, regardless of butter preferences.

Students cheat, and then proctoring tech companies build a tool to catch them. Institutions ratchet up punishments for cheaters. Rinse and repeat. Where will it end? It won't. Not if the people profiting from the conflict have anything to do with it. I fear ADHDers are some of those who might be most tempted to make ill use of this tool and therefore are the most at risk of extreme punishments that disregard the nuances of the teaching and learning process.

Now for some good news. I've already seen interesting innovations that use AI to support ADHDers. AI can take a task list and prioritize it, assigning it suggested times. It can edit your writing for clarity. When I wrote my first book, I used Grammarly, which uses AI, to help me revise my manuscript.

For ADHDers, sometimes getting those first words down when writing is the hardest part. ChatGPT can be a good way to get the juices flowing and to get started. It can eliminate that fear of the blank page. Of course, from what I've seen of its writing, it's formulaic and boring as heck, so I wouldn't want to rely on it too heavily. AI does a good job of giving you some basic, general information that can be a spark toward a bigger, better, more accurate and creative fire. On the flip side, the convenience of simple answers comes with serious concerns about AI's ethics, climate impacts, sexism, and racism.

That all said, don't take my word for it. Let's see what ChatGPT has to say about all of this. I prompted it with the following request: "In one paragraph, using humor, explain to me the pros and cons of AI for ADHD college students."

Ah, AI for ADHD college students, the brainy buddy with some quirks. On the upside, AI can be a game-changer! It's like having a digital personal assistant on hyper-speed, ready to organize your life, zap distractions, and keep you on track like a caffeinated squirrel on steroids. Need reminders? Bam! AI's got your back. Struggling with focus? Pow! AI will whip up a tailored study plan faster than you can say "squirrel." But be warned, my friend, for there are cons lurking in the shadows. When AI gets a little too enthusiastic, you might find yourself drowning in notifications, caught in an endless loop of analysis paralysis. Plus, let's not forget the moment AI decides you're so deep in your studies that it's time for an impromptu dance party to shake things up. So, while AI is a great ally, just remember to keep an eye on it otherwise, you'll be waltzing your way through college while your assignments gather dust.[20]

As you can see here, ChatGPT followed my directions and spit out a response in less than thirty seconds, but at a cost. The stereotype that ADHDers are like squirrels is tired and basic. It's the lowest-hanging fruit to understand the ADHD experience. I could've responded to this response by telling ChatGPT to get its act together and remove the squirrel content. It would've obeyed. But I, as its user, would've had to know enough to prompt it toward a more nuanced response. You get out of it what you put into it. I also have to acknowledge that this simple prompt in this free tool was not free at all. I've read that a few ChatGPT outputs take up the same energy as making a bottle of water. Billions of us using this tool quickly adds pressure to an already overtaxed ecosystem.

As conversations continue about AI's impact on education and learning, I invite you to keep ADHDers and our climate in mind. Raise your hand and ask how decisions about AI might uniquely impact learners (and faculty/staff) with ADHD. Consider that AI might be a helpful tool to offload our thinking and externalize the thinking process, but always remember to ask, at what cost?

Summary

Here's a summary of why external structures are so helpful for ADHDers.

- Teach students to offload brain space to extend minds or create second brains to balance the effects of ADHD's executive function challenges, particularly around working memory limits.
- Checklists can be thought of as assistive devices for the ADHD brain. Use them and use them well.
- Make time visible. ADHDers struggle to perceive the passage of time. Making time visible helps them notice how much time they have to complete a task.
- Outlines are writing maps. All writers can obviously benefit from outlines, but ADHDers in particularly need these maps to avoid getting lost in the woods. Don't just tell students to outline; teach them how and explain why outlines can make their lives easier.
- Google Calendar and Google Tasks are extremely helpful, free resources for time management, scheduling, and life planning. Let's teach our students to use these powerful tools and integrate them into our classrooms.
- Help students understand that scheduling due dates alone is not enough. Instead, scheduling time for do dates in support of those due dates is what's most important.
- AI is a both/and that has the potential to help and harm our ADHDers. Let's be mindful of it while also not letting it consume every conversation about pedagogy. It's one of many conversations we can and should be having about teaching and learning in our current era.

Make as many things external and visible as possible in your classrooms. Trying to hold everything inside our minds (thinking brainbound) is detrimental to ADHD learners. Get it out of their heads to support their working memory and learning experience.

Chapter Seven

Metalearning

Metacognition is the defining characteristic of our species; metalearning is its dynamic epitome.

—National School Improvement Network

The original title of this chapter was "Metacognition," which means to think about thinking. The more I thought about thinking about thinking, which is super meta indeed, the more I realized that this "metacognition" doesn't fit the work we're here to do together, which is to embrace more inclusive ways of being, teaching, and learning.

Metacognition elevates one way of knowing and being, the mental mind, above all else. We are complex human beings, and learning does not only occur via our thoughts. Sarah Rose Cavanagh's work, for example, is rich with evidence that being in touch with our emotions and helping students do the same is the foundation for the type of deep thinking we need to do in education.[1] We don't have an emotional brain and a thinking brain; we have one brain with deeply integrated networks.

We are also gaining an understanding of how our bodies come to "know" things (the field of somatics) that we might not realize at the level of our mind, and out of the field of neurogastroenterology, we have the concept of the enteric brain, also known as the "gut brain."

Our emotions, bodies, and bellies are valuable sources of knowledge and wisdom. I hope this all reminds you of Annie Murphy Paul's contention from chapter 6 that instead of living "brainbound," we can learn through our bodies, environments, and relationships.

Metalearning means to learn about learning and can be seen as a broader paradigm that encompasses metacognition, among other concepts: "Meta-learning covers a much wider range of issues than metacognition, including goals, feelings, social relations, and context of learning."[2] For ADHDers, metalearning is also a healing practice to help us recover from years of exposure to ableism. It is an opportunity to not only notice how we learn but to reclaim our right to learn differently than through the approved norms set forth by schooling and society.

According to the Institute of Education, metalearning includes three important aims:

1. Focus on learning as opposed to performance.
2. Promote a rich conception of learning, and a rich range of strategies.
3. Develop meta-learning to monitor and review.[3]

Let's break each of these down in plain language. First, the goal here is not to ask students to reflect on how to get an A or to avoid an F. That is a performance-based focus. Instead, the goal is to invite students to focus on learning. For those of us (me included) who were trained to see learning and grades as synonymous, we might need to challenge ourselves to uncouple these two concepts to do the work of metalearning with our students. Joshua Eyler provides a roadmap on decoupling teaching and learning from grades that many may find useful.[4]

Second, metalearning is not a narrow, strict, rigid view of what it means to learn or how to best learn. Rather, metalearning is rich and expansive. Having multiple strategies from which they can select empowers learners to feel agile in the face of volatile, uncertain, and changing circumstances. Consider the volatile future we face in light of climate change. We need to prepare our students to adapt to anything as they design better futures for all of us.

Finally, metalearning can absolutely elicit joy, simply from the reflective experience of learning how we learn. However, for the purposes of this book, it needs to be actionable. Students learn about learning to apply that understanding in future and novel circumstances through their ability to monitor how they learn and review the results of their choices.

Here's an example of metalearning in the wild: After months of writing this book, I realized that the book's structure needed to change. Because I was divesting from the medical model and investing in the neurodiversity paradigm, a lot of deep revision was necessary. I needed to pause the writing work for a couple of weeks to reconsider the structure and outline of the book. This was emotionally draining and scary, because using my passion for writing about ADHD is a hyperfocus and talent of mine; structure and outlines are my kryptonite. I needed to work through structural challenges and navigate my emotional reaction to working outside my comfort zone. It affected me mentally, emotionally, and physically. My sleep worsened as I worried over this, and with less sleep, all my systems, cognitive and others, began to shut down. I chose to take a few days off from writing to recharge and then was able to finish the new outline and start writing again.

What I just shared with you is an example of metalearning. Through a deeper understanding of how I think, feel, and know things in body, mind, and spirit, I could better engage with my work and passion in writing this book. I was better able to act in service of creating a better world, the overarching goal of this book. I was better able to take care of myself.

In this chapter, I'll introduce you to strategies to begin or continue to weave metalearning into your teaching. We'll prepare ourselves to anticipate biases that might arise as our students practice an approach to metalearning that might look very different from our own. We'll consider how metalearning can empower our students to become expert learners in any context. Finally, we'll look at some specific metalearning strategies, including metacognitive dialogues, retrieval practice, sentence completers, and checklists/notebooks. Let's get started.

Hike the Metalearning Mountaintop

A quote comes to mind when I think about metalearning: Pema Chö-drön, Buddhist nun and author, is known for sharing a famous directive of her Zen Master, Suzuki Roshi: "All of you are perfect just as you are, and you could use a little improvement."[5] To build inclusive pedagogies for our students, we begin by inviting them to know themselves as learners through metalearning, to simultaneously see themselves as perfect and in need of a little work. Metalearning is not about imposing how we learn best on to anyone else. We can certainly offer our experiences as examples, but we must empower students to find their own paths to the mountaintop, not to follow ours.

Remember, our ADHDers have been exposed to a lifetime of shaming, deficit-based practices. As we invite them to think about their thinking and to learn about how they learn, it is key that we do this with a strengths-based, challenge-aware model in learning communities designed against shame. Our goal here is not for our learners to try to root out so-called "deficits" or to teach them to think and learn more like neurotypical people. We've already established how bad that would be for ADHDers and for a society that's already missed out on ADHDers' creative strengths for too long. Instead, our job is to empower our learners to research, test, and discover how they learn best and then apply that understanding across all aspects of their lives.

Depending on your own neurotype or simply your personality type, at times your students' metalearning reflections may be confusing to you. There might be a temptation to make judgments that equate their differences with deficits. Many of these judgments might be operating under the level of conscious awareness, so it's important that you remain vigilant for their appearance in your teaching.

I'll use myself as an example: one of my coping strategies for my ADHD is to precrastinate. I am so scared of the shame of missing deadlines that I work myself into the ground trying to get as far ahead of deadlines as possible. When my students tell me that they think most clearly when they work on assignments at the last minute, a common strategy of ADHDers, I notice a strong resistance rising within me. I want to tell them that's the wrong approach. I want to tell them that waiting till the last minute will cause them stress and lead to less effective learning. Instead, I've learned to invite them to try working a bit ahead of deadlines and then compare their results to waiting until the last minute. Can you view metalearning as an invitation rather than a requirement?

Many ADHDers use the stress of doing things at the last minute as a motivational tool to help them complete boring tasks. That's not inherently wrong, bad, or deficient. If learners have tried various options and then employed metalearning to reflect upon the most successful strategies for them, it's quite possible that waiting till the last minute could be their best option.

As one of my yoga teachers used to say, "One mountaintop. Many paths up the mountain." Metalearning is not a chance for educators to control students' learning choices but to invite them to reflect on what aspects of their thinking and learning serve them and which they might want to redesign.[6] Metalearning stripped of agency is not metalearning at all; it's poorly disguised indoctrination grounded in bias. Take your own path up the mountain, and let your students discover theirs.

Co-Create Expert Learners

In her book *Antiracism and Universal Design for Learning: Building Expressways for Success*, Andratesha Fritzgerald defines student success as the development of expert learners.[7] Metalearning is the road to that end goal (which is a lifelong learning journey, not a final destination) of helping our students to become expert learners, learners who can apply their metalearning skills in any classroom, any course, any challenge, and any learning opportunity inside or outside of formal schooling and education.

Fritzgerald writes, "Becoming an expert learner is the vehicle that makes learning safe and productive. Learning how to learn is what moves every student forward on this journey in a way that is meaningful and the most enjoyable."[8] She shares the story of a student, Dorian, being welcomed into his expertise as a learner through his teachers' application of universal design for learning (UDL) complemented by an anti-racist lens.

Dorian had long experienced the degrading effects of carceral educational approaches, where he was "punished for being angry about having a stalled car on the expressway of learning."[9] Using UDL, Dorian's teachers invited him, a talented artist, to complete assignments with his artistic skills as the starting point. He was encouraged to listen to audiobooks on headphones in class, and sometimes, "Dorian would forget he had on his headphones, and he would jump out of his seat cheering for the hero of the epic poem."[10] Fritzgerald concludes Dorian's story by saying, "He didn't have access until he found an avenue."[11]

Metalearning helps students discover avenues for adventure, success, and the spaces where they can uniquely contribute to the greater good. This example shows how a limited view of assignment completion via one avenue would've failed Dorian. Taking a broader view that recognized the rich learning possibilities available allowed this student to discover means of learning that matched his skills, interests, and needs. Metalearning is a creative and, more importantly, a co-creative act. Along with his caring teachers, Dorian was discovering and paving the road to learning and success.

To co-create expert learners, we must make learning the focus of our classrooms. This might seem obvious, but in my experience in higher education, this focus is frighteningly limited. Our focus is often less on learning and more on content dissemination. We can look at the "what" of learning (content), then the "how" and "why." A focus solely on the "what" of learning will be fleeting at best and completely ineffective at worst.

As you plan your lessons and courses, consider using this "what, how, why" framework to guide your design and weave metalearning into the fabric of your course and teaching. From this broader approach, you can then drill down to specific assignments and assessments. Moving beyond the "what" into the "how" and "why" will help co-create expert learners like Dorian.

For example, imagine you are asking students to design a meme to illustrate a recent topic discussed in class. Ask students: "What are you creating? How are you creating it? Why are you creating it?" in the time period leading up to that assignment. That will open space for learners to discuss the time and space they'll set aside to work on their memes. Will they create the meme alone or with a partner? What tools will they use to find inspiration and images and to design the actual meme? How will they present it to you and/or their peers? Finally, why are they creating a meme? How will this task contribute to their learning experience in your course, and what skills, knowledge, or wisdom are they developing through this assignment? Some students, for example, might be interested in a marketing career and will see clear value related to their career goal in the assignment. Others might articulate the value of self-expression and creativity for their own sake or for one's mental health and well-being. In other words, co-creating expert learners prioritizes process over product.

The answers (product) are important, of course, but it is the act of learning to ask all these questions, again and again across learning experiences, that will create expert learners who can carry these lessons across courses and life experiences. For your ADHD students, this might be the first chance they've had to express their approaches to learning in a celebratory way without being shamed or feeling like they need to be fixed. Like the student Dorian, who was able to thrive when teachers adapted the learning environment to his needs, rather than trying to force him to adapt to a limited view of learning, co-creating expertise in learning through metalearning with your ADHD students will open a world of possibilities for them that they might've been forced to hide for years within our deficit-based schooling model.

Trust That ADHDers Can Practice Metalearning

True story: an early reviewer of this book, someone who identified with a more traditional clinical background than I do, suggested that I shouldn't recommend metalearning to all of you. He argued that metalearning is "too hard" for ADHDers. He put this in writing unabashedly and questioned my scholarship and legitimacy for recommending metalearning as a strategy in this book.

Metalearning is a challenge for many learners. It's a challenge for ADHDers. However, the idea that we should avoid introducing it to ADHDers because of its challenges is ableist and harmful. As we discussed previously, ADHDers' brains still follow the basic rules of neuroplasticity. We can learn. We can learn anything with the proper support. We can learn to practice metalearning. Metalearning is tremendously beneficial and empowering to ADHD learners.

Be mindful that metalearning will require practice for most students, especially those just starting out, but also know that with practice will come progress. Multiple studies have found positive impacts on ADHD learners' executive functions through metacognitive training,[12] so not only was that reviewer ableist, he was also just plain wrong. I've cited four strong studies here, but know that there are dozens more. Not only can ADHDers practice metalearning, but it also appears to be an even more powerful and helpful intervention for them than for their neurotypical peers.

I share this story to reclaim some territory that this reviewer tried to take from me, but also because I want to remind you that part of the work of designing and teaching for your ADHD students is challenging ableism and neuronormativity. Naysayers are out there in our world and in the field of education. They will ignore the science of learning and attack inclusive strategies to protect the status quo. We must name the science and fight back.

What I love most about metalearning is that it keeps ADHDers in the driver's seat of their lives and learning. Instead of telling them what to do, we ask what they did. We ask whether or how it worked. We ask them to imagine new strategies, and we know that ADHDers have excellent imaginations. I suspect we'll see a lot more about the efficacy of metalearning for all learners in the coming years, and you will now be at the forefront of this work.

To reiterate, do not turn away from this powerful design and teaching tool because of ableism. Remember, ADHDers are capable, resourceful, and creative. Let's rely on their lived experiences and actual research, not ableist opinions about what ADHDers can and can't do.

Engage in Metacognitive Dialogues

In their 2001 review of 100 studies on metalearning through the Institute of Education University in London, the authors use the term "metacognitive dialogues" (or "metalearning dialogues" for our purposes) to explain how teachers can guide students' learning and success.[13] They explore the power of metalearning throughout the lifespan, but I found the questions listed for preschool metalearning particularly interesting. Though most of you are probably working with older students, as the saying goes, everything we need to know we learned in kindergarten. Here's the list for your consideration:

How come we [did X] yesterday?
Did you find out anything you didn't know before?
How did you go about finding out?
Can you find out some more on that by tomorrow?
How would you go about teaching other people all you have learnt about this?[14]

As I've said, I'm a big fan of simplicity and plain language. If you are new to metalearning, these questions are an excellent starting point for weaving it into your classroom. You might also want to design your own metalearning dialogues with your students. What questions do they want to ask their peers about how they learn? What questions do they want to ask you? Themselves? Here are several more questions I think can add value across disciplines:

1. What do you know about this topic? Where/how did you learn or come to know that?
2. Whose perspective is missing? Where are the women? Disabled people? People of color? Low-wealth folks? Trans folks?[15]
3. Does this (information, reading, task, etc.) lead us forward or backward as a society? How so?
4. How might this affect other life forms besides humans living on this planet?

5. How do your unique identity and life experiences influence your understanding of this topic?

For your course, consider designing a metacognitive dialogue through which you can ask the same questions each day or with each module or assignment. Develop the habit of having that dialogue, perhaps at the start of a new module or a week before a major assignment is due. Use these dialogues to simply and sustainably build the habit of metalearning.

Practice Retrieval

Ask 100 students how they study for an upcoming exam, and most will tell you they read over their notes. Unfortunately, reading over notes is a terrible study strategy. By practicing metalearning with your students, you can open the conversation about study skills and introduce students to a more effective method.

Our model of schooling and higher education focuses on getting content into our students' brains. What's more effective, research shows, is to focus on getting information out of their brains through the practice of recall or what some call retrieval practice.[16] The first example of recall I learned about was called "survey, question, read, recall, and review" (SQ3R). I'm still a big fan of this evidence-based study/reading practice, so let's use that as a starting point to illustrate how this recall works.

You have decided that your learners would benefit from reading a chapter on neurodiversity in your course, and you assign them this reading before the next class or online learning unit. One student, Fred, reads through the chapter and highlights words or sections that feel important. A second student, Deanna, uses SQ3R instead. Deanna turns the headings and key points of the reading into questions that they write or type, then they read the entire passage, and then they use those questions to try to recall what they've just read before a final review of the entire process. Research shows that in this scenario, the Deannas of the world will retain more information from the reading than the Freds.

The second R, recall, in this method is the magic of SQ3R. It's that pause, that tug in the brain as we grasp for a word or concept just beyond our reach. It reminds me of the years I spent trying not to fall on my face in a crow pose in yoga class, a pose where you balance your bent legs on your forearms. Nope, nope, nope, still nope. Then, one day, I was flying. That is learning: the moment when the thing we couldn't do is done. The moment when the thing we didn't know is known. That is the power of recall.

In a course where the educator only lectures, trying to put things into their students' brains, there is no space for this magic moment, and often, very little space for authentic learning. Imagine if brief lectures were punctuated with opportunities for students to practice recalling information they'd just learned, and students were then given the chance to practice that recall repeatedly with peers.

Many educators focus on retrieval only at the point of formative assessments or occasional summative assessment checkpoints instead of as part of a regular learning practice. A test, for example, is absolutely an example of asking students to use the recall skill. However, in the original approach of SQ3R and the more modern work of retrieval practice, teachers are meant to use recall with students as an ongoing formative practice and as the foundation of their teaching.

The popular website Retrieval Practice, developed by Pooja Agarwal and colleagues, offers a swath of resources that educators can lean on to weave recall into their courses more regularly. They argue that retrieval practice boosts metalearning because it shows students clearly what they know and don't know. For example, suppose the student in the above example, Deanna, finishes their reading and attempts to answer the questions they created, only to find that they don't know the answers. Deanna can use that powerful piece of feedback to decide what comes next. Perhaps they need to reread the chapter. Perhaps they need to explain it to a peer or listen to an audio version of this chapter. Perhaps they want to take a break before returning to it, or they had too many distractions the first time and will reread in a quiet space. Recall practice is metalearning feedback worth its weight in gold for both students and educators.

Another of their key recommendations is to help students build the habit of asking questions, an approach that complements the metacognitive dialogues we just discussed. Habits are not built in a day. Again, repeated use of recall and metalearning are critical. Keep the word "practice" in mind here. I did not learn to do crow pose in one yoga class, but after years of consistent practice. Your students will learn to become expert learners who are strong in their meta-learning skills over time.

ADHDers are great starters but not so great at consistency, so some external rewards might be a worthwhile incentive to building the metalearning skill of retrieval practice or recall. Consider helping students add a habit tracker to a learning strategies binder and checking a box every time they use recall practice in your course.[17] You might also want to use a habit tracker to hold yourself accountable for regular use of this strategy.

I love stickers as small rewards. Offer gold stars for the students who have an "aha moment" using recall, whether publicly in class or privately, in their reflections and assignments. Rewards can be used mindfully and equitably with a little bit of forethought and consideration for empathetic design choices. In addition to external rewards, teaching students to really tune into that magic moment of recall can be a powerful intrinsic reward. Not knowing something, reaching for it, and then suddenly recalling it into one's mind feels very, very good. Let's give our learners more opportunities for that magical moment.

Share Sentence Completers

I did a bit of crowdsourcing on metalearning via social media, and one of my favorite suggestions was to use sentence completers to promote metalearning. The possibilities here are endless, so let's narrow down a few solutions in the name of simplicity and sustainability.

A sentence completer, or collection of sentence completers, can be used to practice metalearning in a focused container.[18] Examples include:

- When I start to get overwhelmed by my classes, I usually _____.

- In general, I feel _____ about my classes this semester.[19]

The main advantage of sentence completers is that you aren't asking students to reflect too broadly and openly, which can be stressful and overwhelming for some students who might not know where to start. Instead, you are giving them a container to place their reflection. If more open reflections are valuable to you and your learners, you could start with a few sentence completers to "prime the pump" and then open the reflection from there. For ADHDers and other neurodivergent students, some containers will feel too big or too small, and others will feel just right. Talk to your students, and more importantly, listen to them. Perhaps they love sentence completers and find them useful. Others might benefit from broader reflective containers.

What types of sentence completers might work well for your course and learners specifically? Remember to keep that framework of empathy through learning experience design in mind. Who are your learners, and what do they need? Who are you as an educator, and what do you need? Perhaps you'll discover that starting class (or an online module) with sentence completers works well. Others might use them to close out the class. You could obviously do both or weave them into the middle of your lessons.

Keep our strengths-based, challenge-aware approach in mind as you create sentence completers. For example, try: "The learning experience in this course that I'm most proud of is _____," or "I've definitely improved my understanding of _____ over the course of this term." We certainly don't want to use: "I stink at doing _____." Avoid any deficit-based thinking.

Sentence completers can focus on both learning strategies and course content. The goal, remember, is to get students learning about how they learn and to use the constraint of the sentence completers to nudge students into a deeper metalearning awareness. Again, consider working with your students to develop sentence completers that you can reuse repeatedly. For example, perhaps you will always start your class with something like "Today I'm feeling like _____ and my classmates and teacher can support me with _____." That would start your class off with supportive energy and help meet students where they are.

Work with Checklists and Notebooks

Work with students to create a checklist of questions they can use in various conditions, including when reading course texts, evaluating research, and participating in class discussions.[20] For example, a checklist for questions to ask when participating in a class discussion could include: What is the core argument we're discussing here? What are some alternative explanations for this phenomenon? If I were explaining this to a child, how would I help them understand it? Where do I agree with my peers? Where do I disagree with my peers? What's one thing I'm still unsure about and for which I could use additional information?

Invite students to use this checklist when appropriate and normalize the use of external supports. We live in a brainbound culture that likes to reward people who pull things out of their mind, but there's nothing inherently better about that. Help break down the stigma about using tools like checklists to support metalearning and reflection.

If you really want to go to the next level, bring a laminator to class to laminate your students' checklists. Hand out dry-erase markers so that they can check off the questions and otherwise annotate their checklists (or doodle on them; that's okay, too) as they work through them. Students could also use their dry-erase checklists when reading or completing coursework outside of class.

The tactile nature of this activity will help engage your ADHD students in focusing on the task at hand. When I was in college, I rarely spoke in class. Those of you who know me now probably find that incredible, but it's true. My brain would flood with information during class discussions, but not only information about the course topic. I'd be inundated with stimulation from everything else happening in that learning environment, including sounds, smells, and lighting. I couldn't "dig out" the information about the topic because it was buried under an avalanche of information. A checklist like this would've given me a concrete touchstone to help me participate and engage in a much less overwhelmed and anxious way.

Another popular metalearning approach is to offer students reflective options before and after they complete course assessments (e.g., discussions, exams, projects, papers, journals). An evaluation notebook can be a holding space for those reflections. Identify one or more assessments in your course, and after one has been submitted or completed, ask students to write down what strategies they used to complete the assessment. What went well, what challenged them, and how confident are they in their learning? Offer them space to consider what they might do differently in the future.

Written reflections are great, but we can also encourage students to draw or doodle their responses. Maybe a student will make a comic. If done virtually, students could also create a mood board to describe their experience using tools like Padlet, Pinterest, or Canva. They could gather pictures in a virtual bulletin board to document their learning experience.

The evaluation notebook can be used in tandem with the next intervention, a techniques notebook. Ideally, once a student begins to collect some of these post-assessment evaluations, they can pull them out *before* their next related assessment and look over what they did the last time in order to course-correct for the next time.

A techniques notebook is a collection of what works for various assessments and learning experiences. Consider with your students how they might best organize their ideal techniques. Will their notebook be digital or analog? Perhaps they'd like to organize their notebook with one learning experience per page (e.g., a page for essays, a page for exams, etc.). Another option would be to create a mind map of techniques using any one of the free tools or apps available online.

Once they establish a plan to gather their information, students will list their successful learning techniques. This is a great opportunity to balance affirming students' choices with challenging them to consider how they know that technique worked for them. Remember, research into retrieval practice has found that students often overestimate how much they've learned from strategies like reading and highlighting texts. What's more effective is to create questions from readings and then use those questions to recall, or retrieve, key concepts from the text.

To the extent possible, provide students with colorful tools like stickers, markers, and colored paper to use as they design their learning support resources, along with plain options for students who aren't into all that jazz. You can purchase stickers in bulk from a variety of stores; even a gold star here or there can be a fun addition to catch your ADHDers' attention. Online tools like Canva or Google Slides can be used to design colorful and engaging tools.

Imagine that we invite students to consider their assumptions and cognitive biases about learning in a supportive classroom environment, using their own learning as the ground for these experiments. Imagine if students learned to question what they know, seek evidence (including evidence from their own and others' lived experiences), and share and compare their discoveries with peers and a caring professor-guide. Educational entities often state that information literacy is one of their core teaching missions. Well, what better chance to practice those skills than in our own lives and learning?

Along with their other metalearning tools, students can pull out their techniques notebook before assessments and use it to remind themselves of what works best for them. Recently, I sat down and made a similar list in my journal, jotting down what works for me in supporting my well-being and mental health. I am a "throw everything and the kitchen sink at my well-being" kind of person, and I was starting to feel like I had no clear path forward because so many strategies were floating around in my brain.

On one page, so that I could see it all simultaneously, I listed my strengths, challenges, strategies that work, and areas where I still need new strategies. For the past week, I've looked at this page and felt tremendous clarity and relief. I plan to discuss it with my psychotherapist in my upcoming session. Any of us can experience this overload and need for clarity, but it's even more of an issue for ADHDers. Therefore, strategies to help us eliminate the clutter in our minds are even more effective for us.

Your students have accrued a lifetime of inputs on what they should and shouldn't be doing around the topic of learning, much of which probably doesn't work for them. Similarly, I assume you have accrued a lifetime of input about how you should be teaching. Putting our most effective techniques in writing is a bit like the Marie Kondo strategy of cleaning out our drawers and closets. We hold the t-shirt, decide whether it sparks joy, and if not, it gets donated. If it does spark joy, it takes a place of pride in our closet. Technique notebooks invite us to keep what truly serves us and ditch the rest.

Allow me a moment to practice what I've preached by asking you some questions about what you've read so far.

- How do you now define metalearning?
- What are some things we want to be mindful of when using metalearning with our ADHD learners?
- What's one thing you learned from this chapter that you didn't know before?
- What's one thing about metalearning that's still unclear? How could you get clarity about this question?

See? Nothing fancy going on here, just some cool kids learning about learning together to benefit ourselves, each other, and the greater good. Congratulations, you have now boosted your skills in metalearning and are ready to pick one or two strategies from this chapter to test out with your learners, recognizing the power of small shifts. Keep it simple and sustainable.

In chapter 8, we'll turn to infusing our classrooms with a huge ADHD talent: creativity. With metalearning as their foundation, as students cultivate their skills in learning how they learn, they will be well prepared to turn their attention to learning about some of the major strengths of the ADHD neurotype: creative and divergent thinking.

Summary

This chapter focused on the power of metalearning (a broader, more accurate term for metacognition). A summary of what we learned follows:

- Metacognition is thinking about thinking, but learning is not just about thinking. Metalearning speaks to a more holistic, whole-body approach to learning and, therefore, reflects on all aspects of the learning experience.

- Avoid judging your students' metalearning reflections.
- Our job is not simply to teach students content but rather to invite our students to become expert, lifelong learners.
- We can use metacognitive dialogues in our classrooms to help build our students' metalearning skills. These dialogues make the learning process just as transparent as the learning product.
- Retrieval practice focuses on retrieving or recalling what we've just learned. Expert teachers regularly incorporate the power of recall into their classrooms.
- Sentence completers are one of the simplest ways to bring metalearning into your teaching immediately.
- Checklists and notebooks help ADHDers practice metalearning while also staying organized. They allow us to store our metalearning reflections and discoveries so we can easily refer to them in the future.

Take a metalearning inventory of your teaching this term. Just notice what is. How much metalearning are you using? Then, from that space of nonjudgmental awareness, look for one or two places where a metalearning exercise might fit. Start where you are, keep mutualism in mind, and build from there.

Chapter Eight

Get Creative

Creativity is intelligence having fun.

—George Scialabba

I recently attended a meeting by a nonprofit geared toward increasing awareness of the need for accessibility in education. The purpose of the meeting was to invite members of the community to share their ideas and needs in support of this organization's mission. About twelve of us were in the Zoom room, and for an hour, both on camera and in the chat, I shared a ton of ideas with the group.

It was an extremely well-run, inclusive meeting where I could show up as my whole self. In typical meeting settings, I feel like I'm too much, and I consciously "dial myself down" (mask) to match the group's energy. One of the reasons I love an active Zoom chat is that I feel like I can let my ideas flow freely without monopolizing the space. My brain is an idea factory, and in some settings that strength is treated as a gift, whereas in others I get the sense that it's a threat. In this particular meeting, I left on a high note because I felt that I'd offered my creative gifts to this group in service of their greater mission, and I got to do this while remaining true to myself. It was a win-win.

Later that day, while cooking, I put the box of cornstarch in the cabinet with the cleaning supplies, as one does.

If you view me through a lens that judges me based on how I organize, use, and close cabinets, you will see me as an utter failure. But if you instead consider me through the lens of creativity, you will see me as an idea-generating champion, like I was in that well-designed meeting. One of the toughest parts of ADHD is that I have very little control over which of those lenses you choose to use when you and I engage with each other. I cannot control whether or not you choose to see me as a collection of deficits. I cannot control whether you have limited your exposure to education about ADHD to the *DSM* listing of symptoms, a list that excludes strengths. I cannot control whether or not you seek to push yourself to think and feel beyond ableist biases.

I can control what types of spaces I choose to show up to and remain in. Since my ADHD diagnosis, I've realized that there are neuroaffirming spaces where I can be my whole self, like the meeting I just mentioned, and there are deficit-based spaces where I feel forced to mask. In my travels, I'm sad to report that the vast majority of spaces I encounter in education are the latter.

One of the other things I have control over is choosing to write this book to share this message with educators and to influence you to start choosing affirming lenses, to design and teach from a strengths-based, challenge-aware mindset. This chapter will explore the neuroaffirming power of celebrating your ADHD students' creative strengths. I believe that metalearning is the foundation for creative thinking. It sets the tone for the practice of self-reflection, for noticing what works for oneself and what doesn't, and for experimenting with new approaches. With that metalearning habit in practice, your students will be in an excellent position to build their creativity in service of themselves, their communities, and the world. My creativity is one of my favorite parts about myself and one of my favorite parts of the open ADHD neurotype. I hope that this chapter feels inspiring, exciting, and hopeful as you imagine the worlds you can co-create with your ADHD learners.

Understand What Creativity Really Is

A few years ago, my husband, son, and I went to an arts and crafts store so that they could pick up some supplies to make artist's trading cards (ATCs). ATCs are baseball card–sized works of art that people trade online, and this had become a fun father-son bonding activity and creative outlet for them.

I wandered the aisles, and my thought process went something like this:

Creative Me: *Oh, that looks cool. I could make something with that.*

Logical Me: *What would you do with that thing you made?*

Creative Me: *Ummm . . .*

Logical Me: *Would you give it away? Sell it? Display it in our house? Where would you display it?*

Creative Me: *I have no idea. I guess I won't get any supplies after all.*

The bad news is that I left empty-handed. The good news is that, in my experience, the desire to make something, once ignited, rarely disappears. For the next several days, I daydreamed about the paint, canvases, stickers, and paper I'd come across at that store.

Creative Me: *What if "I have no idea" is a good thing? What if that's the point? To make something for the sole purpose of making it, without any logical reason whatsoever.*

We returned to the store the following weekend, and I bought some art supplies. This was several years ago. During the early days of the pandemic, when the whole world was locked down, my messy and illogical creative practice carried me through the worst days. I continue to create for the sake of creating, in some form or another, as often as I can.

That's my personal definition of creativity as a starting point for us: to make something for the sake of making it. Not because you want to sell it (though you can). Not because you want to post it on social media (though you can). Not because you have a place in your house to hang it (though you can). Not to give it as a gift (though you can). Creating for the joy of it.

Examples of this could be baking a pie, cooking a new recipe, playing a steel drum, photographing the moon, doing a puzzle, scribbling with crayons, writing in a journal, carving wood, telling your child a story, doodling, or gardening.

Once you kick your version of Logical Me out of the car and surrender to the sheer whim of your desire to make something, all sorts of benefits start to show up. Creating feels good, eases stress, expresses emotions, connects us to strangers and loved ones alike, and, quite often, benefits people around us, both near and far. I suspect that our creative impulses might be how we'll solve the climate crisis that currently threatens the existence of our species. When I create, I often imagine something fantastical, then design backward, starting with the end product and working my way back toward the first step. I create something that didn't exist. I shepherd it into existence. Isn't that what we're being called to do for our climate and all life on this planet?

Julia Cameron, author of *The Artist's Way: A Spiritual Path to Higher Creativity* and dozens of other creative manuals, is arguably one of the world's leading experts on creativity. Cameron defines creativity as "our true nature," as "like your blood," and a force beyond our understanding that wishes to express itself through us.[1] This is quite different from some of the prevailing cultural messages we've received about creativity, such as that it can only be accessed through an art class or that only visual artists are creative. Creativity is flowing inside all of us, and our job is to remove the blocks to that flow (e.g., the logical mind trained in productivity that wants every choice to result in something useful).

That is the big-picture, generative, open definition of creativity I'll invite us to work with for ourselves and with our students. If we're going to more deeply integrate creative thinking, feeling, and expression into our courses, we've got to ditch the creativity-for-capitalism mindset to start embracing a more inclusive, humane, blood-like definition of a way of being that is our birthright.

Foster Cool Collisions

As I gleefully dove into the research on ADHD and creativity, I reached out to two of the most prominent researchers on this topic. The first was recommended to me as *the* person to talk to about creativity. I sent him my usual introductory email, telling him about my work and this book, and asked if he would be open to discussing the connections between ADHD and creativity. He responded by saying he thought research provided no evidence of a connection between creativity and ADHD. This is a "distinguished professor" from a Research I institution, meaning they are on the cutting edge of academic research and are funded by the federal government to conduct this research. If you'll recall, I shared reams of research in Chapter 2 detailing that ADHDers consistently outperform non-ADHDers on both real-world and lab tests of creativity. Ableism is alive and well in education.

Luckily, I got a very different response from Holly White, the second creativity expert I contacted, an ADHDer herself who has published extensively on this topic in both scholarly and popular outlets. One of the first ways Holly framed this for me was to talk about ravioli. Yes, ravioli.

Early in her work, White was shopping at Costco with a friend who had ADHD, and even though her friend had put her ravioli in the shopping cart, she had neglected to cross it off her shopping list. White wondered if perhaps one element of ADHD that hadn't been explored was what she calls "memory errors." The word "errors" might make that sound like a negative, but for White, it was exciting. Speaking of the types of memory errors she began to observe in folks with ADHD, White says, "Some of them seemed so original and clever. It wasn't just a pattern of deficits. Something else was going on here."[2] White had worked with brain injury patients who were experiencing memory loss. In ADHD, she saw it as "memories operating differently." "The first component of the creative cognition that I uncovered in ADHD was things sort of breaking through memory. With ADHD, you have access to a lot of information, and as soon as somebody's got access to a lot of information, you get a lot of cool collisions between things."[3]

Cool Collisions would've been a great alternate title for this book. I also think that phrase does a good job of speaking to the "condition of paradoxical pairs" concept we learned about earlier from Hallowell and Ratey. Bumping into an old friend while out for a walk could be considered a cool collision. Slamming your car into a telephone pole, not so much. How can we guide our learners to create adaptive and generative types of cool collisions, in recognition of the tons of information that ADHDers hold in our brains, and to mitigate the impacts of the less cool collisions, such as struggling to focus on tasks that will help us meet our self-defined goals?

White is a big fan of strengths-based approaches to ADHD, especially those celebrating our unique creativity. "Your brain is different," she said. "It's not broken."[4] White cited the leadership skills of ADHDers as a potential area of focus for college professors. "They can be a creative catalyst in the classroom, getting other people to think outside of the box."[5] If student engagement, leadership, and out-of-the-box thinking are part of your teaching goals, and I hope they are, learning to support and celebrate the creativity of ADHDers is a great way to meet those goals.

Your invitation, should you choose to accept it, is to name "cool collisions" as a new goal of your teaching. Look for them when students generate them. Publicly celebrate when students make cool collisions. Hand out stickers when a student names and notices their own cool collision. Intentionally combine disparate ideas in your teaching. Let's learn to get a bit messier, to bang some pots and pans together, and celebrate this unique gift of the ADHD brain in service of student learning and engagement.

Encourage Creative Cognition

White distinguishes among three specific elements of creative cognition: "divergent thinking, conceptual expansion, and overcoming knowledge constraints."[6] *Divergent thinking* is typically associated with the ability to generate many potential solutions to a problem or many potential uses for an item. Where divergent thinking is broad, convergent thinking is narrow. An example of divergence would be when you invite your students to create their own final project for your course and mention that one example of this could be a final research paper. Students who lean more heavily on convergent thinking would be more likely to rely on that option and submit a research paper. Divergent thinkers might create a TikTok dance, film a short movie, or even come up with some other submission that you and I can't even imagine.

Conceptual expansion is thinking beyond the boundaries of the categories that often constrain our thinking (e.g., thinking outside the box). For example, I have a Swingline stapler on my desk in front of me as I write these words. If I asked you to list its possible uses, you would probably start with "stapling paper together." You are thinking within the typical concept of a stapler's use. However, if you suggested that I could use the stapler as a backscratcher, you are expanding your concept of what a stapler might be.

A third important element of creativity is the ability to *overcome knowledge constraints*. Some of you might be familiar with this concept as it relates to a type of cognitive distortion called expertise bias, where someone becomes such an "expert" in their field of study that they narrow their thinking to the point where they are closed off from valuable insights and information. One example of this would be a doctor who ignores the symptoms of a patient experiencing a rare type of illness because they are convinced that the patient must have a more common condition. In this example, the physician's knowledge of the probability of the different conditions constrains their ability to view the patient and their symptoms objectively. Creative people are less likely to let expertise and other knowledge constraints limit their views.

Take a minute to assess your current use of creative cognition in your teaching. Here are three questions you can ask yourself to discover your existing creativity teaching strengths and some areas of opportunity.

1. Do you reward or punish divergent thinking?
2. Do you encourage students to recognize "the box" but also to think outside of it?
3. Where might your subject matter or pedagogical expertise limit you as an educator?

For the particularly brave-hearted among us, ask your students to answer these questions about your teaching. Again, many of us have been taught to think about creativity in a very limited way, as if it's only about being a good painter or the like. This three-part definition of creative cognition can help you invite more nuance and clarity about creativity into your teaching and classroom.

Reap Creativity's Benefits

Whether you believe that education's primary purpose is career readiness or not, it's a safe bet that most of you agree that it is at least one element of the work many of us do as educators. In a Conference Board study of employers, 99% of those surveyed agreed that "creativity is increasingly important in U.S. workplaces."[7] Employers ranked "problem identification and articulation" as the number one skill they valued, followed immediately by "ability to identify new patterns of behavior or a new combination of actions."[8] The third highest-ranked skill was "integration of knowledge across different disciplines," and the fourth was "ability to originate new ideas."[9] In short, employers seek folks with skills in divergent thinking, conceptual expansion, and overcoming knowledge constraints, the three components of creative cognition we recently learned from White.

Whether you believe that education's primary purpose is a foundation in the liberal arts or not, I think it's a safe bet that most of you agree that the foundation of a liberal education is at least one element of the work some of us do as educators (see what I did there?). In a recent essay, Mary Dana Hinton, president of Hollins University, makes a compelling case for developing "moral imagination" as the core purpose of higher education. She defines a moral imagination as "the creative energy that enables us to understand, with compassion, other people's struggles and that drives our desire to support meeting their needs."[10] A liberal education is not just about studying the classics or taking courses across various disciplines but rather about learning the habits of body and mind that allow us to imagine new worlds where everyone thrives. I would argue that our current era is also about imagining ways to save the human species.

Activist and author adrienne maree brown describes the necessity and power of creativity and imagination as a type of battle within the broader philosophy of change she practices, a model known as emergent strategy. Brown states, "The world we live in right now is someone else's imagination that we are living inside . . . we are in imagination battles when we choose to live our own truths which go against those constructs . . ."[11] In other words, if we only utilize convergent thinking that thinks within the boxes and constructs in which we already live, we will never be able to imagine better, more humane words into existence. Within brown's battle paradigm, creative thinking is not only a playful expression of our feelings or ideas; it is a matter of life and death for our species.

I'm also reminded here of the work of Andratesha Fritzgerald, which we learned about in the last chapter, and her model of anti-racist universal design for learning in support of co-creating expert learners. My job is not to fill students' heads with a bunch of content. My job is to empower them to become creative thinkers and doers who are ready, willing, and able to face any challenge, circumstance, and possible future. My job is to help them imagine and create better and brighter possible futures. Our ADHD students are uniquely positioned to take the reins and help lead that charge in our classrooms.

Whether you view the purpose of education as career preparation, liberal arts, or engaging in imagination battles, creativity is a core success skill. Have these conversations about the purpose of education with your colleagues, executive leadership, family members, and students. Challenge the idea that protecting the status quo is what we're here to do. Instead, let's reap the many benefits of creativity, including a future for our children and our children's children.

Respect Interest-Based Nervous Systems

As the neurodiversity paradigm continues to gain power over the deficit-based medical model, we are learning new ways to understand ADHD and to explain this neurotype to one another. One of these ways is the descriptor of ADHD as an "interest-based nervous system."

This definition contrasts with other neurotypes that might have more priority-based nervous systems.[12] Here's a quick example to help you understand the differences between the two.

Imagine a room filled with curiosities: art, action figures, toys, antiques, musical instruments, and figurines. At the center of this room sits a large green ball. Two people are tasked with entering the room and retrieving that ball for a researcher (this is not a description of an actual research experiment, just a thought experiment between us).

The first person has a priority-based nervous system. They enter the room, glance around, and find their priority: the green ball. They grab it and exit the room to hand the ball to the researcher. Mission accomplished.

The second person has an interest-based nervous system. They enter the room with the same directions as the first person. They are immediately captivated by the variety of interesting things surrounding them. They are drawn to one object, and then the next, and then the next, led by their interest. After several minutes, they come across a green ball in the center of the room. "Hmmm," they think, "this is okay, but not as cool as that vintage typewriter I was just playing with." Something tugs at the back of their mind, trying to break through their fascination with their surroundings. "The green ball! The researcher!" They suddenly remember the assigned task. They then grab the green ball and exit the room. Mission accomplished, and they've had fun exploring this room of curiosities.

This story plays out in my daily life at least ten times a day. One of the greatest challenges of my ADHD is that when I leave one room of my house to complete a task in another, I don't remember why I'm in the new room. I am instead drawn to whatever catches my interest in the new room. It can be time consuming, exhausting, and frustrating. At the same time, being entranced by what surrounds us in the present moment is a lesson many spiritual traditions teach and can lead to those "cool collisions" that Holly White taught us about. It's not only my movement between rooms, however, that takes extra time. It's also my progress toward any goal, whether it's a microgoal like brushing my teeth, a health goal like making a doctor's appointment, or a life goal like pursuing a new career path. I am often pulled toward all the other fascinating things I see along the road of life.

In the deficit-based medical model, the interest-based nervous system is classified as "easily distracted" and subsequently pathologized. In the neurodiversity paradigm, we recognize this phenomenon as both a strength and a challenge, part of the richness of the human experience. When I think about the interest-based nervous system, I think about the scientist Alexander Fleming, who discovered penicillin after returning from a vacation to discover that mold had grown on one of his bacteria samples. Who is to say that what the interest-based ADHD nervous system is entranced by and drawn to isn't the creative solution for what ails us? Who's to say that our interests won't lead us to the next great American novel, or a cure for cancer, or a loving relationship, or healing for ourselves and our communities? In the example we just considered, both people completed the task of collecting the green ball, but only one person could take in all the other beauty in that room.

A growing body of evidence shows that the interest-based nervous system is tied to differences in how ADHDers process dopamine, the "feel good" neurotransmitter that leads to feelings of pleasure.[13] While other neurotypes are blessed with consistent and strong levels of dopamine in their brains, resulting in consistent and strong "feel good" feelings, ADHDers appear to have lower levels of dopamine. But we're great at adapting, remember—so we adapt to that lack of dopamine by constantly seeking it out by following our interests and pursuing novelty.

In some ADHD communities, folks refer to our neurotype as "dopamine hunters." I'm also seeing a new trend for ADHDers to create "dopamine menus" while completing boring tasks. For example, I might put "Eat Skittles, check Instagram, dance to a Britney song" on my dopamine menu. Then, when completing a boring task like administrative paperwork, I would take breaks every five minutes and reward myself with something from my menu. This is a great example of an ADHDer creating a neuroaffirming approach that honors her strengths and challenges. A dopamine menu provides an external structure to replace missing internal structures for ADHDers. Like many external structures, you can think of a dopamine menu like any other sort of assistive device used by disabled folks. My body doesn't do standing well, so I should use a Rollator or cane with a built-in chair when I travel to public places without reliable seating (I'm still working on using my assistive devices without shame). My brain doesn't do dopamine well, so I can create an assistive device in the form of a dopamine menu that includes motivating rewards.

I suspect that this so-called dopamine "deficit" is, at least in part, what leads to ADHDers' creative strengths. We can't rely on our brains to host the party, so we have to create the party ourselves. We can't rely on our brains to easily and consistently feed us pleasure, so we open our minds (Open Neurotype) to the entire environment to seek pleasure in other ways.

For you as educators, the takeaway is, once again, that this is a difference, not a deficit. Rather than punishing or shaming ADHDers for following their interests and thriving with an external reward system, celebrate our adaptivity. What is the "green ball" of your course? Can you give your ADHD learners time to explore what else is in that room and still gently nudge them back to the green ball? What rewards help your ADHDers stay on track? Can you celebrate your ADHDers using those rewards to complete tasks and assignments? Let's remember that our nervous systems are not "one size fits all" and encourage the creativity born of dopamine hunting. If you like the sound of dopamine menus, consider weaving those into your courses. Some students will benefit; others might find them distracting. Meanwhile, you should continue to empower your learners to practice metalearning and reflect on how to work with their nervous systems, whether they are more priority based or interest based.

Harness Hyperfocus

Another way to work with the ADHD neurotype's creative strengths is through the lens of hyperfocus. In the next section, we'll get a grasp on the benefits and drawbacks of hyperfocus to help you guide your students in making the most of using this skill.

Hyperfocus is defined as "one's complete absorption in a task, to a point where a person appears to completely ignore or 'tune out' everything else."[14] It is discussed very frequently in ADHD circles as one of the strengths of our neurotype, but the research on hyperfocus is still limited. But here's something funny: there's a ton of research on what's called "flow" in the literature. As I learned more about hyperfocus since my own ADHD diagnosis, I started to get a "Spidey" feeling about it. I've read this before somewhere, but where? Then it hit me. Hyperfocus is to ADHDers as flow is to neurotypicals.

"Flow" was popularized by Mihaly Csikszentmihalyi in his book of the same name, so you might be familiar with it via his work.[15] In a recent analysis of hyperfocus, authors Brandon Ashinoff and Ahmad Abu-Akel reviewed and compared the literature on hyperfocus and flow and found that their operational definitions were the same.[16] However, when written about in the psychiatric literature, this phenomenon of complete absorption in a task is often labeled as a "symptom" of clinical conditions such as ADHD, autism, and schizophrenia. In the positive psychology field, it is the valorized and highly sought-after state of flow.

Ashinoff and Abu-Akel cite research that "patients with ADHD experience hyperfocus more often than healthy neurotypical controls."[17] Note the pathologizing language of "patients" and the choice to distinguish neurotypical people as "healthy" compared to the apparently unhealthy nature of ADHDers. Position this against Csikszentmihalyi's popular TED Talk entitled "Flow, The Secret to Happiness."[18] Again, from Ashinoff and Abu-Akel, "flow and hyperfocus are the same phenomenon," their phenomenology is "almost identical," and "there is no evidence to suggest that either flow or hyperfocus are distinct."[19]

This is yet another example of how the truth of ADHD has been twisted through the deficit-based medical model. This strength of our neurotype is renamed, decontextualized from the ADHD experience, and repackaged as a popular self-help strategy. We must stay vigilant and curious about telling the truth of ADHD.

Kat Stephens-Peace, my fellow ADHDer and assistant professor of higher education, spoke at length about the challenges ADHD presents in her daily life—challenges that I, too, know very well. But she also spoke powerfully about its strengths, saying, "On the flip side, there are these other things that happen that are kind of miraculous. Like little miracles every single day. I'm here in this place where there are no barriers. Absolutely no barriers. And I feel like I can do anything."[20]

It is common knowledge among ADHDers and other neurodivergent folks that our ability to hyperfocus is an incredible strength. Again, in the research Ashinoff and Abu-Akel reviewed for their article, ADHDers demonstrate stronger hyperfocus and flow abilities than their neurotypical peers. We need a lot more research on hyperfocus and flow from a strengths-based, neurodiversity paradigm, particularly to include a wider range of diversity to encompass race, class, and gender. However, enough evidence exists to make a firm claim that ADHDers are flow experts and that this strength is likely connected to our creative strengths.

Creating space for ADHDers to hyperfocus can be as simple as giving us some choice in our learning experience. For example, many ADHDers will design a unique, colorful, creative slide deck but struggle to put their ideas into the constraints of an academic paper. This term, in one of the courses I'm teaching, I have expectations for what topics students will address in assignments, but I place zero constraints on the form of their assignments. They can create slides, write papers, make a video, record audio, or come up with other ways to demonstrate their knowledge that aren't even on my radar. This paves the path for the hyperfocus talent or flow state to kick in.

Further, providing students with choices on their topics helps support hyperfocus. I'm teaching a research course this term, and one of my students emailed me today asking for help choosing a topic. My first advice, "Which topic feels like the most fun? I highly recommend following the fun in life." She will learn the research skills no matter what topic she chooses, but if she chooses something that feels fun and exciting, odds are she'll be more motivated to do the work. If possible, give students choices on both content and form in your assignments, and let the amazing talent of hyperfocus flow.

Connect with Your Creativity

I'm of the mindset that we can't teach what we don't know, or at the very least, we can't teach it well. How can we celebrate our ADHD students' creativity and weave it into our pedagogies if our own creativity is blocked, if we carry a sense of shame about expressing our creativity in academia, or if we hold a limited view of creativity that assumes it's only related to painting or drawing? I don't think we can.

As I've explored this research on ADHD and creativity more deeply, I've wondered how many professors are unintentionally shaming the creativity out of their classrooms because someone in academia shamed it out of them. I think now about a quote often attributed to Albert Einstein: "We cannot solve our problems with the same thinking we used when we created them."[21] The same thinking that caused us to reject our own creativity will not be the thinking that helps us support our students'.

I was recently involved in an email thread where a colleague reached out to a couple of her fellow faculty members to inquire how to grade a student's paper for which the student hadn't followed the directions. More specifically, instead of summarizing *one* research article, the student had chosen to summarize *two*. This was what the professor was thinking about deducting points for: a student who had gone above and beyond the assignment requirements. I wrote back and explained that I wouldn't deduct points for this. I noted that I am trying to teach my students to think differently, so as long as they are meeting the course's learning objectives, I stay open to the variety of ways in which they could meet those learning objectives. I would, I told her, celebrate and affirm that student for going above and beyond.

This situation has stuck with me because it felt like a jumping-the-shark moment for higher education.[22] Have we become so concerned with students following directions that we are even willing to lower grades for students who exceed the limitations of those directions? I think we have, and if so, it's important to name it so we can right this ship. Do we really want to reward mindless compliance? Or are we here to teach students to think creatively and to learn how to imagine new solutions to the world's problems? I, for one, am here to do the latter.

Take a walk. Dig up some dirt. Plant something. Bake something. Paint, draw, write—badly if necessary (trust me, I'm right there with you). Create something, anything, to help reclaim that creative energy that has been taught, trained, or drained out of you. It will heal you and help your students, particularly the creative experts and ADHDers.

I spoke to another fellow ADHDer, a business professor and expert on faculty creativity, Lisa Thibault.[23] Lisa works to remind her fellow educators that arbitrary explanations of who is creative and who is not are common in academia. "We want to break that habit of saying, well, she's the creative one because she teaches an art class, but I'm not creative because I teach finance. It's just not useful." Lisa shared that grading practices are an example of creativity, which she defines as something both novel and useful beyond oneself. "Finding ways to have grading take less time is an act of radical creativity," she said. "Having ways to find your pockets of academic freedom, voice, and identity within a syllabus is an act of creativity."

Instead of asking, "Am I creative?" Thibault encourages faculty to ask, "How am I creative?" You might even wish to set this book aside for a minute now and jot down some answers to that question. How are you creative, friend? Naming your creativity will help you better see it and support it in your students.

Be Explicit About Creative Expectations

Many of your learners, both with and without ADHD, probably share some of the same limited beliefs and mindsets about defining and expressing creativity. You might consider a simple poll of your students, asking if they view themselves as creative. As you probe further on that question, you might find that students who have a daily creative practice still won't see themselves as creative because whatever that practice is, it doesn't fit into the box they've been told represents creativity (e.g., painting and drawing).

In the introduction to what is arguably the world's best-selling book on creativity, Julia Cameron describes how people react when she tells them she teaches creativity workshops:

"'How can you teach creativity?' they want to know. Defiance fights with curiosity on their faces. 'I can't,' I tell them. 'I teach people to let themselves be creative.'"[24] Cameron argues that creativity is our true nature and that the things that block our creativity (e.g., the culture of academia) are "an unnatural thwarting" of our natural creative impulses.[25]

There's good news here, and it's no coincidence that Cameron is still selling books by the truckload well into her seventies and famous creators cite her as one of their most powerful muses. Imagining that creativity is some special talent we need to invest ten thousand hours into developing doesn't make it feel terribly accessible to us or our students. Shifting our mindset about creativity and viewing ourselves as inherently, fundamentally creative beings means we don't need ten thousand hours to be creative. Instead, we can slowly and simply start chipping away at the blocks to let our natural state of creativity flow.

Talk to your students about the what, why, and how of creativity. Challenge each other. Point out each other's beliefs about creativity that might not be entirely accurate. Ask each other to consider the implications of who would benefit from a belief that we are inherently creative. On the other hand, who benefits from the common belief that creativity is an exception only bestowed on a precious few?

Consider how you might center marginalized students and populations in this conversation (without making marginalized folks the spokespeople for their entire community). For example, you might ask your students to consider how people from underserved and marginalized communities might have particularly strong and valuable creative strengths. You might, for example, read this section of the book with your students as an example of a person with ADHD speaking on the topic of creativity and connecting it explicitly to her disability. In short, to fully celebrate creativity in your classrooms, redefine and reclaim what creativity really means as your first step.

Balance Direction with Openness

Assignment directions have gone off the rails. Directions used to be a paragraph long, tops. At some point in the mid-aughts, things changed. I regularly come across assignment directions that are two to three pages long, sometimes longer than the expectations of the actual assignment. With a detailed 15-point rubric (not hyperbole) attached. And an example paper attached. And the professor's medical history attached (kidding).

Am I against clear and specific directions? Rubrics? Giving our students examples?

No, of course not. However, we need to keep cognitive load in mind. How much bandwidth are we asking students to invest in the assignment directions before they even get to the assignment? More information does not mean more clarity. Often, the opposite is true. Remember, we want to reduce extraneous cognitive load so students can focus on the heart of the learning experience.

What we typically see in these long directions isn't an exercise in clarity but an info dump. Info dumps are pouring excess information onto our students and then brushing our hands together. "Well, I did my part. I told them everything I possibly could about this assignment. If they screw up, that's not on me." Info dumps can be more about deflecting a fear of blame than actual teaching and learning.

Further, too much information and too many examples constrain our cognition.[26] While ADHDers are better than non-ADHDers at overcoming those constraints, it's important that we balance explanation, support, and directness with openness and flexibility.

We can certainly be too open as well, without sufficient direction. I once took an undergrad philosophy of religion course, the only course I ever withdrew from in college. The syllabus showed that we would write two papers in the course, each worth 50% of our final grade. The directions were about a sentence long and were something along the lines of: Discuss and analyze a key concept in this course in a five-page essay.

That was it. No guidance. No scaffolding. No examples. I felt overwhelmed and lost, unwilling to risk my GPA because of this professor's inequitable grading scheme.

Can we find a happy medium? The middle path? Can we learn to balance direction with openness to support all our students' creativity?

Edit your directions. Edit some more. Then, edit one more time for good measure. This might seem like too big of a time investment, but clarity always pays off. In the long run, it will cut down the time you spend answering questions. It will result in higher-quality assignments that excite you as an educator. Clarity is your best friend. Invest some time in achieving it.

Road-test your directions with creativity in mind. Here's how: if all your students' assignment submissions look pretty much alike, you've been too prescriptive. Open things up a bit. One of my yoga training teachers once told me that if I looked out at my class and everyone's poses looked alike, I'd failed. My job as a yoga teacher was always to invite each student into the posture that best served their body and needs. I designed my posture cues with that idea in mind. I'd never say, "Stand like this." Instead, I might say, "Find your expression of tree pose. Perhaps one foot remains on the floor. Maybe you'd like to take tree pose seated. Some of you might wish to play with closing your eyes." You get the idea. My job was to create a warm, supportive environment where students could create their own trees.

There's also data showing that mind-wandering is connected to creativity and creative problem solving,[27] so consider how much time you allow for your students' minds to wander. Creating time for mind wandering can feel like a waste of time. But what if it isn't? What if you devoted just five minutes at the start of each class, played some classical music, and had designated mind wandering time together? Just five minutes per class. Or maybe even five minutes once a week (can you tell I'm trying to negotiate with you?). Test it out and see what happens. It just might be the best five minutes of teaching you've ever done, and it will boost your creativity along with your students'.

Picture openness and direction as a continuum, and practice being intentional about where you fall on that continuum. The answer might shift depending on the assignment, the season, and the students in your classroom, but try to balance the complementary energies of openness and direction to best support your students' creativity.

Try Term-Long Creative Projects

Offering a term-long creative project opportunity can help your ADHD students realize they can stick with something with the appropriate support. First and foremost, a creative project allows ADHDers to harness and celebrate their strengths. Consider being very clear about your goals here, perhaps even naming the assignment, "Term-Long Creative Project." The very word "creative" will catch their attention and get their creative juices flowing. No need to hide what we're doing. Let's start using the word "creative" more often and more intentionally.

Next, this is a chance for ADHDers to build persistence. One of our gifts is that we have a plethora of ideas and bring immense passion to many of those ideas. One of our challenges is that we often run out of steam quickly, and the idea we were so passionate about on Monday seems incredibly boring to us on Friday. Starting things without finishing them isn't always the worst thing in the world, but if we *never* finish anything, this can weigh on our self-esteem. Give your ADHD students the chance to realize they can finish things with the right amount of support.

Finally, ADHDers think and move fast. Remember, as we learned earlier, we have racecar brains with bicycle brakes. This isn't true for all ADHDers, but many of us are the first ones in class to finish the project or quiz. In many classrooms, that leaves us to sit and twiddle our thumbs until the next learning activity. Giving students access to a term-long project will offer them something to work on, should they finish certain tasks sooner than other students.

A term-long project could be as simple as having students create a Padlet to post one key learning takeaway from the course each week. You could call this their "Creative Learning Journal." This has structure, but it also gives students a fair amount of leeway on the type of content they post each week. They could write a brief reflection or share videos, podcasts, or other examples of what they've learned.

Another way to approach this is from the angle of service. Term-long projects are a great way to help students understand and apply the "why" of your course. Work with students to develop a term-long project that serves their local community or advances a cause that matters to them, braiding this service together with your learning objectives. One example from an infinite number of possibilities would be asking students to design resources on "x topic" to be used as a community resource. They could put together a YouTube playlist, record a series of TikTok videos (I'll assume TikTok hasn't been banned by the time you read this), or create a Google Site, all geared toward explaining the principles they've learned in your course to their chosen community as a form of service.

For those of us who make use of external platforms to support our students' creativity, it's worth mentioning that these platforms are not guaranteed to stick around, and even if they do, they do not belong to us. As I write this at the start of a new administration in the United States, I'm reminded that we all need to be more careful about what we do and communicate online, and that we cannot trust apps and social media sites, period. If you and your students are creating in these spaces, tread lightly, save your work in a place where you have power to access it, and know that anything created that's at odds with the platforms' owners' interest could potentially place you at risk.

One final suggestion is to spend some time at the start of the term asking students to put their vision for this project in writing. As we learned in Chapter 6, we've got to put it in writing and make it external. Don't expect ADHDers to hold their vision for their project in their minds, because that's a challenge for most of us. Putting it in writing will help us stay on track throughout the term and finish what we've started. If you're helping your students work with Google Calendar and Tasks, you might also have them plug deadlines and tasks into their calendar and planning tools.

Reward Divergent Thinking

I told the story earlier about the educator thinking of docking points on a student's assignment because they did more than was asked of them. While I found this deeply concerning, it was not shocking. When I think of higher education, divergent thinking is not the first thing that pops into my mind—not even close, which seems odd to me. Doesn't it seem odd to you? "Higher education" to me implies thinking beyond limitations and binaries. If that's not the type of higher ed that we work in now, it can still be the type of higher ed that we create. One way to do this is to celebrate our students' creativity by rewarding divergent thinking.

Take a look at your current pedagogies, lessons, and assignments. Are you asking students to arrive at a predetermined correct answer, or are you offering them space to make the answers that may not even exist yet? You might find that you're doing one or the other or a mixture of both. If you've been leaning more heavily or completely on convergent thinking in your pedagogy, could you create 10% more space for divergent thinking?

One specific example of divergent thinking I'm loving lately is what some professors are calling "the unessay."[28] How fun does that sound? My next book might be an unbook. In the unessay, students have autonomy over expressing themselves and their learning in your course (e.g., through making a quilt instead of writing a paper), and you get a break from reading twenty-seven essays on the same topic. It's a win-win example of mutualism if I've ever heard one. Instead of a traditional essay emphasizing convergent thinking (e.g., please bring together these theories in a cohesive essay), the unessay creates space for divergent thinking through its open nature. What else can we "un" in education?

Offer Choice Condiments

Let's imagine you are teaching a political science course. In Module 4 of the course, your primary goal is for your learners to compare and contrast capitalism and socialism. You offer a few short lectures combined with some small group activities to engage your learners. You'd like to require students to complete a summative assessment for this module. Your reasons for that are twofold: first, you want to give them an opportunity to reflect and integrate what they've learned in the module. Second, you view assessments as a chance to get data on your own teaching. Did your students learn what you wanted them to learn? If not, you can offer some additional instruction on this topic.

The most obvious, traditional solution here would be to require your students to write a brief essay comparing and contrasting these two political systems. If you're like me, and you love to write, and you generally write pretty well and pretty quickly, you'd love that assignment. If you loathe writing and your writing pace is very slow, that assignment is very bad news.

The goal that we started with, remember, is not to assess whether students can write about capitalism and socialism, right? The goal is to assess whether they can describe those systems. Writing is one way to explain something—one of many ways. One could argue that there are an infinite number of ways you could assess this learning objective. What if you offered students more options to demonstrate their understanding of that learning objective than just an essay? Would it be better to actually offer your students a dozen options, particularly for your ADHD students? Well, hold on for a minute.

You've probably heard the phrase "the tyranny of choice" (also called the paradox of choice). This is the idea that having too many choices can make it harder to choose. Offering your students too many options might have great intentions behind it, but it's likely to fail in its execution, particularly for your ADHD learners. We have a tough time making decisions because of our open cognitive profile. We're already getting all the information about every possible choice and thinking about a hundred other angles that our neurotypical peers haven't considered. We're already overwhelmed.

When I was in a doctoral program, the one I dropped out of, I sailed through my coursework. I didn't have a lot of choices there. Take this class. Take the next class. When I hit the dissertation phase, that's when I bottomed out. Why? In part because I had too much choice. My dissertation topic was completely up to me. I had an infinite amount of choice. I would settle on a topic, start reading on that topic, and that reading would lead me to another interesting idea. New topic. I repeated this cycle about a dozen times. What I needed at that time, something I didn't get, was a compassionate, caring guide who understood ADHD and could explain to me that my curiosity was a huge asset to my research. And I was letting my curiosity get the best of me. I needed to balance my desire to know and explore everything in the history of the world with the desire to earn my doctorate. I needed to decide and stick with it. One very practical thing I could've done at that time would've been to start an "ideas file" where I stored all the extra ideas that kept coming to me. I have one of those now in Notion. It allows me to have all these ideas without feeling that I have to pursue them all. I also know that my ideas are safe and sound in Notion, waiting for me for another time.

How can we provide our students with choices within caring structures that help them to achieve their goals?

Use choice like your favorite condiment. What's yours? Mine is, unapologetically, full-fat mayonnaise. I love it on French fries. Sue me. But it's on the side. It's the dip. You won't catch me eating a bowl of mayonnaise (although never say never).

A recent study reviewing 129 syllabi found that 70% of professors offered their students some choices with assignments, however, those choices were typically only in selecting a topic, not in the type of assignment a student could complete.[29] For example, most professors offer students a choice about the topic of a research paper they're assigned to write, but they don't offer them a choice of writing a paper or creating a podcast. This is important research because it shows us that we have room to grow in offering choices, not only in topic but also in content, to our learners.

Consider offering students two options for one or more assignments in your course, and make sure you're offering choice in both the content of the assignment and the topic. If you've never offered any choices before, starting with one assignment is great. You can eventually work up to a place where all your assignments incorporate an element of choice.

ADHDers and our open minds, which love to practice divergent thinking, are not fans of rigid boxes such as assignments with only one path forward. Any amount of choice you can dovetail into your classes will empower us to celebrate our creativity. Remember, use this approach sparingly, like mayonnaise.

Connect Through Crisis

Have you ever heard of the acronym VUCA? I've been using it a lot lately. VUCA comes from the business field and stands for volatile, uncertain, complex, and ambiguous. Many argue that we are living in the VUCA era. I might've leaned toward another four-letter word, but VUCA will work for our purposes.

A current refrain in higher education is that we are in a "student disengagement crisis."[30] Nah, I say. It's VUCA.

The students are fine. Which is not to say that the things professors are reporting aren't real. Lower attendance. More students out sick and missing class more often for mental health concerns. An increase in general malaise. A "what's the point" vibe.

Too often, I see folks treating these symptoms as the disease. As if "students today," a phrase I hear on repeat, are fundamentally flawed.

Perhaps what we're seeing isn't some random social virus that's infected our current students, but instead, students very clearly communicating to us that they no longer wish to be isolated in any ivory towers. The planet is burning. Species are dying. Why should I sit in this classroom instead of fighting to protect our planet? More unhoused people are living on the streets of my community than at any other point in my lifetime. Why should I sit in this classroom instead of helping create affordable housing options? Someone was killed by gun violence on this very campus last week. Why should I sit in this classroom when my government officials refuse to protect me through enacting sane gun laws? My friend is in a mental health crisis. Why should I sit in this classroom instead of comforting them?

The scales have tipped. These questions have always existed, but they've been put in bold. Highlighted. Size 100 font. Global pandemics and massive collective traumas do that. They are a crisis of both health and meaning. Whereas before these questions might've been whispers for many students, now, they are shouted through a megaphone to all students. They cannot be ignored.

Those "why" questions I just asked are not rhetorical. I want us to answer them for and with each other and our students. If the only reason

I can articulate for a course I teach is that it checks a box for the registrar on the degree plan, that's not a good enough reason—not anymore.

Are students disengaged? I have a hard time believing that when I see images of students marching on the state senate in Nashville demanding gun control legislation, showing up at school committee meetings to protest book bans, and staging silent protests in campus administrative buildings to hold racist leaders accountable for their actions. Disengaged? Absolutely preposterous.

Partner with your students. Talk to your students. Listen. Work together to refine your course "why" in the VUCA era. How can students use calculus, philosophy, or graphic design to answer the most pressing questions facing our species? Your courses and discipline are relevant to this time; I know they are. But we could also use a little work to tweak our teaching and content to make that purpose more tangible and clearer for our students.

Your ADHD learners are ready and willing to help you. They are justice oriented, they are passionate, and they love nothing more than generating ideas. Connect with your students, all students, by facing the crisis, together.

Summary

Creativity is a huge strength of ADHDers. Let's review what we learned about celebrating this strength in your classrooms:

- Creativity encompasses much more than painting or drawing. Expand your view of creativity and view yourselves and your learners as creative beings.
- Creativity has benefits for career preparation, liberal arts, and moral imagination.
- ADHDers have interest-based nervous systems. Harnessing the power of our ADHD learners' interests can boost learning and engagement.

- Hyperfocus (often denigrated) is equivalent to the flow state (often celebrated). Celebrating both hyperfocus and flow allows us to apply a strengths-based, challenge-aware approach to this aspect of the ADHD experience.
- Spend some time getting your creative juices flowing to best support your learners' creativity.
- Be clear about what you mean when you talk to your students about creativity. Many of them will bring limiting views of creativity into the classroom. Create spaces for more open definitions to guide the learning experience.
- Balance being direct and clear on assignment directions with allowing space for choice and openness.
- Give the fast-paced ADHD brains in your class a space to work and be creative during class downtime through term-long creative projects.
- Seek out, celebrate, create, protect, and reward divergent thinking.
- Use choice like a condiment: sparingly.
- Invite learners to engage creatively with our often scary, volatile present and futures.

What would our world look like if creativity were valued and celebrated, particularly among people with ADHD? I, for one, would like to find out.

Chapter Nine

Flexible Structure

_____

A tree that won't bend easily breaks in storms.

—Lao Tzu

If you've practiced yoga, you've probably spent some time in tree pose. Even if you've never set foot in a yoga studio, it's pretty easy to picture it: one foot is flat on the floor. The opposite leg is bent at the knee, and the foot of that bent leg is placed on the inside of the thigh of the straight leg. Palms are pressed together in front of the heart or hands are held overhead to mimic the branches of a tree.

Do you want to know the secret to tree pose from someone practicing yoga for over thirty years?

You've got to bend so you don't break.

Many yoga students assume that to be a tree, they must stay perfectly still, but think about it. Look or walk outside on a windy day. Trees aren't still at all. They're swaying, riding the waves of the wind. If they tried to stay completely still, the wind would break them.

Let yourself bend in tree pose. Let yourself sway a bit. Don't panic when you start to move, because accepting that movement will actually prevent you from falling. And if you do fall, then that's part of the practice, too. Learning to fall without judging oneself? What a gift.

There's been much talk about how flexible or structured we should be as educators,[1] especially since the pandemic began. I've worked with thousands of students and thousands of educators. I've seen classrooms with total flexibility, classrooms with extremely rigid structures, and everything in between.

What works best? A combination of flexibility and structure, which can often feel like an oxymoron to many educators. How can I be flexible and structured, they wonder. The natural environment provides us an answer: be like a tree. Who would accuse a tree of not being highly structured? Preposterous! And at the same time, trees are almost always in motion, not only through growth but also through flexibility. They move with the elements around them, bending so they do not break. Keep the vision of a tree moving in the wind in mind throughout this chapter as we explore how this model of flexible structure can benefit ADHD learners. And if the tree analogy doesn't work for you, try a portmanteau (combining two words into one fun, new word) instead. Might I suggest "flexure" or "structible," two words I just created? Whatever you decide, continue returning to this realization that you don't have to be all flexibility or all rigidity. Instead, you can balance between the two for your own good and the good of your learners.

Teach Like a Tree

Designing courses for ADHD learners requires a thoughtful balance of flexibility and structure, ensuring both accessibility and rigor in service of the right kind of challenge to motivate and excite students. Flexible structures give students the freedom to learn in ways that work best for them, but without clear guidelines, they can feel lost. Remember that ADHD learners, in particular, have less highly structured brains than neurotypical peers, so while flexibility can benefit them, too much flexibility does not provide enough support to create balance for those with open neurotypes.

Faced with a lack of structure, students might simply "float" away in a learning environment that's too flexible. Or, they might make incorrect assumptions when educators don't provide clarity. The Yale Poorvu

Center for Teaching and Learning emphasizes, "When not enough structure is built into a course, students make assumptions about requirements," which can disproportionately affect underrepresented and first-generation students.[2]

The article "Getting Under the Hood: How and for Whom Does Increasing Course Structure Work?" explores how adding structure to college courses can reduce achievement gaps, especially for underrepresented students. By introducing more structured activities like regular quizzes and clearly defined expectations, the study found that students from underrepresented groups—particularly Black and first-generation students—improved significantly in their learning. The authors note that this approach "halved the achievement gap between Black and White students."[3] We need more research on flexible structure for ADHD learners, but this compelling data can serve as a motivation and model for this work.

One common criticism of the flexibility movement is that it waters down learning, offending the sensibilities of those who claim to stand for rigor. However, the opposite is actually true. "Flexible approaches to teaching preserve this notion of rigor by reducing barriers so that all learners can engage in deep, meaningful learning."[4] The flexibility you build into your structured classroom will allow students to be challenged more deeply. It will bring a wider range of voices into the classroom discourse and challenge students who need less flexibility.

One specific example of research on flexible structure for ADHD learners that we can consider is using extended time for tests and assignments as a standard accommodation for ADHDers. This is one of the most common formal accommodations we use and see for ADHD students. But does it work? The data, thus far, is mixed.[5] Extra time provides greater flexibility for these students. But without the necessary structure, it can often draw out the struggles of ADHD without nudging them toward a resolution. A friend of mine once told me that our job is not necessarily to give ADHD students more time for assignments but to "help them land the plane." Picture a plane circling endlessly in the sky without a clear directive from air traffic control. What would happen to that plane if it circled too long? This is not, to be clear, a suggestion for you to ignore or deny any students' learning accommodations. Never do that. However, we can build structure into our classes for all students to complement existing norms in ADHD accommodations. In the meantime, I hope that continued discussion of this topic and additional research will give our disability and accessibility services better information about the types of evidence-based accommodations that result in student well-being and learning success.

Finally, flexible structure is an example of mutualism, a win-win for both educators and students. "Planned flexibility eliminates the need to negotiate every extension and exception."[6] I work as an adjunct at multiple institutions, mostly with new-traditional learners, and I've been teaching since 2006. Building flexible structure into my course design and teaching "like a tree" has been one of the best things I've ever done for myself. For the first five years or so of my teaching, I went with a more old-school, traditional, structured approach with limited flexibility, unless students provided proof of a serious crisis. I cringe now to read those words and remember that time. But when we know better, we do better. Shifting toward greater flexibility has helped me flow with the winds of change in education and in the world. More of my students complete my courses successfully with less effort on my part to manage the myriad exceptions I used to try to juggle or gatekeep. I can honestly tell you that if not for my approach of flexible structure, I don't think I'd still be teaching. I'd have burned out years ago. It's good for me and good for them. It can be good for you and your learners, too.

So, you're on board with the "be like a tree" way of life—Now what? How can you design and teach for the open neurotype of ADHDers using this model? In this next section, I'll outline suggestions for this approach within my simple and sustainable design and teaching model. As always, I must remind you to take what you need and leave the rest. I work as an adjunct at several institutions, teaching many new-traditional learners. What works for someone who teaches mainly eighteen-year-old students at an Ivy League institution might not work for me, and vice versa. During the early COVID-19 days, I worked with an educator who had one thousand students enrolled in her emergency remote online course. I didn't dare give her any advice, only my support and empathy. Take what you need, leave the rest, and remember to embrace the power of small choices for big impacts.

Move Your Mindset

Many of us who teach and work in higher education were ourselves once taught through rigid teaching styles with very little flexibility. It's tempting to see our existence as professors in higher education as evidence that those old models are successful. But remember, learning experience design (LXD) prompts us to consider the students in front of us at this moment, to consider the most recent evidence about the science of teaching and learning, and to then balance that with our needs. In short, many of us might need to give some attention to our mindsets before effectively implementing a flexibly structured class.

Take a minute to name your mindset. Simple noticing and naming that you have a mindset with beliefs and assumptions about flexibility and structure can be a powerful shift. Rather than going through the motions and teaching how you were taught, you get to choose how you want to teach for yourself and your learners. What a gift. From there, call to mind a variety of learners. Do your assumptions about flexibility and structure change due to a student's race, class, gender identity, sexuality, or disability status? What about a student's personality type or parental status? Just notice without judgment at first; from there, you can get curious about which of your assumptions are grounded in stereotypes and which are about meeting the needs of the students in front of you. For example, a highly motivated, gregarious extrovert might need less flexibility than an introverted, ADHD mother of three. Equity in our mindsets about teaching like a tree does not mean we try to apply one-size-fits-all solutions. Get to know your students, meet them where they are, try new things, revise, adapt, and repeat.

Finally, give yourself grace in your approach to doing this work. If you were taught under the model of toxic rigor and have relied on it for years in your teaching, weaving in greater flexibility will take some getting used to. It will feel uncomfortable at times. You will feel like you're failing at times. But as I always tell my students, F.A.I.L. stands for "first attempt in learning." Be patient with yourself, take your time, and give it time. Mindsets usually don't change overnight, but if you're willing, they will change, and you and your students will be better for it.

Care for Your Community

Once you've reflected on your mindset about teaching like a tree, it's time to look at the foundations of your courses. Think of this as examining the soil before you plant a new hydrangea bush. You can spend a pretty penny on a new hydrangea, get a super variety, and plant it in crappy soil that dooms it to failure. The soil of your course is the classroom community you create with and for your students. If you create a strong community, flexible structure will bloom and thrive. If you have a weak or disordered community, flexible structure will wilt and struggle, and so will you and your learners.

I wrote a lot about caring, shame-free communities in chapter 5, so I won't belabor that point here. In short, a welcoming classroom community is a place where we show up as humans first, educators and students second. We use each other's names. We challenge each other because we believe in one another's abilities and gifts. We support one another because life happens to all of us. In specific practice, that might look like sending a welcome email a week before the course starts, greeting students at the door (whether the one made of wood or the virtual one), and sharing appropriate personal details with your students (and vice versa). If you teach online like I do, community means interacting with my students, being present most days of the week in the online classroom, and providing evidence of care to my learners. I do a lot of this through video but also through simply showing up and learning with my students consistently.

Most of the time, this creates the right conditions for flexible structure to work. If I don't have a strong community of care, flexible structure can go south, make no doubt about it. If students don't feel you are present and invested in the course, guess what? They won't be present and invested, either. You'll likely see an uptick in late submissions.

Ditch Hard Due Dates

Now it's time to talk about one of the most hotly debated topics in higher education: to due date or not to due date. That is the question, apparently. People are generally quite nice to me on social media (knock on wood), but this topic has gotten me the most heated pushback. It's a sensitive subject, so stay in touch with your emotions and experiences as we work through this.

I run a course with a flexible structure, which means that I have due dates. I teach online asynchronously, so that typically means two deadlines per week: one for an initial discussion post and a second for discussion responses and any other assignments for that week. These due dates are published in the course calendar and repeated throughout the course in my emails, announcements, and task lists. I have due dates!

And I accept late work without any grade penalty until the last day of the course.

Can you picture me, a big old pine tree, swaying in the wind? It's glorious up here! Come join me.

What does this look like in practice? Is it chaotic, you ask? Not in the slightest. Not even a little. I have a system (because we ADHDers are great at designing creative systems to scaffold the needs of our open neurotypes). My system looks like this: I enter "0" grades for any students with missing work the day after an assignment is due. I enter a comment along with the grade, asking students to submit the missing work and to email me with any questions. Then, in addition to the grade comment, I send out weekly outreach emails reminding students of their missing work and asking them to respond to my email, letting me know when they plan to submit it and what help they need from me. Again, I put an ask in my email to them in addition to the missing work reminder. Our brains handle questions differently than statements, and I want to engage them with my questions and pull them toward an email contact so that we can be in dialogue about their missing work.

I've been doing this for about ten years with thousands of students. Anecdotally, I can tell you that about 20% of my students miss due dates consistently. Sixty percent of those students submit the missing work within a couple of days of receiving that reminder from me. Another 20% might take longer to submit the work, but they eventually get it submitted. Now, we've got 20% of students who've missed the due date remaining in our anecdotal sample. About half of them, 10% of students who missed the original due date, wait until the course's final week and submit a bunch of work in one fell swoop. Another 10% remain lost to me and don't get their work submitted. Remember, I'm not talking here about all the students I teach. I'm talking about one in five who are even falling behind at all, so in a course of thirty students, that's about six students total with the varying outcomes above. Typically, only one or two students are cramming in late work during the last week of the course, so this does not become a grading burden for me at all. I wouldn't do it if it were a problem, because self-sacrifice does not make for good teaching or learning.

I am free from toxic rigidity. You can be, too.

When I get a frenzied email from a student at the start of a term explaining that someone is sick, lost, or harmed, I get to respond the same way: "I'm so sorry to hear that. I trust you, and I don't deduct points for lateness. Please take care of yourself and submit when you can." Again, most submit quickly after that. Life happened, and they just needed another day or two. If they've got ADHD, they might very well gain motivation via urgency, so they waited till the eleventh hour. However, they underestimated how long the assignment would take. They just needed that extra day. I don't really need to know why they need the extra time. It's none of my business. I trust my students to know what they need to do in their own lives.

Free, I tell you. This has saved me so much time in trying to figure out what work is late and what isn't, how many points to deduct, and wondering whether or not I should grant an extension for this student but not for that student. I don't need to use my increasingly limited and precious bandwidth for any of that. Because my students are smart and don't want to create unnecessary stress for themselves, the vast majority who miss a due date will course-correct very quickly. Only a couple of students submit a large chunk of work at once, and that's very manageable for my grading routine.

Finally, my sense from students' responses to this approach is that they feel trusted, seen, challenged, and supported. The idea that saying to students, "This is your life and your education, and I trust you to manage it as you see fit" is somehow "dumbing down" their education is silly. Micromanaging due dates is treating students like untrustworthy children. My students are adults, and my trust empowers them to take ownership of their lives and to pay attention to how their habits help or harm them. That's challenge. That's support. That is the gift of teaching like a tree, for me and for them.

Accept Challenges

Let's take a minute to walk through a brief case study example of a prototypical student with ADHD to illustrate how I address challenges when using flexible structure. As you can tell, I'm a huge proponent of this work and have no plans to stop doing it anytime soon. It works for me and my students, but some nuances are worth considering to help you plan for all possibilities.

Say you decide to follow the model of due dates combined with acceptance of late work without grade penalty through the final day of the course. One of your students, who disclosed their ADHD to you at the start of the term, misses the first due date. You contact them to nudge them toward submission. They reply that they have been overwhelmed but plan to submit soon. A few days go by. Now you're getting into new content, so new assignments are due soon, on top of the missing work. A few more days pass. The student does not submit the missing work or the new work. You nudge them again. And the cycle repeats. The student is showing up to your onsite sessions or if they're online, they're posting in the weekly online discussion, but they're not submitting assignments. Has the tree model failed you?

Not so fast. First, we have no reason to believe that flexible structure caused the student to fall behind. It's quite likely that the student would not have submitted even with hard due dates. And if you had hard due dates, they might be failing your course with little help of passing as three weeks of zeroes accumulated. Flexible structure is keeping the door to success open for this student.

This situation has occurred occasionally in my teaching, and I always handle it the same way. First, I get a clear line of communication open with the student. If that means texting them (I use Google Voice, not my private number), texting it is. I also document everything in email so both of us can read a written summary of our conversations as a reference.

Second, I ask the student what's going on. That can be as simple as, "I'm concerned about your missing assignments. I'm wondering what's going on and how I can help. I'd love to help you come up with a plan to get back on track." I don't force the student to disclose personal information, but I want to be a resource for the student if they have an unmet need. Unfortunately, I've had students who confided to me that they were sleeping in their cars, fleeing an abusive ex, or caring for children who have been trading a virus for three weeks in a row. Sometimes, students identify as perfectionists, and they're afraid to submit the assignment because they're feeling afraid they'll get something wrong. A little information can go a long way to creating a plan together with our students.

Finally, I aim to get the student to the next, smallest, simplest step. I'll explain to them (via text or phone) what that next step is, and then I'll also tell them I'm emailing them with those directions, reminding them to check their email. I will then write out a clear plan with the student for when they'll complete the work and submit it. Perhaps most importantly, I will ask them to text or email me when they've submitted. I've noticed that this type of accountability seems to work well for a lot of students. I express this in a warm tone, not a scary tone. It's more "Email me when you're done so we can move on to the next step" and not at all "do this or else."

Once students get that first small task completed, and most do with this level of direction, I get them to the next step and then the next. Typically, by that point, they have enough confidence and momentum to keep moving forward with less directed support. This takes time, of course, but this kind of intensive support is very rewarding. Again, a small proportion of my students need this one-on-one advising. Some institutions have academic coaches for all students, and some provide coaches as part of ADHD students' learning accommodations. In the absence of that support, communicating with the student, assessing their needs, and being directive about a simple next step can help them thrive. All of this is, of course, still done within the model of flexible structure, accepting the student's work after the deadline and trusting that they submitted the assignment when it was best for them to do so.

Answer This Call to Action

If you're ready to start instituting flexible structure in your design and teaching, I suggest you start with one course and focus on two key tasks. First, clarify how this course is a community of care for you and your learners. If there's room for improvement in how you communicate that message, implement that before you start going hog wild with flexible structure.

Once you've established that community foundation, try implementing flexible structure in one course. To be clear, I didn't do this. My too-structured approach wore me down over the first few years, and I had a "to heck with it" epiphany and booted rigidity from all my courses at the same time. If you're there and want to get free from rigidity all at once like I did, have at it. But I know many of you prefer a gradual, measured approach. This will allow you to compare and contrast your experiences and your students' experiences. Generally speaking, I wouldn't recommend switching to a flexible structure in the middle of a term, but I do think you're better off doing so late instead of never. If you take this approach, be transparent with your students. I'd recommend emailing them to let them know you've thought over your hard deadlines and decided they don't work for you or your learners. Explain the new expectations, encourage students to still submit by the due dates, and tell them why staying on track will benefit them. Finally, if you switch halfway through, you will likely need to accept a flurry of late assignments and take back previous zero grades. That feels a bit chaotic to me, so again, if possible, make this shift at the start of a new term.

Give yourself grace as you move through this process. It can take a bit of getting used to for both educators and students. But I promise you, it has been one of the best, if not *the* best thing I've ever done for myself as a human being and a teacher.

Summary

This chapter urged educators to "be like a tree" by keeping a very clear structure in their courses while still "swaying with the wind."

- Remember, trees bend so they don't break. How can you bend in service of your well-being and your students' well-being?
- Research shows us that flexible structure is a path to equity. Too much flexibility and too much structure (rigidity) tend to impede student learning, particularly for marginalized learners. Strike a balance between the two.
- Examine your own mindset about flexible structure before starting this work. Be open to teaching the way you really want to and in alignment with what we know works for student and faculty success; this is not necessarily how you were taught when you were a student.
- Flexible structure works best when balanced on a strong foundation of caring community.
- Use suggested due dates instead of hard deadlines. Communicate warmly and clearly to nudge students to completion. Consistent outreach to students is a key element of this approach.
- If students struggle to get work submitted, open several communication channels, including email and text, evaluate their issues and needs, and be directive about a simple first step to help them build momentum.

Remember, wobbles in tree pose are part of the work. And if you should fall, fall with a smile on your face, then simply begin again.

Conclusion

The Future of ADHD

We will either find a way, or make one.

—Hannibal

I have spent twenty-three years as a student in formal education, count-
ing my pre-school through post-secondary years. Twenty-three years. At
the time of this writing, that's nearly half my life. Do you want to know
how many of my teachers and professors identified to me that they had
ADHD?

None. Not one.

We've learned about how shame is often considered to be the most
debilitating aspect of ADHD. Lacking role models we can look to in order to say, "Okay, she did that. Maybe I can do that, too," is deeply inter-
woven with our shame and self-doubt. Representation matters. To be
clear, this is not the fault of ADHDers. First, we lack role models partly
due to women not getting access to a diagnosis. Second, ADHDers are
choosing to keep their diagnosis private to protect themselves from real
and persistent threats. Remember how Hallowell and Ratey used the
word "sadistic" to describe the treatment of kids with ADHD? Ableism is
life-threatening.

That said, since I've been diagnosed with ADHD, I've made it a practice to disclose it when the benefits outweigh the risks. The level of risk varies with the setting. Do I have some privileges that protect me from taking those risks? Yes. My whiteness protects me. Being cisgender protects me. Being married to someone with a stable job that affords my family access to health insurance protects me. I use those privileges to allow me to take risks that benefit me and my fellow ADHDers.

I cannot tell you the fullness of spirit I feel when I tell a new student who has ADHD, "Hey, guess what. Your professor has ADHD, too." That all my students, especially my ADHDers, get to know that people with ADHD can become college professors is deeply healing for me and for my students, too, I hope.

I had zero role models. They have at least one. That's not perfect, but it's progress.

I have a vision for the future where every kid with ADHD on this planet has multiple ADHD role models from all walks of life. A vision for the future where folks with ADHD who want to share their neurotype with others feel safe and empowered to do so. A vision for the future where ADHDers are celebrated as creative leaders and experts and also supported in their many challenges.

As we turn toward the future of ADHD in this concluding chapter, it's our chance to imagine and dream a better world into existence. What does the future hold for ADHDers in education? How can we make choices today that will give us the best shot at creating a world where ADHDers can thrive? What barriers and threats should we anticipate as we do this work? Finally, we'll end our time together imagining a future where ADHDers live, learn, and work beside their fellow neurodivergent and neurotypical peers, leaning on one another's strengths and mitigating one another's challenges, a world that I like to think of as populated by a combination of architects and builders. We've never needed this ace team of changemakers more.

The climate change era is no longer a scary future we're reading about in our school textbooks, confident that our parents will figure out a way to prevent that collapse. The climate change era is here, and our most creative minds and most caring hearts must be carried forward to the front lines of this work and wholly supported once they're there. As we've learned, our ADHDers are humanity's creative experts, and I believe we are the ones who can best imagine and create a better future for all life on this planet. With deficit-based models dismantled and replaced by a strengths-based, challenge-aware model of ADHD, a.k.a., the Open Neurotype, we can and will design and teach for ADHD students' success. We can and will empower our ADHD learners to lead us into these brighter futures.

Straining at the Seams

To create this brighter future, we need not only classroom educators but also researchers to start recognizing the reality of the ADHD experience in all its fullness. Fortunately, this shift is beginning to take hold in the research community. In a recent commentary on the state of ADHD research, Jessica Agnew-Blais and Giorgia Michelini write, "As new research expands our understanding of ADHD, a more conventional conceptualization of ADHD is straining at the seams."[1] They cite increased information streams via holistic and strengths-based approaches to ADHD, often with more inclusion than ever before from neurodivergent voices as some of the reasons behind this shift. The old ways are dying. Positive change, led by ADHDers, is happening.

Many will fight this shift in the research; they will try to push ADHD and ADHDers into boxes that have never been sufficient to hold the complexity of any human experience. But time and the realities of our rapidly changing world are not on their side. This movement to better understand, explain, and support the ADHD experience is here, right now, and we're not going back.

I shared with you earlier in the book how a so-called distinguished professor in higher education at a major research university told me there was no correlation between ADHD and creativity. While ADHDers and our allies are pushing at the seams that have long held us in, ableism and ignorance persist. Recently, I've been thinking that when this book appears in the world, it's very likely I will hear from some researchers, clinicians, and educators who are unwilling to let go of deficit-based approaches. I think it's probable that they'll accuse me of bias when writing this book. They'll ask: How can I, someone with ADHD, write objectively about ADHD? That non-ADHDers have been writing inaccurate, deficit-based, heavily biased research for decades will be of no concern to them. I know this has happened, because it has already happened to me and other neurodivergent writers and researchers.

If you're joining me in this work, whether as a fellow ADHDer or ally, as an educator or researcher, I don't want you to go into this thinking everyone will welcome this shift with open arms. Let's stay vigilant as we continue to imagine a better world. Let's stay focused on our end goal, never letting them slow down our forward progress. Your willingness to press forward, straining the seams with me, will benefit not only you and your students but all ADHDers, as well as the future of human life on this planet.

Beyond the *DSM*

The *DSM* is dying. Let it.

There are so many ways the deficit-based *DSM* has done harm. In addition, many of the *DSM*'s diagnoses are beginning to collapse under the weight of neurodivergent folks' lived experiences. Increasingly, overlap between disorders is causing many to question how accurate these diagnoses really are and to what extent placing people into these restrictive boxes provides any actual benefit. In my own clinical diagnosis journey, my neuropsychologist used the *DSM* to diagnose me, but in her explanation of the diagnosis, she completely switched to a strengths-based paradigm. She recognized that to explain my diagnosis to me using the *DSM* would be harmful. If that's the case, it begs the question, why are we still using the *DSM* at all?

Sonny Jane Wise, whose work I've shared throughout this book, continues to refine their understanding of neurodiversity and generously share their work with the world. At the time of this writing, Wise has just published a new framework[2] to provide an alternative to DSM diagnoses. It's called "The Neurodiversity Smorgasboard." Rather than listing diagnoses, Wise groups common traits and differences around areas such as empathy, communication, memory, and stimming.

Using memory as an example, we can recognize that autistic folks might struggle with paying attention to anything, such as small talk or discussing the weather on a surface level, that is not one of their areas of intense interest. Someone with ADHD might also struggle with paying attention because their default mode network is activated, keeping them in reflective mode, which can be a barrier to any work that requires their task-positive network's resources. For someone with anxiety or depression, anxious or depressive thought patterns can serve as distractions. We could go on and on listing ways that various neurotypes affect how we express our attention while moving through the world.

What best helps people to honor their unique minds and meet their goals? I suspect that in the next twenty years, we'll see the continued death of the *DSM* as people continue to answer that question in a more inclusive, neuro-affirming way, led by neurodivergent folks themselves. As more of us receive dual or multiple diagnoses across what were once believed to be distinct conditions, the usefulness of a discrete diagnosis starts to become very suspect indeed.

Intersectionality

Intersectionality is a concept from critical race theory that explains how our identities connect to political and social realities.[3] For me, intersectionality is just common sense. I have a bunch of identities. I live in a society. I'm never just one of those identities. Rather, they all intersect and influence how I live my life, how society treats me, and what resources I get to access. Again, it seems like common sense to me.

We cannot talk about the future of ADHD without talking about intersectionality. Some people will try, and I wish them all the best, but that doesn't make any sense to me. ADHD, by its very nature, defies explanation. It blasts out of any box you try to put it in. I sometimes call my ADHD "galaxy brain." It's just not going to be contained. So, to imagine that we can talk about ADHD as though it exists in some sort of weird, impossible vacuum doesn't make any sense to me. ADHD coexists with our gender, our race, our access to high-quality health care, our employment status, our housing status, our sexuality, and, of course, with disabilities and illnesses.

Kat Stephens-Peace, whom I was so grateful to interview for this book, studied the experiences of Black women with ADHD for her doctoral dissertation. This type of work is the future of ADHD. Stephens found that first, Black women with ADHD were largely ignored in the literature on ADHD, practically erased, and that interventions focused on white boys and men often fell short in adequately supporting the needs of Black women. Further, Stephens studied graduate students, a population she implored me to mention in this book, as they are often forgotten in higher education.

The future of ADHD will not leave anyone behind. The future of ADHD will not erase any parts of our identity. We ADHDers have been shamed, erased, and harmed by deficit-based models throughout our existence. Our way forward cannot be built on doing the same to members of our community or to anyone else.

As you make design and teaching decisions, practice some good old-fashioned common sense by using the concept of intersectionality to get curious about all the identities our learners hold. Pay attention. Educate yourself. Center marginalized voices. If you don't know something, go find out, and then when you know better, do better. The future of ADHD must be intersectional. Period!

Positionality and Public Disclosure

I started this chapter sharing my own decisions about public disclosure, and now, I want to return us to that conversation, because again, if we're going to create a better world, we need to first create a world where ADHDers feel safe in publicly disclosing and leading us forward. Let's consider some of the opportunities and barriers to this work.

Should we disclose our ADHD identities to our students and colleagues? What benefits does disclosure offer us and others? What threats hover around disclosure? If you're an ally, how can you be mindful of these concerns?

One way that disclosures can occur is through positionality statements. For those unfamiliar, a positionality statement describes our identities and privileges, along with spaces in our lives where systemic oppression and discrimination marginalize us. That was a mouthful. I much prefer to think of it as simply "sharing my story."

For example, yes, I have ADHD, and I'm also white, straight, and cisgender. I have chronic illnesses that are a total pain in the butt, and I grew up in a middle-class family where both of my parents had attended college. There's a lot more to the story, but for brevity's sake, we'll pause there. You can see from this brief example that in American society, I have privileges. I live within identities that give me access to resources and that protect me from state-sanctioned violence. And other aspects of my identity push me out from the center, a center that I think of as a little cornucopia of resources and protection. Pull. Push. Repeat.

In terms of my neurodivergence, it's complicated. How does my whiteness impact how people view my ADHD? How does my having graduate degrees influence perceptions of my disability? The impulsivity component of ADHD may be seen as "quirky" for a white woman and "dangerous" or "brash" for a woman of color. Same behavior—different rules.

Kat Stephens-Peace shared with me how she's navigated the disclosure of her ADHD. In the year prior to our interview, Stephens-Peace was on the academic job market. She did not disclose her ADHD. "I never disclose on applications or anything," she told me. "I don't know. I keep moving. I never asked for things in that nature."[4] The idea that we just need to keep moving, keep our heads down, and not bother anyone with these traits of ours that influence every aspect of our days and lives pervades the ADHD experience. Imagine that someone as bright and creative as Kat felt safe enough to share her story in more spaces. Imagine that her ADHD was viewed as an asset on the job market, with potential employers motivated to co-design a neuroaffirming workplace with Kat. How cool would that be?

It's important that we share our positionality and stories so we can better understand the complexities of the human experience and so we can take effective action against societal harms. Personal and political benefits can follow positionality statements and public disclosures. It's also true that forcing disabled people to disclose their disabilities doesn't feel like an ideal solution. Threats coexist with potential benefits.

Bradley Irish is an associate professor of English and literature at Arizona State University. Irish received adult diagnoses for both ADHD and autism, the combination, mentioned earlier, often referred to as AuDHD. Irish told me that he believes a big barrier to him accessing a diagnosis (and therefore access to correct care and community) is that "academia is a place that encourages overwork and internalizing one's difficulties."[5] He went on to say, "I wasn't even aware that my work could be easier for me or that it was more difficult for me than it may have been for others."[6] For Irish, that internalization of his challenges led to a period of extended burnout where he described himself as "just frozen."[7]

Irish now works to be a voice for neurodivergent support in higher education. In his research, he told me he's found that "50% of neurodivergent professors don't disclose to their university based on fear of discrimination. But I thought, for me, being authentic to myself was worth that risk."[8] In March of 2023, Irish wrote a piece for the *Chronicle of Higher Education*, one of higher ed's most popular trade publications, sharing his diagnosis story and neurodivergent status.[9] That article is how he and I connected and continues to be a resource I share often, particularly for more information on AuDHD.

As you can see, ADHDers have a lot to consider as they make their choices about disclosure and positionality. As we imagine our new world into creation, these tensions and frictions are never the end, only the beginning, nudging us to think more deeply about our navigation decisions on the road forward.

Neurodiversity Centers

Bradley Irish, whom you just met, also shared a wish for the future of higher education and our world when we spoke. "Neurodiversity is a form of diversity that needs to be honored and cultivated to the same extent as other categories of identity. We spend a lot of time doing mandatory training on other types of diversity, and neurodiversity is seldom included. Awareness is a key need, and I think that explicitly acknowledging neurodiversity and taking it seriously is something that is a fundamental platform on which other, more pointed and targeted initiatives can grow."[10]

Neurodiversity centers appear to be one of the greatest areas of opportunity to raise awareness on campus, to support neurodivergent students specifically, and to help us transition into a more strengths-based, challenge-aware era. In this section, we're going to get a quick refresher on the terms "neurodiversity" and "neurodivergence," and then I'm thrilled to share insights for you from two folks who are currently directing one of these centers.

I continue to see a lot of folks misusing language, albeit with very good intentions. Neurodiversity is about all of us. It includes neurotypical and neurodivergent folks. It includes ADHD, autism, bipolar, anxiety, and many other neurotypes. Neurodivergence is about those of us who diverge from mainstream norms. A neurodivergent person is someone who doesn't adhere to neurotypical systems and structures.

As we talk about the potential for creating a neurodiversity center on your campus, keep that language in mind. Get clear on your goals, and then choose the appropriate language to convey your goals. A neurodiversity center on campus is about all of us. It includes neurotypical and neurodivergent folks. It educates every person on campus about the vast variety of neurotypes and how none of those neurotypes is better or more deserving of resources than another. It's important that we include neurotypical folks in this work to educate them about reducing bias, while we also celebrate neurodivergent folks' strengths and mitigate their challenges.

If you want to create a neurodivergence center, that would be a different focus, likely aimed solely at serving the needs of your neurodivergent students. Again, get clear on your goals, and then choose the appropriate terms in service of those goals.

Most campuses have disability resource centers (sometimes renamed as accessibility services). These are most typically charged with managing the formal accommodations process that we learned about in chapter 2.

A neurodiversity center is a different model. Again, all students are welcomed in these spaces, so for example, a student who suspects they have ADHD but doesn't have formal accommodations in place would be able to receive support, education, and community through a neurodiversity center. A neurotypical ally would be encouraged to attend a neurodiversity center's programming to learn more about neurodiversity and neurodivergence. A neurodiversity center's mission is much broader and not coupled with the deficit-based medical model.

Very few neurodiversity centers exist today in higher education. I hope this book helps us imagine and create many more. In the face of shifting norms about diagnosis and disclosure, I suspect our students are going to start or continue to demand more inclusive support and communities. You know what would make my day? If you set this book down after finishing it and sent an email to get the ball rolling on creating a neurodiversity center on your campus. Imagine if one of you did that. Imagine if a hundred of you did that. Remember, small is all.

Chiara Latimer and John Woodruff are co-directors of the Rowan University Center for Neurodiversity in southern New Jersey, coincidentally about thirty minutes away from the small town where I grew up. They were kind enough to share their work with me, including how the center came into existence. They've also given me their blessing to pass along that they are open to being resources to guide those of you who wish to start your own neurodiversity centers.

John shared with me that the Rowan center was born out of a diversity task force that was aiming to be more inclusive by including neurodiversity in its charge (many diversity initiatives sadly fail to do so). The task force researched and wrote a white paper and ran a campus climate survey across Rowan's main and satellite campuses to assess the state of affairs on campus for neurodivergent students. Along with some other shifts on campus, John called this time "the perfect storm," which led the team to recognize the need for a neurodiversity center and then find a physical space to house it (in an old first-year student residential hall).

Chiara and John impressed me with the description of the work the center does for all students on campus, including academic coaching, a popular speaker series with neurodivergent presenters, and a sensory-friendly room where students can hang out. Many of their speakers are hosted virtually so that folks from outside of Rowan can also attend.

For those of you seeking to build your own neurodiversity center, John and Chiara's specific tips include:

1. Find on-campus partners and allies. Again, at Rowan, the center was born from a diversity task force with representation from across campus.
2. Start with programming and training for faculty, staff, and students. Book talks and other events are often low-risk entry points for people to start getting comfortable in the neurodiversity space and to learn with one another.
3. Survey your students. Chiara told me, "Each campus is going to have its own culture. If you launch this, will students show up? If there's an overarching stigma that exists in your campus environment, even if you designate a space for this, what if no one feels comfortable in coming? And that's not just for students; it's faculty and staff too. How are you going to make sure people will want to be there?"[11] Surveys can give you a better idea of the overarching climate in which your center will sit.
4. Consider connections with first-year experience (FYE) type courses. Both Chiara and I teach first-year seminars and agreed that neurodiversity-affirming sections of FYE that explicitly invited all neurotypes could benefit students and help spread the word about a neurodiversity center.

I hope hearing this success story inspires you to think about taking that next best step on your own campus. Remember, small is all. Your center does not need to be built in a day. Rather, what is the next, smallest, best step you can take toward this vision?

Interdependence

When I was pregnant with my son, I read a parenting book that challenged its readers to identify one or two hopes for our children. Parenting would sometimes be overwhelming and chaotic, so we could use those two hopes as touchstones to guide us forward and provide us with clarity. For my son, I wished two things: first, that he would always know how loved he is, and second, that he would be independent. I suspect these were two things I lacked myself, and their absence was profoundly challenging in my life.

Over the past fifteen years of parenting him and reparenting myself, that hope for independence has shifted. Now, I hope for and practice interdependence with him and with myself. Interdependence is the balance point between dependence and independence. In one of the recovery programs I've participated in, led by author and teacher Laura McKowen, Laura identifies nine reminders for the sober life. They include these two truths: "You can't do it alone. Only you can do it."[12] That is interdependence in a nutshell. It is, I believe, a fundamental truth of what it means to be human. We are here in these separate bodies to have a human experience, and it's also true that we are inextricably all woven together in a giant sea of humanity. We are both the wave and the ocean.

I long for a future where we increasingly cultivate, protect, and celebrate our interdependence. The current climate change and global warming era will force our collective hand. We will wake up from the dream (nightmare) of rugged individualism. We will realize that we are responsible for our life choices and simultaneously tied to a massive web of other humans and their life choices. We will finally deeply understand that what we do to others is done to us and is done to our children. What we do to our ADHDers is done to all of us. When we celebrate our ADHDers and support them in living full lives that encompass their challenges and strengths, the entire web of humanity will reap the benefits.

Author adrienne maree brown has written extensively on interdependence as one of the core tenets of emergent strategy. She describes four practices she uses in her daily life to practice interdependence: (1) Be seen. (2) Be wrong. (3) Accept my inner multitudes. (4) Ask for, and receive, what I need.[13] We, too, can begin or continue to practice our interdependence, with our students, in our classrooms.

Be seen. Brown writes that being seen requires that "your capacity and need are transparent."[14] In one of my favorite workshops I've ever facilitated for educators, I asked them two questions: What do you need? What do you have to offer others? There was so much power in answering those two questions next to one another. So many of us are scared to say what we need or have been told that our needs don't matter. There's great power in starting a sentence with the words "I need." On the other side of that coin, many of us are so tired of not having our needs met that we cut ourselves off from giving our offerings to the world. Giving can be draining in many contexts, of course, but when done in loving community, giving to others can actually fill us with energy. My art practice, for example, provides me with a great deal of energy. What do you need? What can you offer others? Ask these questions of your students. Teach them to ask these questions for themselves.

Be wrong. I love being proven wrong. Why wouldn't I want to know the whole truth? If I'm wrong, I'm missing out on the truth, and I don't like missing out.

Brown writes, "The easier 'being wrong' is for you (the faster you can release your viewpoint), the quicker you can adapt to changing circumstances."[15] I love this vision of releasing your viewpoint. I'm picturing that moment when you touch a hot pan by accident. The more quickly you pull your hand away, the less likely it is that you'll be burned. But if your mind resists what your body knows and stubbornly hangs on for a second or two, you'll probably burn yourself. In the coming era of severe climate change effects, we must be more willing to be wrong more quickly to adapt to our volatile era.

This is a tough one for higher education. Much of academic culture is hyperfocused on avoiding mistakes and always proving ourselves right. Instead, teach your students how to make mistakes and be wrong. Show them the joy of discovering the truth. Model mistakes for them. Celebrate the mistakes. Laugh at them together. I once heard in a recovery meeting, "The point of making a mistake is to learn how to make more," and I'll never forget that. Mistakes will be made. How quickly can we learn to embrace them?

Accept your inner multitudes. Brown explains interdependence as related to her recovery from an ectopic pregnancy. She describes herself simultaneously leaning toward the healing practices that her body needed, only to turn away from those needs in the next breath. How often have you gone to bed at night with a promise that tomorrow you'll start that thing you know you need, only to set that need aside at the break of day? How often have you promised yourself, "Enough, now," in that harmful relationship, only to later break that promise?

There is something deeply human about the journey of learning to stop betraying ourselves. Personally, it has taken me four and a half decades.

This is work that cannot be done alone. I have found that surrounding myself with people who are also working on keeping their promises to themselves and who are willing to do the hard work of building a new habit of self-honesty and self-leadership helps me to be more honest with myself, too. At the end of each day, I am the only one who can keep these promises, and it's also true that I cannot do this work alone. Our ADHD students, like all of us, contain inner multitudes of challenges and strengths, of self-honoring and self-betrayal. Our ADHDers, like all of us, are on this journey of self-leadership, of learning to be true to ourselves both at night and at the break of day. We can practice this complex work of being human together in our classrooms.

Finally, **ask for and receive what you need**. One of the first things I learned in the early days of my recovery and sobriety process was how to name what I need. This might seem like a small thing, but trust me, there was an entire world in that sentence. The ability to identify what I needed was taken from me at a very young age and replaced with the needs of others. As a recovering adult, I have learned to say, "I need to make my bed now," or, "I need to have a snack now." It was even more challenging to state my needs to others: "I need you to give me a hug and tell me it will be okay" or "I need you to be quiet now so that my brain can rest."

The advanced version of that lesson is that you might have to ask more than once, and you might have to ask more than one person. We don't always get our needs met, and we don't always get our needs met by a particular person. This is why recognizing the web of humanity is so important for us social animals (even us introverts).

In the climate change era that is upon us, our needs will be increasingly urgent. We will need food, shelter, energy, and love. Our ability to access those needs is expected to shift rapidly in the coming decades, and many make catastrophic predictions about what that might look like.

I choose curiosity over catastrophe.

I am curious about how we will rise to this challenge. How can I get incredibly skilled at identifying my needs? How can I get incredibly skilled at meeting the needs of my loved ones and my community? As an ADHDer, I feel uniquely poised for this work. I trust that I am an expert in needs-meeting. Many of your ADHD learners are, too. Talk about needs in the classroom. What can this course teach your students about meeting their needs and the needs of our world? Teach your students how they might also choose curiosity over catastrophe.

I often like to use what I call course keywords with my students. For example, in a course I'm teaching about social justice, I use the keyword "respect." That word shows up in all of my communications to students, and at the end of the course, I'm always so thrilled when I get to thank my students for remaining true to our shared course keyword.

Perhaps "interdependence" could be your next course keyword.

Freedom

In one of the learning spaces I facilitate, I am often working to help my learners break out of negative framing to scare their clients/users into action. Instead, I invite them to frame their work generatively, answering the question: How will your work help your clients be more free? I use this kind of generative framing when doing climate action consulting. Telling people they better start voting for Green candidates because if they don't, "We're all gonna die," won't work. It will terrify people into avoidance. Instead, we can support people into action by telling them how climate action will lead them to greater freedom.

The idea of education as a practice of freedom is not new, but I wish to restate it here in the context of the future of ADHD in education. I want to braid in one of my favorite things written recently about freedom, the work of Marcie Bianco, author, feminist, and cultural critic, in her recent book *Breaking Free: The Lie of Equality and the Feminist Fight for Freedom*.[16] Bianco argues that women should stop fighting to be equal to men and start dreaming of and creating better worlds where everyone is free. She writes, "Feminists need a tool, a new guiding idea, that allows us to build a society on something other than patriarchal values and to cultivate lives not circumscribed by them. One that finds dignity in difference, and from that recognition helps us create a society that cherishes independence and interdependence; autonomy and belonging; accountability, care, and justice. And that idea, I believe, is freedom."[17]

I don't want what neurotypicals have. I don't want to be a productive worker bee who never misses an appointment. I don't want to be a dutiful first daughter anymore. I don't want to always stay on the paved path and miss out on the beauty of the scenic route. I don't want to ignore all the cool collisions happening in my brain because they don't match what's on my to-do list for the day.

I want to be free. I want all my fellow ADHDers, and all my fellow humans, to be free, too. The goal here is not equality for ADHDers; at least that's not *my* goal. My goal is bigger. My goal is to imagine and create a more vibrant, colorful, caring world for all life on this planet. My goal is freedom. As you finish this book, I invite you to think deeply about what it is you are fighting for, both on behalf of ADHDers and also on behalf of all marginalized folks on this planet. I hope you'll join me in dreaming and fighting for freedom.

Architects and Builders

Ocean Vuong writes, "We often tell our students, the future's in your hands. But I think the future is actually in your mouth. You have to articulate the world you want to live in, first."[18] I want to end our time together by articulating the world I want to live in. We have to get better at this. I want us to get better at doing this with our students and, honestly, to make this what higher ed does: envisioning and creating the world we want to live in. I want to live in a world where more of us believe in the power of our imaginations to create better worlds. I want to work in a higher education field where it is common practice to use our courses to imagine and create those worlds in partnership with our students.

There is a possible future where ADHDers and their non-ADHD peers work and learn together in a complementary ecosystem of care. In that future, we ADHDers are creative leaders. We are celebrated for our many gifts. Our Open Neurotype is recognized as one of many ways to experience and know the world, and that neurotype is accepted for its multitudes of strengths and challenges.

In that future, our non-ADHD peers have many gifts and challenges, too. Many non-ADHDers with more defined neurotypes excel at working with details, naming immediate needs, and addressing those needs with both focus and concentration. Where ADHDers might excel at generating creative ideas, non-ADHDers might excel at prioritizing those ideas and then bringing the highest priorities to fruition.

In this possible future, neither of these groups is labeled or considered deficient. Rather, the complementary nature of all neurotypes is honored, respected, and celebrated. On a practical basis in our daily lives, we will work in partnership with other neurotypes, each of us working within our strengths and then using each other's strengths to alleviate challenges.

In the future, workplaces and classrooms will be less interested in rigid titles or roles and more interested in weaving together this web of strengths so that every member of their community feels a clear sense of care and purpose. I, for example, am an imagineer. With my high creative energy and idea generation skills, I am partnered with an engineer, someone with high executive function skills who can prioritize the value of those ideas and then develop concrete plans of action to enact them. Together, we tack back and forth between openness and definition.

In this possible future, we partner together as architects (the big picture, creative starters) and builders (the detail-oriented, convergent closers), neither deficient nor superheroes but rather complex humans who recognize this paradox: that we can't do it alone and that we alone must do it.

I like to spend time in this possible future. But it's not where I live. As a sober person, I have learned to live inside this day, this one right here, the one that I was gifted with this morning when I woke up. If I try to live in the future (or in the past) instead of just visiting, I lose all my power. Instead, I visit those places, then return to this present moment, the moment where all my energy lives. Now, from here, I ask myself, what is the next best thing I can do? It is inside that choice that I stay present with this moment and also begin to take small steps toward creating a better world for all life on this planet.

It reminds me of one of my favorite old stories. A person is lost in the woods at night. They stumble upon an old cabin. A wise old soul answers their knock at the door and hands the lost traveler a lantern. As the traveler turns to walk away through the woods, they realize something and turn back. "I can only see a few steps ahead of myself with this lantern," they say. And the wise old soul responds, "That's all you need to see."

I've shared a lot of ideas, information, and inspiration with you in this book. You might be feeling a bit lost in the woods. Of course, add that overwhelm to the overwhelm of living in this era of equally abundant information and crisis. It's a lot.

You might feel lost. How to proceed? Here is your lantern. None of us can see the end of this journey. Not one of us knows what the future holds. But we do have access to the next step forward and the next after that. We do have the power to walk toward a possible future where people with ADHD are supported in their full humanity, where they are recognized as creative leaders, and where we design classroom learning environments where our ADHDers can show up as their whole selves. And for now, that is all you need to see.

Notes

Introduction

1. Elie Abdelnour, Madeline O. Jansen, and Jessica A. Gold, "ADHD Diagnostic Trends: Increased Recognition or Overdiagnosis?" *Missouri Medicine* 119, no. 5 (2022): 467-73, https://pmc.ncbi.nlm.nih.gov/articles/PMC9616454.

2. Darby E. Attoe and Emma A. Climie, "Miss. Diagnosis: A Systematic Review of ADHD in Adult Women," *Journal of Attention Disorders* 27, no. 7 (2023): 645-57. https://doi.org/10.1177/10870547231161533; Children and Adults with Attention-Deficit/Hyperactivity Disorder (CHADD), "Bias About ADHD Leaves Many Women with a Late Diagnosis," *ADHD Weekly,* March 2, 2022, https://chadd.org/adhd-weekly/bias-about-adhd-leaves-many-women-with-a-late-diagnosis/.

3. Anthony Yeung, Enoch Ng, and Elia Abi-Jaoude, "TikTok and Attention-Deficit/Hyperactivity Disorder: A Cross-Sectional Study of Social Media Content Quality," *Canadian Journal of Psychiatry* 67, no. 12 (2022): 899-906, https://doi.org/10.1177/07067437221082854.

4. Ellie Middleton, *Unmasked: The Ultimate Guide to ADHD, Autism, and Neurodivergence* (Penguin Life, 2023), 127.

5. Gabor Maté, *Scattered Minds: The Origins and Healing of Attention Deficit Disorder* (Penguin Random House, 1999).

6. Edward M. Hallowell and John J. Ratey, *ADHD 2.0: New Science and Essential Strategies for Thriving with Distraction - from Childhood through Adulthood* (Ballantine, 2021), xv.

7. "Data and Statistics about ADHD," Centers for Disease Control and Prevention, accessed June 18, 2024, https://www.cdc.gov/adhd/data/?CDC_AAref_Val=https://www.cdc.gov/ncbddd/adhd/data.html.

8. Stephen V. Faraone, Joseph Biederman, and Eric Mick, "The Age-Dependent Decline of Attention Deficit Hyperactivity Disorder: A Meta-Analysis of Follow-Up Studies," *Psychological Medicine* 36, no. 2 (2006): 159-65, https://pubmed.ncbi.nlm.nih.gov/16420712/.

9. Claire Sibonney, "With a Diagnosis at Last, Black Women with ADHD Start Healing," *KFF Health News,* July 20, 2021, https://kffhealthnews.org/news/article/black-women-adhd-attention-deficit-hyperactivity-disorder-underdiagnosed/.

10. Terrie E. Moffitt and Maria Melchior, "Why Does the Worldwide Prevalence of Childhood Attention Deficit Hyperactivity Disorder Matter?" *American Journal of*

Psychiatry 164, no. 6 (2007): 856–58, https://doi.org/10.1176/ajp.2007.164.6.856; Guilherme Polanczyk et al., "The Worldwide Prevalence of ADHD: A Systematic Review and Metaregression Analysis," *American Journal of Psychiatry* 164, no. 6 (2007): 942–48, https://doi.org/10.1176/ajp.2007.164.6.942.

11.   CHADD, "More Fire Than Water: A Short History of ADHD," *ADHD Weekly*, 2018, https://chadd.org/adhd-weekly/more-fire-than-water-a-short-history-of-adhd/.

12.   José Martinez-Badía and José Martinez-Raga, "Who Says This Is a Modern Disorder? The Early History of Attention Deficit Hyperactivity Disorder," *World Journal of Psychiatry* 5, no. 4 (2015): 379–86, https://doi.org/10.5498/wjp.v5.i4.379.

13.   Klaus W. Lange et al., "The History of Attention Deficit Hyperactivity Disorder," *Attention Deficit and Hyperactivity Disorders* 2, no. 4 (2010): 241–55, https://doi.org/10.1007/s12402-010-0045-8.

14.   Marco Catani and Paolo Mazzarello, "Grey Matter Leonardo da Vinci: A Genius Driven to Distraction," *Brain: A Journal of Neurology* 142, no. 6 (2019): 1842–46, https://doi.org/10.1093/brain/awz131.

15.   Royce Flippin, "Hyperfocus and the ADHD Brain: Intense Fixation with ADD," *ADDitude*, January 21, 2023, https://www.additudemag.com/understanding-adhd-hyperfocus/.

16.   Corita Kent and Jan Steward, *Learning By Heart* (Allworth Press, 2008).

17.   Jay Timothy Dolmage, *Academic Ableism* (University of Michigan Press, 2017), 32.

18.   Adrienne Maree Brown, *Emergent Strategy: Shaping Change, Changing Worlds* (AK Press, 2017), 10.

Chapter 1. What Is ADHD?

1.   "DSM-5 Changes: Implications for Child Serious Emotional Disturbance," Substance Abuse and Mental Health Services Administration (SAMHSA), 2016, https://www.ncbi.nlm.nih.gov/books/NBK519712/table/ch3.t3/.

2.   Gary Greenberg, *The Book of Woe: The DSM and the Unmaking of Psychiatry* (Penguin, 2014); Peter Simons, "Medscape Article Reviews the Fatal Flaws of the DSM," Mad in America: Science, Psychiatry, and Social Justice, December 28, 2020, https://www.madinamerica.com/2020/12/medscape-article-reviews-fatal-flaws-dsm/#:~:text=Criticisms%20leveled%20at%20the%20DSM,the%20manual%20despite%20these%20criticisms.

3.   "DSM-5 Changes," 2016.

4.   "APA Dictionary of Psychology," American Psychological Association, 2018, https://dictionary.apa.org/attention.

5.   "Attention (n.)," Online Etymology Dictionary, accessed November 1, 2023, https://www.etymonline.com/search?q=attention.

6.   Les Fehmi and Jim Robbins, *The Open-Focus Brain: Harnessing the Power of Attention to Heal Mind and Body* (Trumpeter, 2007).

7.   Fehmi and Robbins, *The Open-Focus Brain*, 12.

8.   Cal Newport, "The Frustration with Productivity Culture," *The New Yorker*, September 13, 2021, https://www.newyorker.com/culture/office-space/the-frustration

-with-productivity-culture; Jenny Odell, *How to Do Nothing: Resisting the Attention Economy* (New York: Melville House, 2019).

9. James I. Charlton, *Nothing About Us Without Us: Disability Oppression and Empowerment* (University of California Press, 1998).

10. Edward M. Hallowell and John J. Ratey, *ADHD 2.0: New Science and Essential Strategies for Thriving with Distraction—From Childhood Through Adulthood* (Ballantine, 2021), 5.

11. Hallowell and Ratey, *ADHD 2.0*, xvii.

12. Hallowell and Ratey, *ADHD 2.0*.

13. Hallowell and Ratey, *ADHD 2.0*, 6.

14. Hanh Nguyen, "The Daniels on the ADHD Theory of 'Everything Everywhere All at Once,' Paper Cuts and Butts," *Salon*, April 17, 2022, https://www.salon.com/2022/04/17/everything-everywhere-all-at-once-daniels-adhd/.

15. Mads Dengsø, "Wrong Brains at the Wrong Time? Understanding ADHD Through the Diachronic Constitution of Minds," *Advances in Neurodevelopmental Disorders* 6 (2022): 184–95, https://link.springer.com/article/10.1007/s41252-022-00244-y.

16. F. Xavier Castellanos and Erika Proal, "Large-Scale Brain Systems in ADHD: Beyond the Prefrontal-Striatal Model," *Cognition in Neuropsychiatric Disorders* 16, no. 1 (2011): 17–26, https://pmc.ncbi.nlm.nih.gov/articles/PMC3272832/.

17. Mads Dengsø, in discussion with the author, 2022.

18. Lisa A. Friedman and Judith L. Rapoport, "Brain Development in ADHD," *Current Opinion in Neurobiology* 30 (2015): 106–11, https://pubmed.ncbi.nlm.nih.gov/25500059/; Jacob Levman et al., "Cortical Thickness Abnormalities in Attention Deficit Hyperactivity Disorder Revealed by Structural Magnetic Resonance Imaging: Newborns to Young Adults," *International Journal of Developmental Neuroscience* 82, no. 7 (2022): 584–95, https://doi.org/10.1002/jdn.10211; P. Shaw et al., "Attention-deficit/hyperactivity disorder is characterized by a delay in cortical maturity," *Proceedings of the National Academy of Sciences* 104, no. 49 (2007): 19649–54, https://pubmed.ncbi.nlm.nih.gov/18024590/.

19. Kimberlé Crenshaw, "Demarginalizing the Intersection of Race and Sex: A Black Feminist Critique of Antidiscrimination Doctrine, Feminist Theory, and Antiracist Politics," *University of Chicago Legal Forum* 140 (1989): 139–67, https://www.taylorfrancis.com/chapters/edit/10.4324/9780429500480-5/demarginalizing-intersection-race-sex-black-feminist-critique-antidiscrimination-doctrine-feminist-theory-antiracist-politics-1989-kimberle-crenshaw.

20. Kat Stephens, "The Gendered, Racialized, & Dis/abled Experiences of Neurodivergent Black Women Graduate Students Across Higher Education" (PhD diss., University of Massachusetts, 2022), Scholarworks.

21. Courtney Sobers (professor) in discussion with the author, May 2023.

22. Teddy G. Goetz and Noah Adams, "The Transgender and Gender Diverse and Attention Deficit Hyperactivity Disorder Nexus: A Systematic Review," *Journal of Gay & Lesbian Mental Health* 28, no. 1 (2024): 2–19, https://doi.org/10.1080/19359705.2022.2109119.

23. "Autism and ADHD: How They're Connected," Healthline, last modified January 10, 2023, https://www.healthline.com/health/adhd/autism-and-adhd#research.

24. Camille Hours, Christophe Recasens, and Jean-Marc Baleyte, "ASD and ADHD Comorbidity: What Are We Talking About?" *Frontiers in Psychiatry* 13 (2022): 891866, https://www.ncbi.nlm.nih.gov/pmc/articles/PMC8918663/.

Chapter 2. ADHDers' Strengths

1. Tracey Tokuhama-Espinosa, *Mind, Brain, and Education Science: A Comprehensive Guide to the New Brain-Based Teaching* (W.W. Norton & Company, 2010).

2. Oriana R. Aragón, Sarah L. Eddy, and Mark J. Graham, "Faculty Beliefs About Intelligence Are Related to the Adoption of Active-Learning Practices," *CBE—Life Sciences Education* 17, no. 3, 1–9, https://doi.org/10.1187/cbe.17-05-0084.

3. Anne-Laure Le Cunff, "Distractibility and Impulsivity in ADHD as an Evolutionary Mismatch of High Trait Curiosity," *Evolutionary Psychological Science* 10 (2024): 282–97, https://doi.org/10.1007/s40806-024-00400-8.

4. Mads Dengsø (researcher and lecturer) in discussion with the author, May 2023.

5. Mads Dengsø (researcher and lecturer) in discussion with the author, May 2023.

6. Holly A. White and Priti Shah, "Uninhibited Imaginations: Creativity in Adults with Attention-Deficit/Hyperactivity Disorder," *Personality and Individual Differences* 40, no. 6 (2006): 1121–31, https://doi.org/10.1016/j.paid.2005.11.007.

7. Anna Abraham et al., "Creative Thinking in Adolescents with Attention Deficit Hyperactivity Disorder (ADHD)," *Child Neuropsychology: A Journal on Normal and Abnormal Development in Childhood and Adolescence* 12, no. 2 (2006): 111–23, https://doi.org/10.1080/09297040500320691.

8. Holly A. White and Priti Shah, "Creative Style and Achievement in Adults with Attention-Deficit/Hyperactivity Disorder," *Personality and Individual Differences* 50, no. 5 (2011): 673–77, https://doi.org/10.1016/j.paid.2010.12.015.

9. Nienke Boot, Barbara Nevicka, and Matthijs Baas, "Subclinical Symptoms of Attention-Deficit/Hyperactivity Disorder (ADHD) Are Associated with Specific Creative Processes," *Personality and Individual Differences* 114 (2017): 73–81, https://doi.org/10.1016/j.paid.2017.03.050.

10. Holly A. White and Priti Shah, "Scope of Semantic Activation and Innovative Thinking in College Students with ADHD," *Creativity Research Journal* 28 (2016): 275–82, https://doi.org/10.1080/10400419.2016.1195655.

11. Christa L. Taylor et al., "Divergent Thinking and Academic Performance of Students with Attention Deficit-Hyperactivity Disorder Characteristics in Engineering," *Research Journal for Engineering Education* 109, no. 2 (2020): 213–29, https://doi.org/10.1177/1042258719890986.

12. Curt Moore, Nancy McIntyre, and Stephen E. Lanivich, "ADHD-related Neurodiversity and the Entrepreneurial Mindset," *Entrepreneurship Theory and Practice* 45, no. 1 (2021): 64–91,
https://doi.org/10.1177/1042258719890986.

13. Holly White, "The Creativity of ADHD," *Scientific American Mind* 30, no. 3 (May/June 2019), 5–7.

14.   Edward M. Hallowell and John J. Ratey, *ADHD 2.0: New Science and Essential Strategies for Thriving with Distraction—From Childhood Through Adulthood* (Ballantine, 2021), 11.

15.   Gregor Kohls, Beate Herpertz-Dahlmann, and Kerstin Konrad, "Hyperresponsiveness to Social Rewards in Children and Adolescents with Attention-Deficit/Hyperactivity Disorder (ADHD)," *Behavioral and Brain Functions* 5, no. 20 (2009): 1–20, https://doi.org/10.1186/1744-9081-5-20.

16.   L. M. Schippers, C. U. Greven, and M. Hoogman, "Associations Between ADHD Traits and Self-Reported Strengths in the General Population," *Comprehensive Psychiatry* 130 (2024): 1–9, https://pubmed.ncbi.nlm.nih.gov/38335571/.

17.   Schippers, Greven, and Hoogman, "Associations Between ADHD Traits and Self-Reported Strengths," 5.

Chapter 3. ADHDers' Challenges

1.   Ilan H. Meyer, "Prejudice, Social Stress, and Mental Health in Lesbian, Gay, and Bisexual Populations: Conceptual Issues and Research Evidence," *Psychological Bulletin* 129, no. 5 (2003): 674–97, https://doi.org/10.1037/0033-2909.129.5.674.

2.   Monique Botha and David M. Frost, "Extending the Minority Stress Model to Understand Mental Health Problems Experienced by the Autistic Population." *Society and Mental Health* 10, no. 1 (2018): 20, https://doi.org/10.1177/2156869318804297/.

3.   Edward M. Hallowell and John J. Ratey, *ADHD 2.0: New Science and Essential Strategies for Thriving with Distraction—From Childhood Through Adulthood* (Ballantine, 2021), xv.

4.   "New Research Suggests Untreated ADHD Reduces Life Expectancy," CHADD, January 8, 2019, https://chadd.org/advocacy-blog/new-research-suggests-untreated-adhd-reduces-life-expectancy/.

5.   Allison Inserro, "Psychologist Barkley Says Life Expectancy Slashed in Worst Cases for Those with ADHD," *AJMC*, January 14, 2018, https://www.ajmc.com/view/psychologist-barkley-says-life-expectancy-slashed-in-worst-cases-for-those-with-adhd.

6.   Substance Abuse and Mental Health Services Administration, "Adults with Attention Deficit Disorder and Substance Use Disorders," *SAMHSA Advisory* 14, no. 3 (Fall 2015), https://store.samhsa.gov/sites/default/files/d7/priv/sma15-4925.pdf.

7.   Judit Balazs and Agnes Kereszteny, "Attention-Deficit/Hyperactivity Disorder and Suicide: A Systematic Review," *World Journal of Psychiatry* 7, no. 1 (2017): 44–59, https://doi.org/10.5498/wjp.v7.i1.44

8.   Nathalie Brunkhorst-Kanaan et al, "ADHD and Accidents Over the Life Span—A Systematic Review." *Neuroscience & Biobehavioral Reviews* 125 (2021): 582–91, https://doi.org/10.1016/j.neubiorev.2021.02.002.

9.   Greg Grillo, "ADHD and Dental Care: Guidance for Parents and Caregivers," CHADD, December 2019, https://chadd.org/attention-article/adhd-and-dental-care-guidance-for-parents-and-caregivers/.

10.   George DuPaul et al., "College Students with ADHD: Current Status and Future Directions," *Journal of Attention Disorders* 13 (2009): 234–50, https://doi.org/10.1177/1087054709340650.

11.   Mary Rooney, Andrea Chronis-Tuscano, and Yesel Yoon, "Substance Use in College Students with ADHD," *Journal of Attention Disorders* 16, no. 3 (2012): 221–34, https://doi.org/10.1177/1087054710392536.

12.   Barbara Shaw-Zirt et al., "Adjustment, Social Skills, and Self-Esteem in College Students with Symptoms of ADHD," *Journal of Attention Disorders* 8, no. 3 (2005): 109–20, https://doi.org/10.1177/1087054705277775.

13.   Russell A. Barkley, *Executive Functions: What They Are, How They Work, and Why They Evolved* (Guilford Press, 2012).

14.   Lisa LaCroix, "Tales of an ADHD Adult," TikTok, November 15, 2020, https://www.tiktok.com/@lisa_lacroix/video/6895449935731281158.

15.   Francisco Xavier Castellanos et al., "Characterizing Cognition in ADHD: Beyond Executive Dysfunction," *Trends in Cognitive Sciences* 10, no. 3 (2006): 117–23, https://doi.org/10.1016/j.tics.2006.01.011; A. Christakou et al., "Disorder-Specific Functional Abnormalities during Sustained Attention in Youth with Attention Deficit Hyperactivity Disorder (ADHD) and with Autism," *Molecular Psychiatry* 18, no. 2 (2013): 236–44, https://pubmed.ncbi.nlm.nih.gov/22290121/.

16.   Hallowell and Ratey, *ADHD 2.0*, 24.

17.   "Is Time Blindness an Ableist Term?," ADHD Homestead, accessed June 20, 2024, https://adhdhomestead.net/is-time-blindness-an-ableist-term/.

18.   Hallowell and Ratey, *ADHD 2.0*, 39.

19.   Harvard Health Publishing, "Co-Regulation: Helping Children and Teens Navigate Big Emotions," *Harvard Health Blog*, April 3, 2024, https://www.health.harvard.edu/blog/co-regulation-helping-children-and-teens-navigate-big-emotions-202404033030.

20.   "Neurodivergent Friendly Workbook of DBT Skills," Lived Experience Educator, accessed May 15, 2023, https://www.livedexperienceeducator.com/store/p/neurodivergent-friendly-workbook-of-dbt-skills.

21.   William Dodson, "3 Defining Features of ADHD That Everyone Overlooks," *ADDitude*, April 8, 2024, https://www.additudemag.com/symptoms-of-add-hyper arousal-rejection-sensitivity/.

22.   William Dodson, "New Insights into Rejection Sensitive Dysphoria," *ADDitude*, December 20, 2023, https://www.additudemag.com/rejection-sensitive -dysphoria-adhd-emotional-dysregulation/.

23.   Ying Deng (ADHD coach and meditation teacher) in discussions with the author, May 2023.

Chapter 4. Transitioning from Old to New Models of ADHD

1.   Edward M. Hallowell and John J. Ratey, *ADHD 2.0: New Science and Essential Strategies for Thriving with Distraction—From Childhood Through Adulthood* (Ballantine, 2021), 16.

2.   Hallowell and Ratey, *ADHD 2.0*, 16–18.

3.   Leah Lakshmi Piepzna-Samarasinha, *Care Work: Dreaming Disability Justice* (Arsenal Pulp Press, 2018).

4.   Richard R. Valencia, *Dismantling Contemporary Deficit Thinking* (Routledge, 2010).

5. Lori Patton Davis and Samuel D. Museus, "What Is Deficit Thinking? An Analysis of Conceptualizations of Deficit Thinking and Implications for Scholarly Research," *NCID Currents* 1, no. 1 (2019), http://dx.doi.org/10.3998/currents.17387731.0001.110.

6. Hallowell and Ratey, *ADHD 2.0.*

7. "Education Crisis: Neurodiversity-Affirming Teacher Training Needed," Autistic Realms, accessed January 23, 2025, https://autisticrealms.com/education-crisis-neurodiversity-affirming-teacher-training-needed/.

8. Zaretta Hammond, *Culturally Responsive Teaching and the Brain: Promoting Authentic Engagement and Rigor among Culturally and Linguistically Diverse Students* (Corwin, 2015), 59.

9. Hallowell and Ratey, *ADHD 2.0*, 128.

10. Djoerd Hiemstra and Nico W. Van Yperen, "The Effects of Strength-Based versus Deficit-Based Self-Regulated Learning Strategies on Students' Effort Intentions," *Motivation and Emotion* 39, no. 5 (2015): 656–68, https://doi.org/10.1007/s11031-015-9488-8.

11. Brené Brown, "Shame vs. Guilt," January 15, 2013, https://brenebrown.com/articles/2013/01/15/shame-v-guilt/.

12. Matthew D. Lieberman, *Social: Why Our Brains Are Wired to Connect* (Broadway Books, 2013).

13. Kathleen Cushman, "3 Ways to Keep Shame from Blocking Deeper Learning," *Education Week*, January 19, 2016, https://www.edweek.org/leadership/opinion-3-ways-to-keep-shame-from-blocking-deeper-learning/2016/01.

14. Cushman, "3 Ways to Keep Shame from Blocking Deeper Learning."

15. Kim M. Baldwin, John R. Baldwin, and Thomas Ewald, "The Relationship Among Shame, Guilt, and Self-Efficacy," *American Journal of Psychotherapy* 60, no. 1 (2006): 1–21, https://doi.org/10.1176/appi.psychotherapy.2006.60.1.1.

16. Penny Jane Burke, "Difference in Higher Education Pedagogies: Gender, Emotion and Shame," *Gender & Education* 29, no. 4 (2017): 430–44, https://doi.org/10.1080/09540253.2017.1308471; Vik Loveday, "Embodying Deficiency through 'Affective Practice': Shame, Relationality, and the Lived Experience of Social Class and Gender in Higher Education," *Sociology* 50, no. 6 (2016): 1140–55, https://doi.org/10.1177/0038038515589301; Luna Dolezal and Matthew Gibson, "Beyond a Trauma-Informed Approach and Towards Shame-Sensitive Practice," *Humanities and Social Sciences Communications* 9, no. 1 (2022): Article 1, https://doi.org/10.1057/s41599-022-01227-z.

17. Carol A. Lundberg, Young K. Kim, Luis M. Andrade, and Daniel T. Bahner, "High Expectations, Strong Support: Faculty Behaviors Predicting Latina/o Community College Student Learning," *Journal of College Student Development* 59, no. 1 (2018): 55–70, https://doi.org/10.1353/csd.2018.0004.

18. Kat Stephens-Peace (assistant professor) in discussion with the author, May 2023.

19. Kat Stephens-Peace (assistant professor) in discussion with the author, May 2023.

20. Courtney Sobers (associate teaching professor) in discussion with the author, May 2023.

21. Apparently, the Foucault Pendulum was removed from the Smithsonian in 1998. Sad! https://www.si.edu/spotlight/foucault-pendulum

22. "About Universal Design for Learning," CAST, Accessed April 13, 2023, https://www.cast.org/impact/universal-design-for-learning-udl.

23. Jay T. Dolmage, *Academic Ableism: Disability and Higher Education* (University of Michigan Press, 2017).

24. Adria Battaglia, "'Plus-One' Thinking: A Framework for Inclusive Teaching," Center for Teaching and Learning, University of Texas at Austin, accessed January 29, 2025, https://ctl.utexas.edu/news/plus-one-thinking-framework-inclusive-teaching.

25. A few months after writing this section, I read that the early developers of the neurodiversity concept likened it to biodiversity. My understanding of this connection arose from first learning about biodiversity in my climate action work, and then recognizing the similarity. I find it interesting and hopeful that this connection arose organically for me, a nice sign that I/we are on the right track.

26. "Biodiversity," *National Geographic,* accessed November 1, 2023, https://education.nationalgeographic.org/resource/biodiversity.

27. Monique Botha et al., "The Neurodiversity Concept Was Developed Collectively: An Overdue Correction on the Origins of Neurodiversity Theory," *National Autistic Society*, 2024, https://doi.org/10.1177/13623613241237871.

28. University of Massachusetts, "Neurodivergence," Inclusive by Design, accessed April 4, 2025, https://www.umassp.edu/inclusive-by-design/who-before-how/understanding-disabilities/neurodivergence.

29. Sonny Jane Wise, "About," Lived Experience Educator, accessed June 7, 2023, https://www.livedexperienceeducator.com/about-1.

30. James I. Charlton, *Nothing About Us Without Us: Disability Oppression and Empowerment* (University of California Press, 1998).

31. Adrienne Maree Brown, *Emergent Strategy: Shaping Change, Changing Worlds*. (AK Press, 2017), 10.

32. Niels Floor, "Empathy Map for Learners," LXD, September 21, 2023, https://lxd.org/news/empathy-map-for-learners-and-learning-experience-design/.

Chapter 5. Designing and Teaching Against Shame

1. Hallowell regularly encourages ADHDers to get a pet, and I second this. Our pets love us unconditionally, and we ADHDers really need that kind of love.

2. Edward M. Hallowell and John J. Ratey, *ADHD 2.0: New Science and Essential Strategies for Thriving with Distraction—From Childhood Through Adulthood* (Ballantine, 2021), 50.

3. I often hear people tell me they try to show up to work or school in a way that "leaves their emotions at the door." Unlike shoes, emotions cannot be left at the door. It's simply not possible. For more on the reality of emotions in our classrooms and how to view this as an opportunity rather than a weakness, check out Sarah Rose Cavanagh's book *The Spark of Learning* at https://www.sarahrosecav.com/books/.

4. Karen Costa, *Creating Simple and Sustainable Educational Videos* (Stylus Publishing, 2022), https://www.amazon.com/Creating-Simple-Sustainable-Educational-Videos/dp/1642670855.

5. Hallowell and Ratey, *ADHD 2.0*, 73.

6. Hallowell and Ratey, *ADHD 2.0*, 65.

7. Temma Ehrenfeld, "ADHD May Come and Go in Adults," *Psychology Today*, September 17, 2021, https://www.psychologytoday.com/us/blog/open-gently/202109/adhd-may-come-and-go-in-adults.

8. ADDitude Editors. "PMS and ADHD: How Menstrual Cycle Hormones Intensify Symptoms." *ADDitude*, November 17, 2022, https://www.additudemag.com/pms-adhd-hormones-menstrual-cycle/.

9. Marcus Buckingham and Ashley Goodall, "The Feedback Fallacy," 2019, accessed February 2024, https://edevlearn.com/wp-content/uploads/2021/02/Why-Feedback-Rarely-Does-What-Its-Meant-To.pdf.

10. Colleen Flaherty, "Even 'Valid' Student Evaluations Are 'Unfair,'" *Inside Higher Ed*, February 26, 2020, https://www.insidehighered.com/news/2020/02/27/study-student-evaluations-teaching-are-deeply-flawed.

11. Buckingham and Goodall, "The Feedback Fallacy."

12. David Nicol, "Principles of Good Assessment and Feedback," REAP Project, accessed January 23, 2025, https://www.reap.ac.uk/reap/public/papers/Principles_of_good_assessment_and_feedback.pdf.

13. Rebecca Pope-Ruark, *Unraveling faculty burnout: Pathways to reckoning and renewal* (Johns Hopkins University Press, 2022), https://www.press.jhu.edu/books/title/12574/unraveling-faculty-burnout.

14. Margaret Price, *Crip Spacetime: Access, Failure, and Accountability in Academic Life* (Duke University Press, 2024), https://www.dukeupress.edu/crip-spacetime.

Chapter 6. Externalizing Everything

1. Tiago Forte, *Building a Second Brain: A Proven Method to Organize Your Digital Life and Unlock Your Creative Potential* (Atria, 2022).

2. Jason Frand and Carol Hixon, "Personal Knowledge Management: Who, What, Why, When, Where, How?" May 16, 2007, Internet Archive, https://web.archive.org/web/20070516142458/http://www.anderson.ucla.edu/faculty/jason.frand/researcher/speeches/PKM.htm.

3. Annie Murphy Paul, *The Extended Mind: The Power of Thinking Outside the Brain* (Mariner Books, 2022).

4. Ken Robinson, "Do Schools Kill Creativity?" TED Conferences, February 2006, https://www.ted.com/talks/sir_ken_robinson_do_schools_kill_creativity?language=en.

5. Paul, *The Extended Mind*, 9.

6. Paul, *The Extended Mind*, 9.

7. Paul, *The Extended Mind*, 48.

8. Paul, *The Extended Mind*, 115.

9. Paul, *The Extended Mind*, 97.

10. Paul, *The Extended Mind*, 216.

11. David A. Rosenbaum and Edward A. Wasserman, "Pre-crastination: The Opposite of Procrastination," *Scientific American*, June 30, 2015, https://www.scientificamerican.com/article/pre-crastination-the-opposite-of-procrastination/.

12. Courtney Sobers (associate teaching professor) in discussion with the author, May 2023.

13. Gawande, Atul. *The Checklist Manifesto: How to Get Things Right* (Picador, 2010).

14. Karen Costa, "Trauma-Aware Teaching Checklist," 100 Faculty, May 15, 2023, https://bit.ly/traumachecklist.

15. Radek Ptacek et al., "Clinical Implications of the Perception of Time in Attention Deficit Hyperactivity Disorder (ADHD): A Review," *Medical Science Monitor: International Medical Journal of Experimental and Clinical Research* 25 (2019): 3918–24, https://doi.org/10.12659/MSM.914225.

16. "Sarah Madoka Currie," Google Scholar, https://scholar.google.com/citations?user=AgenjGIAAAAJ&hl=en.

17. Ying Deng (ADHD coach and meditation teacher) in discussions with the author, May 2023.

18. Camila Domonoske, "AI Brings Soaring Emissions for Google and Microsoft, a Major Contributor to Climate Change," *NPR*, July 12, 2024, https://www.npr.org/2024/07/12/g-s1-9545/ai-brings-soaring-emissions-for-google-and-microsoft-a-major-contributor-to-climate-change.

19. Dr. Seuss, *The Butter Battle Book* (Random House, 1984).

20. ChatGPT (November 17 version), OpenAI, accessed 2023, https://chat.openai.com/chat.

Chapter 7. Metalearning

1. Sarah Rose Cavanagh, *The Spark of Learning: Energizing the College Classroom with the Science of Emotion* (West Virginia University Press, 2016).

2. Institute of Education University of London, "NSIN Research Matters: Learning about Learning Enhances Performance," 2001, http://complexworld.pbworks.com/f/Metacognition.pdf.

3. Institute of Education University of London, "NSIN Research Matters," 2.

4. Joshua Eyler, *Failing Our Future: How Grades Harm Students and What We Can Do about It* (Johns Hopkins University Press, 2024), https://www.press.jhu.edu/books/title/53857/failing-our-future.

5. Pema Chödrön, "The Ultimate Kindness," *The Sun*, September 2006, https://www.thesunmagazine.org/issues/369/the-ultimate-kindness.

6. Note that metalearning has nothing to do with the flawed concept of learning styles. Learning styles argue that some students have a primary preferred mode of learning: visual or kinesthetic, for example. No research supports the theory of learning styles, and some evidence has shown that teaching students to identify a preferred learning style actually impedes learning.

7. Andratesha Fritzgerald, *Antiracism and Universal Design for Learning: Building Expressways to Success* (Cast, Inc., 2020).

8. Fritzgerald, *Antiracism and Universal Design for Learning*, 23.

9. Fritzgerald, *Antiracism and Universal Design for Learning*, 24.

10. Fritzgerald, *Antiracism and Universal Design for Learning*, 29.

11. Fritzgerald, *Antiracism and Universal Design for Learning*, 30.

12. Marah Butzbach et al., "Metacognition in Adult ADHD: Subjective and Objective Perspectives on Self-Awareness of Cognitive Functioning," *Journal of Neural Transmission* 128 (2021): 939–55, https://doi.org/10.1007/s00702-020-02293-w; Agnese Capodieci et al., "The Efficacy of a Training that Combines Activities on Working Memory and Metacognition: Transfer and Maintenance Effects in Children with ADHD and Typical Development," *Journal of Clinical and Experimental Neuropsychology* 41 (2019): 1074–87, http://dx.doi.org/10.1080/13803395.2017.1307946; Leanne Tamm and Paul A. Nakonezny, "Metacognitive Executive Training for Young Children with ADHD: A Proof-of-Concept Study," *ADHD Attention Deficit and Hyperactivity Disorders* 7 (2015): 183–90, https://doi.org/10.1007/s12402-014-0162-x; Lynda Thompson and Michael Thompson, "Neurofeedback Combined with Training in Metacognitive Strategies: Effectiveness in Students with ADD," *Applied Psychophysiology and Biofeedback* 23 (1998): 243–63, https://doi.org/10.1023/a:1022213731956.

13. Institute of Education University of London, "NSIN Research Matters."

14. Institute of Education University of London, "NSIN Research Matters," 3.

15. I was taught to ask, "Where are the women?" in my introductory women's studies course in college, and it has been a life-changing question.

16. Li-Kai Son, Natalia B. Furlonge, and Pooja K. Agarwal, "Metacognition: How to Improve Students' Reflections on Learning," Retrieval Practice, accessed January 31, 2024, https://pdf.retrievalpractice.org/MetacognitionGuide.pdf.

17. Tons of free habit tracker printables and apps are available for free online, or design one with your students in Google Docs or Sheets.

18. "Using Sentence Completion Activities to Promote Academic Belonging," https://bit.ly/scforadhd.

19. Thank you to Michael McCreary for sharing this resource.

20. The ideas for the question-asking checklist, evaluation notebook, and techniques workbook come from the NSIN Research Matters metalearning brief previously discussed in this chapter (Institute of Education University of London, "NSIN Research Matters."). Discussion of how you can implement them in the course come from me. According to NSIN, all three of these interventions have been found to boost learning comprehension along with learners' sense of control and purpose over learning.

Chapter 8. Get Creative

1. Julia Cameron, *The Artist's Way: A Spiritual Path to Higher Creativity*, 10th anniversary edition (J. P. Tarcher/Putnam, 2002), xxiii.

2. Holly White (PhD and cognitive scientist) in discussion with the author, May 2023.

3. Holly White (PhD and cognitive scientist) in discussion with the author, May 2023.

4. Holly White (PhD and cognitive scientist) in discussion with the author, May 2023.

5. Holly White (PhD and cognitive scientist) in discussion with the author, May 2023.

6. Holly White, "The Creativity of ADHD," *Scientific American*, March 5, 2019, https://www.scientificamerican.com/article/the-creativity-of-adhd/.

7. Mary Wright, Christopher Woock, and James Lichtenberg, *Ready to Innovate: Are Educators and Executives Aligned on the Creative Readiness of the U.S. Workforce?*, The Conference Board, October 10, 2008, 1, https://www.americansforthearts.org/sites/default/files/ReadytoInnovateFull.pdf.

8. Wright et al., *Ready to Innovate*, 1.

9. Wright et al., *Ready to Innovate*, 1.

10. Mary Dana Hinton, "The Work of Moral Imagination," *Liberal Education*, Fall 2022, https://www.aacu.org/liberaleducation/articles/the-work-of-moral-imagination.

11. Jonathan Van Ness, host, *Getting Curious with Jonathan Van Ness*, podcast, "Are We Imagining a Better Future into Existence? With Adrienne Maree Brown," November 11, 2020, https://podcasts.apple.com/us/podcast/getting-curious-with-jonathan-van-ness/id1068563276.

12. William Dodson, "ADHD & the Interest-Based Nervous System," *ADDitude*, June 29, 2023, https://www.additudemag.com/adhd-brain-chemistry-video/.

13. Kenneth Blum et al., "Attention-Deficit-Hyperactivity Disorder and Reward Deficiency Syndrome," *Neuropsychiatric Disease and Treatment* 4, no. 5 (2008): 893–918, https://doi.org/10.2147/ndt.s2627.

14. Brandon K. Ashinoff and Ahmad Abu-Akel, "Hyperfocus: The Forgotten Frontier of Attention," *Psychological Research* 85, no. 1 (2021): 1–19, https://doi.org/10.1007/s00426-019-01245-8.

15. Mihaly Csikszentmihalyi, *Flow: The Psychology of Optimal Experience* (Harper-Collins, 2008).

16. Ashinoff and Abu-Akel, "Hyperfocus." Though not mentioned in the Ashinoff and Abu-Akel article, I would argue that Cal Newport's concept "deep work" is also a mainstream, non-pathologizing example of hyperfocus.

17. Ashinoff and Abu-Akel, "Hyperfocus," 10.

18. Mihaly Csikszentmihalyi, *Flow, the Secret to Happiness*, video, TED Conference, 2004, https://www.ted.com/talks/mihaly_csikszentmihalyi_flow_the_secret_to_happiness?language=en.

19. Ashinoff and Abu-Akel, "Hyperfocus," 5.

20. Kat Stephens-Peace (assistant professor) in discussion with the author, May 2023.

21. StackExchange, "Did Einstein Say 'We Cannot Solve Our Problems with the Same Thinking We Used to Create Them'?," accessed May 3, 2024, https://hsm.stackexchange.com/questions/7751/did-einstein-say-we-cannot-solve-our-problems-with-the-same-thinking-we-used-to.

22. Jumping the shark refers to the episode of *Happy Days* where Fonzi water skis and jumps over sharks, which is really random and weird. To jump the shark means to

stretch beyond credulity. You've run out of decent ideas so you substitute random weirdness for actual creative quality.

23. Lisa Thibault is a pseudonym. This interviewee expressed concern about publicly identifying as ADHD and the impacts that could have on her personally and professionally.

24. Cameron, *The Artist's Way*, xxi.

25. Cameron, *The Artist's Way*, xxiii.

26. Anna Abraham et al., "Creative Thinking in Adolescents with Attention Deficit Hyperactivity Disorder (ADHD)," *Child Neuropsychology: A Journal on Normal and Abnormal Development in Childhood and Adolescence* 12, no. 2 (2006): 111–23, https://doi.org/10.1080/09297040500320691.

27. Benjamin Baird et al., "Inspired by Distraction: Mind Wandering Facilitates Creative Incubation," *Psychological Science* 23, no. 10 (2012): 1117–22, https://doi.org/10.1177/0956797612446024.

28. Jodie N. Mader, "The Unessay Experiment: Moving Beyond the Traditional Paper," *Faculty Focus*, July 22, 2020, https://www.facultyfocus.com/articles/course-design-ideas/the-unessay-experiment-moving-beyond-the-traditional-paper/.

29. Christine Harrington, "How Much Assignment Choice Do Students Have? A Descriptive Study of Syllabi," *Currents* 14, no. 2 (2024): 6–15.

30. Jeffrey R. Young, "Student Disengagement Has Soared Since the Pandemic. Here's What Lectures Look Like Now," *EdSurge*, December 13, 2022, https://www.edsurge.com/news/2022-12-13-student-disengagement-has-soared-since-the-pandemic-here-s-what-lectures-look-like-now#:~:text=We've%20been%20hearing%20that,is%20worth%20doing%20at%20all.

Chapter 9. Flexible Structure

1. Ann Gagné, "Flexible Profession: How Much Can We Bend?," *English Studies in Canada* 44, no. 4 (December 2018): 47–50, https://muse.jhu.edu/pub/79/article/787129/pdf.

2. Poorvu Center for Teaching and Learning, "Flexible Structures in Course Design," Yale University, accessed September 6, 2024, https://poorvucenter.yale.edu/strategic-resources-digital-publications/managing-classroom/flexible-structures-course-design.

3. Sarah L. Eddy and Kelly A. Hogan, "Getting Under the Hood: How and for Whom Does Increasing Course Structure Work?," *CBE—Life Sciences Education* 13, no. 3 (2014): 453–68, https://doi.org/10.1187/cbe.14-03-0050.

4. "Balancing Flexibility and Rigor to Advance Equity in Course Design," Teaching@Tufts, September 3, 2021, https://sites.tufts.edu/teaching/2021/09/03/balancing-flexibility-and-rigor-to-advance-equity-in-course-design/.

5. Lawrence J. Lewandowski et al., "Extended Time Accommodations and the Mathematics Performance of Students With and Without ADHD," *Journal of Psychoeducational Assessment* 25, no. 1 (March 2007): 17–28, https://eric.ed.gov/?id=EJ803225; Laura A. Miller, Lawrence J. Lewandowski, and Kevin M. Antshel, "Effects of Extended Time for College Students With and Without ADHD," *Journal of*

Attention Disorders 19, no. 8 (April 16, 2013): 697–704, https://doi.org/10.1177
/1087054713483308; Alison Esposito Pritchard et al., "Academic Testing Accommodations for ADHD: Do They Help?," *Learning Disabilities Research & Practice* 21, no. 2
(2016): 67–78, https://doi.org/10.18666/LDMJ-2016-V21-I2-7414.

6. "Balancing Flexibility and Rigor to Advance Equity in Course Design," Teach-
ing@Tufts, September 3, 2021, https://sites.tufts.edu/teaching/2021/09/03/balancing
-flexibility-and-rigor-to-advance-equity-in-course-design/.

Conclusion. The Future of ADHD

1. Jessica Agnew-Blais and Giorgia Michelini, "Taking Stock of the Present and
Looking to the Future of ADHD Research: A Commentary on Sonuga-Barke et al.
(2023)," *Journal of Child Psychology and Psychiatry* 64, no. 4 (2023): 533–36, https://doi
.org/10.1111/jcpp.13758.

2. Sonny Jane Wise, "Understanding Neurodiversity Beyond the DSM," LinkedIn,
accessed October 2, 2024, https://www.linkedin.com/pulse/understanding-neuro
diversity-beyond-dsm-sonny-jane-wise-nmdlc/?trackingId=BGsz02zB7q1QAY3v4YY
AAA%3D%3D.

3. Kimberlé Crenshaw, "Demarginalizing the Intersection of Race and Sex: A
Black Feminist Critique of Antidiscrimination Doctrine, Feminist Theory, and
Antiracist Politics," *University of Chicago Legal Forum* no. 1 (1989): 139–67, https://
www.google.com/url?sa=t&source=web&rct=j&opi=89978449&url=https://chicago
unbound.uchicago.edu/cgi/viewcontent.cgi%3Farticle%3D1052%26context%3Duclf&
ved=2ahUKEwiH9reclaaMAxWbKFkFHad7GTUQFnoECAkQAQ&usg=AOvVaw36y
PHMVpAK8DAWsflgm7Yw.

4. Kat Stephens-Peace (assistant professor) in discussion with the author,
May 2023.

5. Bradley Irish (associate professor) in discussion with the author, May 2023.

6. Bradley Irish (associate professor) in discussion with the author, May 2023.

7. Bradley Irish (associate professor) in discussion with the author, May 2023.

8. Bradley Irish (associate professor) in discussion with the author, May 2023.

9. Bradley J. Irish, "How to Make Room for Neurodivergent Professors,"
Chronicle of Higher Education, March 2, 2023, https://www.chronicle.com/article/how
-to-make-room-for-neurodivergent-professors.

10. Bradley Irish (associate professor) in discussion with the author, May 2023.

11. Chiara Latimer (co-director, Rowan University Center for Neurodiversity), in
conversation with the author, March 2024.

12. Laura McKowen, "The 9 Things," The Luckiest Club, accessed April 27, 2024,
https://www.theluckiestclub.com/about.

13. Adrienne Maree Brown, *Emergent Strategy: Shaping Change, Changing Worlds*
(AK Press, 2017), 93–95.

14. Brown, *Emergent Strategy*, 93.

15. Brown, *Emergent Strategy*, 94.

16. Marcie Bianco, *Breaking Free: The Lie of Equality and the Feminist Fight for
Freedom* (PublicAffairs, 2023), https://www.hachettebookgroup.com/titles/marcie

-bianco/breaking-free/9781541702448/. Fun fact: Marcie grew up across the street from me, on Queen Ave. in Pennsville, NJ. We remain friends to this day.

17.   Bianco, *Breaking Free*, 5.

18.   OnBeing, "Ocean Vuong: A Life Worthy of Our Breath," *On Being with Krista Tippet*, May 3, 2023, https://onbeing.org/programs/ocean-vuong-a-life-worthy-of-our-breath-2022/.

Index

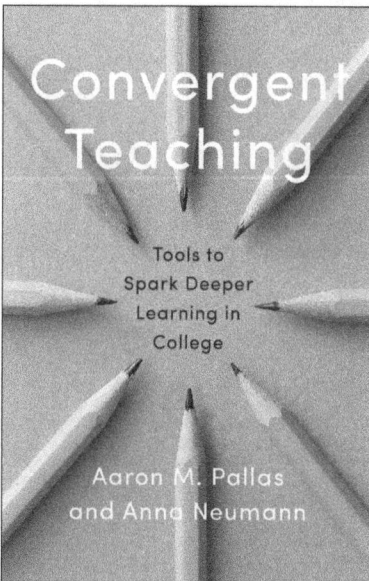

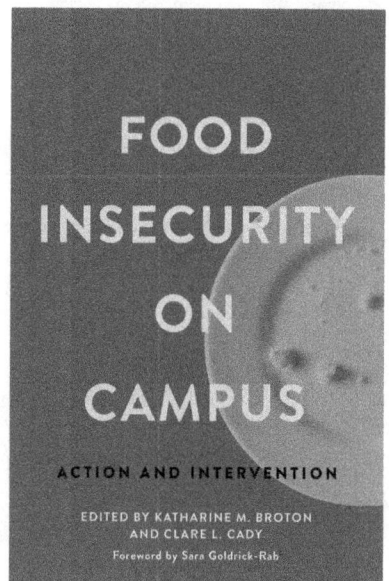